INEQUALITY, BOOM, AND BUST

There is enormous inequality between the income and wealth of the richest 1 percent and all other Americans. While the top 1 percent own 42 percent of all wealth in America, the lower half on the income ladder has only 2 percent of all of the wealth. This book develops a viewpoint contrary to the prevailing conservative paradigm, setting out both reasons for this inequality and the impact of this.

To explain inequality, conservative economists focus on individual characteristics such as intelligence and hard work. This book puts forward new evidence to show that changes in economic inequality are primarily due to characteristics inherent in the standard operation of capitalist institutions. Furthermore, the authors seek to explain the cycle of boom and bust by considering political and social factors often overlooked by conservative economists. This book also explores how wealth influences political policies in a way that increases economic inequality even more than its present level.

Through analysis of American political and economic institutions, *Inequality, Boom, and Bust* presents concrete steps for an activist, progressive policy to greatly reduce inequality through free healthcare, free higher education, and reduced unemployment.

Howard J. Sherman is Professor of Economics Emeritus at University of California, Riverside, and is Visiting Researcher at the Political Science Department of the University of California at Los Angeles, USA.

Paul D. Sherman is a computer engineer in Silicon Valley (USA) with concerns for the problems of the people of the world.

INEQUALITY, BOOM, AND BUST

From Billionaire Capitalism to Equality and Full Employment

Howard J. Sherman and Paul D. Sherman

Routledge
Taylor & Francis Group

LONDON AND NEW YORK

First published 2018
by Routledge
2 Park Square, Milton Park, Abingdon, Oxon OX14 4RN

and by Routledge
711 Third Avenue, New York, NY 10017

Routledge is an imprint of the Taylor & Francis Group, an informa business

© 2018 Howard J. Sherman and Paul D. Sherman

British Library Cataloguing-in-Publication Data
A catalogue record for this book is available from the British Library

Library of Congress Cataloging-in-Publication Data
Names: Sherman, Howard J., author. | Sherman, Paul D., author.
Title: Inequality, boom, and bust: from billionaire capitalism to
    equality and full employment / Howard Sherman and Paul D
    Sherman.
Description: New York: Routledge, 2018. | Includes bibliographical
    references and index.
Identifiers: LCCN 2017045946 (print) | LCCN 2018002306
    (ebook) | ISBN 9781351210904 (Ebook) | ISBN
    9780815381280 (hardback: alk. paper) | ISBN 9780815381297
    (pbk. : alk. paper) | ISBN 9781351210904 (ebk)
Subjects: LCSH: Income distribution—United States. | United
    States—Economic conditions—21st century. | Full employment
    policies—United States.
Classification: LCC HB523 (ebook) | LCC HB523 .S5327 2018
    (print) | DDC 339.2/20973—dc23
LC record available at https://lccn.loc.gov/2017045946

ISBN: 978-0-8153-8128-0 (hbk)
ISBN: 978-0-8153-8129-7 (pbk)
ISBN: 978-1-351-21090-4 (ebk)

Typeset in Bembo
by Swales & Willis Ltd, Exeter, Devon, UK

DEDICATED TO
SENATOR BERNIE SANDERS
FOR HIS INSPIRATION
AND
IN MEMORIAM TO
BARBARA L. SINCLAIR

For over 40 years, Barbara's life and my life were intertwined. At her death in 2016, Barbara's position was "Distinguished Professor Emeritus of Political Science, University of California Los Angeles (UCLA)." My position was "Professor Emeritus of Economics, University of California Riverside (UCR)" and "Visiting Researcher in Political Science, UCLA." Our work was close enough that we could read what each other wrote and could discuss it, but not close enough to risk doing detailed studies together.

Barbara published eight widely acclaimed books on the United States Congress, plus a large number of articles on the Congress. She was on four or five panels and conferences each year. She answered innumerable questions about Congress from the *New York Times* and the *Washington Post*. She gave testimony to Congress, including a detailed statement of the problems caused by the Senate filibuster.

Barbara was a caring and helping person. Her graduate students greatly appreciated her help, especially the detailed letters of reference and recommendation she wrote over their careers. She helped me not only by her love and support, but also by her solution to some econometric problems I had, plus her constructive criticism when I wrote on politics beyond my limited knowledge of its details.

To help Barbara with her work, I mostly gave her my love, support, and enthusiasm. The only exception was her book called *The Women's Movement*; it went through three editions, providing a comprehensive view of the fight for women's rights. Most of it was written on a long summer's vacation. We each read all of the useful books available on the struggle for women's rights, and then discussed them, after which Barbara wrote each chapter. My only direct contribution was to give her economic data for the chapter on economic discrimination.

We worked long hours, but we took long vacations.

CONTENTS

FIGURES

TABLES

PREFACE

This book is revolutionary in two respects. It finds that in the American economy, there have been continuing increases in inequality as well as a falling percentage of people in the labor force compared to the population. As a result, it finds that a number of very major changes are needed, such as free healthcare and free higher education. To achieve these goals would require a democratic or political revolution through the election system.

Furthermore, the viewpoint of the book is contrary to the prevailing conservative paradigm in economics. It argues that greater inequality will not increase the rate of growth, but will tend to cause stagnation, recession, or depression. Thus, the viewpoint developed in the book is contrary to conservative economics, and its vision is a progressive one.

In the past, there have been many progressive movements in America attempting to create a high level of income equality and full employment, including the highly successful campaign for the Democratic nomination for President in 2016 by Senator Bernie Sanders. What does the future offer?

A vision of the future

The four long years of the Trump Administration produced many measures that were racist, sexist, and helpful to the income of billionaires. The resulting harm to the middle class created a large protest movement that became part of the progressive movement. The poor availability of good jobs and the great increase in economic inequality in the years before 2020 resulted in a storm of anger among the American people. In the election of 2020, that anger was expressed in a flood of votes that elected a progressive President, Senate, and House of Representatives.

The new government enacted programs that reflected all of the promises of their campaign. Income inequality was reduced in several ways. The Medicare program became free and provided care to everyone. All Americans who could qualify for higher education were able to attend for free. A minimum, living wage for all American workers was passed.

Having access to free medical care and free education along with a living wage for the lowest paid worker raised the real income of the middle class and the poor. This helped close some of the income gap between the average American and the wealthy. This change reduced the possibility of recessions and unemployment.

The new government also passed measures so that everyone who was qualified and wanted to work was entitled to a job. A large stimulus to the economy was enacted, which included public money for infrastructure, expansion of public health facilities and staff, and public education facilities and staff.

Other legislation was approved to help the 12 million illegal American residents begin the road to citizenship. The Department of Justice worked to stop all local and state laws that were unconstitutional and prevented people from voting.

The other issues dealt with successfully by the government included: the enforcement of stronger anti-discrimination laws against both racism and sexism by the future government; public disclosure of anyone wanting to buy a gun; a pardon for all federal prisoners held for nonviolent crime; a program for strict climate control; and a voting franchise for prisoners who had served their time. (The illustration on the book cover reflects the Women's March of January 2017, the day before the Trump inauguration; this march was the largest protest march in American history, and it focused on discrimination against women and many other issues, all of which are causes of inequality.)

Power was switched from Wall Street and the largest non-financial corporations, which are owned by the wealthiest 1 percent, to democratic public ownership, as well as cooperative employee ownership.

The road to the future

The future, unfortunately, is not yet here. What are the problems that must be faced today? The focus here will be on the problems of inequality in income, wealth, and opportunity, as well as the problems of unemployment, stagnation, and recession. At the present, some human beings are trying to end these problems.

The fight to combat inequality and unemployment

There is enormous inequality between the income and wealth of the wealthiest 1 percent and all other Americans. Most of the wealth of the wealthiest 1 percent comes from their ownership of stocks, bonds, and other kinds of real property. On the other hand, most of the income for the other 99 percent of Americans is from wages and salaries. The wealthiest 1 percent own 40 percent of all wealth in America. The lower half on the income distribution ladder in America has only 2 percent of all of the wealth. The percentage of all income received by the middle class has been slowly shrinking.

America has suffered from repeated bouts of recession and unemployment during the last two centuries. Excluding periods of war, the normal expansion of the economy lasts for three to seven years. Then it falls into a recession or deep depression. Human misery increases as unemployment rises, as in the Great Depression when 25 percent of all working people were unemployed and had no unemployment compensation. In 2007 to 2009, there was a Great Recession in which 11 percent of the labor force was unemployed.

A capitalist institution, such as giant corporations, banks, and the labor markets that they control, causes increasing inequality in every peacetime business expansion. The increasing inequality eventually leads to constricted growth of consumer demand, which leads to a recession and higher unemployment.

The drastic improvements in the economic system needed to achieve equality and full employment can be achieved by a peaceful, democratic political revolution.

What's new in this book?

To explain inequality, conservative economists focus on individual characteristics, such as intelligence and hard work. This book reveals new evidence to show that changes in economic inequality are primarily due to the usual operation of the institutions of capitalism in each business expansion.

To explain the cycle of boom and bust, which causes most unemployment, conservative economists focus on non-economic factors, such as government mistakes. This book will reveal evidence showing that the most important factor causing business expansions to turn into contractions, recessions, and depressions is the rise of economic inequality. The rise of inequality in expansions is a reflection of the fact that wages stagnate while profit soars.

Most economists looking at the business cycle use the framework of rises and falls in GDP to measure everything else. Although the turning points in GDP are important, this book focuses attention on the behavior of the main economic sectors relative to the expansion and contraction profits because profits are the key variable causing expansion or contraction of the capitalist economy.

Finally, conservative economists argue for elimination of government services to the middle class and the poor, as well as elimination of all regulations governing the risky profit seeking of the banks and other corporations. This book will present concrete steps for an activist, progressive policy to greatly reduce both unemployment and inequality.

Evolution and excitement

Most students find economics books to be extraordinarily dull. The main reason is that most economics books for students assume a set of unreal assumptions, which always yield the conclusion that capitalism has always existed and will always exist because it is the only possible economic system. They deny any evolution from one system to another.

Economics books based on an evolutionary view tell an exciting story of the past and the exciting possibility of a far better society in the future. Chapter 1 will explain and illustrate the evolutionary view from the prehistoric era to capitalism. Other chapters will examine the evolution of the American political economy, the evolution of thought about inequality, and the evolution and use of the concept of effective demand. Chapters 5 to 14 will examine how the economy evolves within each cycle of boom and bust, as well as from cycle to cycle. On this basis, policies are proposed for the evolution to a better society through revolutionary changes in the present economy in Chapter 15.

Language

To simplify the language used in this book, the term United States of America will sometimes be called America. The citizens of the USA will sometimes be called Americans. When we use the term Americans, there is an implied apology to Latin Americans, Central Americans, or other North Americans, all of whom have a right to this term. When we are not talking about the USA, it will be made clear which part of the Americas we are discussing.

Appendix to the Preface

Poem on poverty

Prejudice based on wealth is called classism. Classism asserts that the wealthiest capitalist class is better than other people because they are wealthy. The class prejudice states that a person who is a billionaire must be superior in all qualities to a person who is middle-class or poor, not just in terms of money, but in general. A wonderful poem by Robert Burns in 1795 attacks the prejudice of classism:

A MAN'S A MAN FOR A' THAT

Is there for honest Poverty

That hings his head, an' a' that;

The coward slave-we pass him by,

We dare be poor for a' that!

For a' that, an' a' that.

Our toils obscure an' a' that,

The rank is but the guinea's stamp,

The Man's the gowd for a' that.

What though on hamely fare we dine,

Wear hoddin grey, an' a' that;

Gie fools their silks, and knaves their wine;

A Man's a Man for a' that:

For a' that, and a' that,

Their tinsel show, an' a' that;

The honest man, tho' e'er sae poor,

Is king o' men for a' that.

Ye see yon birkie, ca'd a lord,

Wha struts, an' stares, an' a' that;

Tho' hundreds worship at his word,

He's but a coof for a' that:

For a' that, an' a' that,

His ribband, star, an' a' that:

The man o' independent mind

He looks an' laughs at a' that.

A prince can mak a belted knight,

A marquis, duke, an' a' that;

But an honest man's abon his might,

Gude faith, he maunna fa' that!

For a' that, an' a' that,

Their dignities an' a' that;

The pith o' sense, an' pride o' worth,

Are higher rank than a' that.

Then let us pray that come it may,

(As come it will for a' that,)

That Sense and Worth, o'er a' the earth,

Shall bear the gree, an' a' that.

For a' that, an' a' that,

It's coming yet for a' that,

That Man to Man, the world o'er,

Shall brothers be for a' that.

ACKNOWLEDGEMENTS

The author, Howard J. Sherman, wrote every word of this book in the initial draft by himself. He used no sentence or paragraph from any previous book or article.

This book could not have been written without my son, Paul D. Sherman. He did all of the research, improved the program for describing the path of variables over the business cycle, calculated all of the data, and made all of the figures and tables.

Lisa Sherman, my daughter, contributed enormously to the quality of the manuscript. She copyedited every chapter, getting rid of an amazing number of mistakes and awkward sentences.

Harvey Sherman, my nephew, used his extensive knowledge of the financial world to improve this book. He also was a tremendous help by doing in–depth final editing while working directly with the author to improve style and remove repetitious or ambiguous sentences.

This book has been strongly influenced by many economists of the past. These include John Maynard Keynes and his followers, especially Joan Robinson; Karl Marx and his followers, especially Michael Kalecki and Paul Sweezy; and Thorstein Veblen and his followers, such as Wesley Mitchell. Their contributions are discussed in Chapter 3.

My work has been influenced by many excellent progressive economists from the twenty–first century, especially those writing in three journals: *Journal of Economic Issues*, *Journal of Post Keynesian Economics*, and *Review of Radical Political Economics*.

Several people have also greatly helped the book through their constructive criticism of earlier drafts, articles, and parts of previous books. Michael Meeropol has written extensive criticisms on each chapter and also spelled out exactly how to make the improvements. A lecture by Richard Wolff also inspired an important change in the book.

The criticisms by William Dugger and Robert Pollin forced the author to make changes in this book's basic focus and policy statements. Charlotte Furth, Kenneth Korman, and Nicholas Massoni also gave me extensive constructive criticisms over the past several years.

We previously published an article called "Inequality and the business cycle" (Sherman and Sherman, 2015). It represented our first attempt to publish on the subject of inequality, so we are grateful to the editor, Jeffrey Madrick, and the journal, *Challenge*, for publishing it. We have, however, changed many of our views, and have used none of the writing or data from that article in this book.

Finally, the campaign of Senator Bernie Sanders for President of the United States in 2016 was exhilarating and a sign of hope for most progressive economists. His campaign gave this author the strength to finish this book.

Howard J. Sherman

ABOUT THE AUTHORS

Howard J. Sherman is Professor of Economics Emeritus at University of California, Riverside, and is Visiting Researcher at the Political Science Department of the University of California at Los Angeles. He was chair of the Economics Department at the University of California, Riverside, for a total of five years, in which he tried to build a department of the highest possible academic quality combined with freedom for anyone to participate in activism according to their views.

When he was a small child, Howard heard many denunciations of facism, racism, sexism, and unemployment. All of his life, he has been an activist against those evils. Some of the activism has been in demonstrations and speeches, but some has been in books. Sherman has published 21 books, all of them attempting to change the world as part of his activism.

He wrote a brief autobiography explaining his life, "Making of a radical economist" (Sherman, 2006b). For the critical views of many economists on his work and how it developed, see *Capitalism, Socialism, and Radical Political Economy: Essays in Honor of Howard J. Sherman* (Pollin, 2000). See all works at https://works.bepress.com/howard_j_sherman/. For a contemporary analysis of his work, an anonymous review by another economist to the editor of this book at Routledge is given below:

> Professor Howard Sherman has had a long and distinguished career as a professor of economics and author of numerous books on political economy. Many of his books have sold widely and influenced people both inside of and beyond academia. His books have been successful because of a unique combination of features. These include the following:
>
> 1. He is an extremely clear writer. He has an ability to boil down complex ideas into very readable prose. His writing is typically fully accessible to any reader of, say, the *New York Times*, or a first- or second-year undergraduate.
> 2. He is open about his leftist political convictions. As Joseph Schumpeter explained, all economists come to their work with what he called a

"pre-analytic vision." These pre-analytic visions shape the way economists see the world and ask questions. Most economists pretend that their work is strictly objective and scientific, thereby diminishing the legitimacy of their work precisely because they are suppressing the reality that they are guided by pre-analytic visions. By contrast, with Howard Sherman, precisely because he is totally open about his convictions, his writings possess a level of verve and authenticity that is generally absent in the economics literature.

3. He has a wide breadth of knowledge, and, in particular, a strong command of economic history. He uses that broad knowledge to good effect in his writings.

4. Unlike many generalists, Sherman is also a technical specialist in the field of business cycle research. He is thus able to skillfully synthesize his depth of technical knowledge on business cycles with his breadth of knowledge in illuminating ways.

As with many of Sherman's previous books, *Inequality, Boom, and Bust* effectively brings together these four major features of Sherman's work. With this book, in particular, Sherman combines these features in a unique way to address the issue of inequality in the U.S. economy. Of course, there has been a lot written already about the trend of rising inequality in the U.S., including, most prominently, the recent books of Thomas Piketty and Joseph Stiglitz. What Sherman's work brings out that is not featured in these other books is the connection between inequality and instability, as represented, in particular, through the ups and downs of the business cycle—i.e. through the periodic swings of recessions and booms.

To my knowledge, there are no other recent extensive treatments on this link between rising inequality and increasing instability. This is surprising. After all, it is a central feature of the one of the two or three most famous and influential books on political economy ever written, i.e. Marx's *Capital*. In *Capital*, Marx strongly emphasizes that recessions and the connected rise in mass unemployment are necessary to the operations of capitalism, to prevent workers from obtaining excessive bargaining power through which their wages will be driven up. Capitalists' profits will correspondingly fall when workers' wages rise. Thus, in Marx, changes in the distribution of income—i.e. increases and decreases in inequality—are completely bound up with business cycle fluctuations.

Especially given this background, Sherman's book fills a significant gap in the literature . . .

Paul D. Sherman is a computer engineer in Silicon Valley with concerns for the problems of the people of the world. He has played an active role in the evolution of the data storage industry for the past 25 years. He has published at least 21 articles with the SAS Institute user group community on statistical problems, co-authored five articles and books on progressive economics issues, and received four U.S. patents for inventions on testing and manufacture of data storage devices.

1

EVOLUTION OF CAPITALISM, INEQUALITY, AND UNEMPLOYMENT

The present economy, with its inequality and cycles of boom and bust, can only be understood by examining the long, twisting road from the beginning of society to modern capitalism. This chapter attempts to explain just how capitalism developed out of earlier societies in a way that made inequality and cyclical instability an essential part of it.

From 2007 to the present (2017), many countries have had continuing significant unemployment. It is a tragedy when one person is involuntarily unemployed. When 10 million people are unemployed, that is a national calamity. When hundreds of millions of people are unemployed all over the world, it is a disaster with more human misery than the author can fully describe. The present problems of inequality and unemployment take place under the economic system called capitalism.

The evolution of capitalism

What was the behavior and extent of inequality during each stage of economic history? How has inequality developed over the history of capitalism?

How did capitalism come to be our present economic system? Why did the cycles of boom and bust become the usual form of economic change under capitalism? Why does this terrible process keep repeating itself, with corporations and governments making the same mistakes every time? What is the role of vested interests, such as the wealthiest 1 percent of wealth owners? How can we permanently get rid of this terrible system of boom and bust?

How it began

Many sciences today are based on an understanding of how their subject matter evolved from its beginnings. For example, geologists go back to the beginning of the earth's history to trace how it changed and evolved for billions of years to produce today's continents, lakes, mountains, and valleys.

Similarly, in biology, in order to understand all modern species of animals, including human beings, biologists trace the development of animals from the simplest one-celled organisms through the dinosaurs and all the stages of evolution until today. In society, there was a similar process of change to what was found in biology and geology.

There were tremendous struggles to prevent these new theories in geology, biology, and society from being known by everyone. This attempt to hold back the progress of social and natural science was because the political and economic elite wanted no change in knowledge that might threaten their rule. The elite worried that if the average person realized that vast changes were part of the ordinary process of development in the physical and biological worlds, they might get the subversive notion that change is possible in society.

The prehistoric clan economy

There are four aspects of society that can be used describe how it changes and evolves: economic, political, technological, and ideological.

In the prehistoric era, the basic working group consisted of a clan of 20 to 35 people, all of whom were members of an extended family. In what is called the Old Stone Age, the clan used the earliest stone implements as their technology. These tools and weapons were sufficient for the hunter-gatherer type of economy. Most women would gather fruits and vegetables. Most men would hunt for animals. All of the food was then consumed collectively by the entire clan.

This type of economy, relying on collective action and collective consumption, was not designed by a bunch of philosophers. On the contrary, it arose out of utter necessity. Only a hard-working collective of all members of the clan could possibly bring in enough food to feed everyone. Food, clothing, and shelter all depended exclusively upon the labor of the entire clan. There was little or no trading with other clans. If all went well in the hunting and gathering, then the clan could achieve just enough food to prevent starvation.

This type of collective economic unit was naturally ruled by the collective social unit of all the adults in the clan. A leader might be elected from time to time with limited duties and powers, either to rule on disputes or to lead the clan in its economic activities. There was no other government.

The general viewpoints or ideology of the clan arose on the basis of this collective economic and political activity. The strongly held view of the clan was that each person had to contribute their share of labor in order to get their share of the food, clothing, and shelter. Anyone who did not cooperate, or who tried to accumulate a private hidden reserve out of the collective output of the clan, would be exiled. Since the full strength of the clan was needed to produce enough for each person's subsistence, exile was a sentence of death.

Because the whole economy consisted of collective action and sharing within the clan, there was no market exchange, no money, private business, or private profit. Therefore, there could be no economic downturn caused by lack of aggregate demand, as there is in the modern business contraction. The only reason for an economic contraction in the prehistoric era was external calamities, such as floods or drought.

There was no economic inequality for more than 100,000 years because everyone in the clan was forced to work together in order to survive. Therefore, they collectively owned and consumed all the products of their labor. There was no business cycle of boom and bust because the present cycle of the modern capitalist economy is based on money, sales, and profit, which did not exist in the prehistoric society.

How did this 100,000-year-old economy ever change to something new and different?

From collective clans to slavery and feudalism

The prehistoric economy of *Homo sapiens* lasted for 100,000 years or more. Its technology changed at such a slow pace as to be almost unobserved. Then, about 10,000 years ago, the Neolithic Revolution in technology began. The term Neolithic simply means "new stone." In this New Stone Age, there were some improvements made in the stone tools and weapons that were used in some areas, such as the Middle East. These improvements, which appear modest to modern eyes, were enough to allow some new economic patterns to emerge.

With improved tools, the group of women who collected fruits and vegetables were now able to cut away the weeds and preserve the desirable crops. This led to the first farming.

The men, who had done the often dangerous and sometimes unsuccessful hunting, now became herders able to surround, direct, and to some extent control large groups of animals, such as cows or horses.

The new farming practice of the women, although still with crude implements, provided a much higher level of productivity. The new practice of herding by the men also provided a far more stable diet and larger amounts of meat. The community now had enough food to give up its previous nomadic existence and form a stable village. With a relatively stable food supply and home area, the population began to increase. There was also enough food to feed some people who did no farming or hunting, but specialized in producing better tools and weapons. Under this new system, the technology began to improve significantly.

The larger and more stable production also meant that a few people could specialize in being chiefs and their armed retainers. These people did no subsistence work, but only supervised the activity of the whole clan.

At first, these chiefs had only limited powers and a limited term. Since, however, they had legitimate access to the food supply of the clan, they were able to hire armed followers, expand their powers, and increase their term limits. It took a couple of thousand years from the beginning of the Neolithic Revolution until these new forms of political and economic life emerged.

Once a permanent village was established, and the productivity of the clan was greatly enhanced by the new tools and weapons, the population grew more rapidly. The village might turn into a small town, while the elected chief might turn into a powerful, permanent chief.

In the Old Stone Age, a war against another clan was always unprofitable. Since the tribes were nomadic, they did not accumulate well-made furniture or fancy dwellings. Moreover, in the Old Stone Age, they had no herds.

The capture of slaves in the Old Stone Age did not help a chief. In the Old Stone Age, any given individual could only produce enough goods for the tribe to provide subsistence for all of its members, including that individual. So the slaves could not produce any surplus for a chief.

That situation changed with the Neolithic Revolution. Productivity rose because of improved stone tools and weapons, so that an individual could produce a surplus above their own needs. The chiefs and their armed followers could then use captives from a successful war as slaves. The slaves could then produce their own subsistence plus enough goods and services to allow the chief to live at a much higher standard of living.

Slavery meant that one person could tell another person what to do and the owner had the right to use anything the slave produced. The slaves were a type of labor that was coerced by armed strength and had no personal freedom.

On the foundation laid by the Neolithic Revolution, there followed the Bronze Age and Iron Age. During those ages, humanity expanded from small villages to towns to large cities, and from large cities eventually to empires.

During the Hellenistic/Roman Age, there were various types of labor. These ranged from slaves to serfs to free workers, as well as every combination in between. Some empires, such as Egypt, Greece, and Rome, used a larger percentage of slaves. Some empires in the Middle East, such as Persia, used more serfs.

The operation of slavery

The Roman Empire consisted mainly of large plantations using slaves, though there were some large cities. The cities encompassed about 5 percent of the population. Slavery allowed a small wealthy class to live in luxury. The cities were also able to find enough slave labor to build immense monuments for religious deities and governing kings and emperors.

Slavery, however, also led to many problems. Slavery exhausted the land because it could utilize only the simplest techniques and the same type of crop in most of the plantations. Any more complex situation made it impossible to keep order and to supervise the slaves. Therefore, Roman agriculture became more systematic, but hardly ever increased its productivity per slave.

Another problem was that slavery produced an ideology which claimed that all work was servile, so the master class should indulge only in the arts and in politics.

Thus, the entire class that had the leisure time to work on new inventions did not do so because any kind of work was considered beneath the status of the master class.

Because of the continued use of the simplest technology in farming, there was always a need to expand by conquering new lands. Furthermore, the lifetime of a slave was limited because of the hard work in poor conditions for most agricultural slaves, combined with insufficient food. To replace those slaves who died, it was necessary to conquer new areas from which large numbers of slaves could be taken.

To conquer other peoples, the Romans needed a large army. The army was also necessary to defend Rome from large nomadic tribes on its frontiers. These tribes were envious and wanted to conquer the luxurious homes and monuments of the Roman cities.

Yet it became more and more difficult to maintain a large army. Slaves could not be used for an army because they would have to be armed, and armed slaves were the great nightmare of Rome. So the Romans conscripted almost all of the free farmers who remained outside the plantations. As those farmers remained in the Roman army or were killed in war, the Romans ran out of replacements.

Heavy taxation was also needed to finance the wars. Therefore, the farmers that were left behind became poorer and poorer from taxation. These impoverished farms often ended when they were taken over by the larger slave plantations.

Since the Romans could not rely on the slaves as soldiers, and since there were few free farmers remaining, the Romans were forced to pay members of the hostile nomadic tribes to become soldiers. Such armies became less and less reliable at fighting against the other tribes on the frontiers. Moreover, these armies began to exercise their power in the sport of taking over the Empire and creating a new Emperor.

Slavery is the most exploitative and unequal society. The slave owner has complete control of all production, although the owner normally allows the slaves just enough goods and services to exist at a subsistence level during a brief lifespan. The high degree of inequality meant that the national market for consumer goods was always limited, because slaves produced all of their food, clothing, and shelter on the plantation.

A capitalist type of market economy never developed for most of the society as inequality remained so great within the Roman Empire. Most of the Roman population remained on large slave plantations until near the end of the Empire. Therefore, most goods and services were used with the slave economy on these plantations, but were not sold in markets. As a result, there was no cycle of boom and bust, but rather a long stagnation that finally resulted in a decline and fall.

Roman power and living standards declined from the second to the fifth century AD, then fell completely apart in the fifth century. As a substitute for the slave plantations, the ruling group slowly turned toward the society known as feudalism and the labor form known as serfdom. Some small amount of slavery continued to exist in Europe during feudalism.

The complex story of the end of the prehistoric period and the rise of slavery is in the Pulitzer Prize winning book *Guns, Germs, and Steel* by Jared Diamond (1997).

The operation of feudalism and serfdom

Feudalism slowly became dominant in Western Europe, starting about 500 AD and reaching its peak in 1200 to 1500 AD. In feudal society, the law said all land belongs to the King. The King was the strongest of the nobles. He gave large estates to the other nobility, which they could use so long as they agreed to furnish soldiers to help him in his wars. The great lords in turn gave some of their lands to lesser lords and knights, who retained the right to use these lands as long as they gave military support to their particular lord.

At the bottom of this pyramid of power were the serfs. The serfs worked on the estates of the lords and the knights. Under the feudal system, each serf must work a certain number of days for the lord of the estate. The male serfs did agricultural labor as well as making some roads and other infrastructure. The female serfs often worked in the lord's castle, doing domestic activities of all types. They were frequently exploited sexually by the lord, his sons, or his armed retainers.

The aggregate economy of slavery and feudalism

It is worth emphasizing that 90 to 95 percent of the population worked on the land in both slave and feudal societies. Each of the plantations or estates was largely self-sufficient. The slaves or serfs produced all of the food, clothing, and shelter that were needed.

The Roman masters brought only a small percentage of their output to market. Although the Romans had a few major cities with markets in them, most plantations produced mainly for themselves, with a relatively small surplus sent to market.

Roman bankers mostly loaned money for long-distance trade or for military purposes. Few people in agriculture ever saw money. Finance and long-distance trade did sometimes have problems of lack of demand or inflation. The basic economy of the plantations, however, was self-sufficient. Therefore, it could not be harmed by lack of aggregate demand.

The feudal lords of Western Europe used almost everything on their own estate, leaving next to nothing to be brought to market. As a result, at the peak of feudalism in about 1200 to 1500 AD, there were few markets, little use of money or credit—except in a few long-distance transactions—and no private profit to be made in most of the transactions that were within a single estate.

Since there were few or no markets, no money or credit, and no private profit, there was no business as defined in modern capitalist societies. Since there was no business and no need to sell anything, there were no cycles of boom and bust. There could be no lack of aggregate demand within a single self-sufficient estate.

The problems of Western European feudalism included both natural and man-made ones. Lack of sanitation and medical knowledge made it possible for plagues to wipe out as much as half of the population. Wars between the feudal lords, or between the kings, often produced devastation of wide areas and tremendous loss of life.

In addition to these problems, the use of serfs produced some of the same problems as had weakened the slave plantations of Rome. Each person on the lord's estate had their own tasks and was never allowed to consider changing their status in life. This frozen society could not easily change its production process or innovate in new ways.

The lords needed to produce enough food, clothing, and shelter for themselves and their retainers, but seldom had the means to focus on producing a surplus. Each serf had a small farm of their own on which they attempted to produce enough food for their own family. To try to take a small surplus a long way to an unknown market was too dangerous.

The focus was therefore self-sufficiency, not production of profitable commercial goods for a market. In order to protect the power of the feudal lords, the ideology produced by the Church said that every present custom and technology was designed by God. Therefore, all change was considered dangerous. Since there were few incentives and many dangers in attempting new methods of production, feudal technology remained at the same low level for many centuries.

There continued to be a high level of inequality under feudalism, although serfs had somewhat greater rights than slaves. From the available historical data, it appears that the wealthiest 1 percent of the Roman population under slavery held perhaps as much as 80 or 90 percent of all wealth. Feudalism was somewhat more decentralized, so many lords and knights held some measure of wealth. In fact, most serfs possessed a small plot of land so long as they fulfilled their duties on the lord's land. The conclusion appears to be that serfdom produced a high level of inequality, but not as high as that of slavery.

The feudal manor was isolated from other economic units and there was little market activity. Since there was almost no use of money or markets, the self-sufficiency of the feudal lord and of the peasants left no room for a lack of aggregate demand to reduce the products of feudalism. The feudal economy suffered declines only from floods, droughts, wars, and epidemics. These disasters often caused devastation to the feudal economy. Since these economic crises were not based on a lack of aggregate demand, however, they did not resemble the modern business cycle.

From British feudalism to capitalism

By the fifteenth century, there were still some countries of the world with clan hunter–gatherer societies, as well as some with slavery as the dominant system. In Western Europe, there was about 10 percent slavery, but the society was mainly feudalism with its serf form of labor.

In England, the fourteenth and fifteenth centuries had seen plagues and wars that had greatly reduced the supply of labor. The feudal lords had to compete in order to attract labor by offering more freedom and less feudal services. The serfs also used armed revolt to further broaden their freedom. The result was a countryside that slowly saw the emergence of a class of farmers who were working to sell their surplus at the market.

As markets emerged for agricultural goods, the free farmers started to plant more and more commercial crops designed for the market. There emerged in the countryside a set of economic relations based on buying and selling goods and services. Some farmers owned their own land, while others were tenants who paid rent, but that did not change their place as commercial farmers in the market economy. This capitalist system of agriculture slowly replaced all of the vestiges of feudalism in the sixteenth, seventeenth, and eighteenth centuries.

Since most farmers, including former serfs, now practiced a commercial agriculture designed to bring goods to the market, they no longer had the food and clothing needed for their families. As they sent their food into the towns, they used that money to buy necessary consumer goods and tools in the cities. This gave new growth to the towns as centers for handicraft and merchant sales to the countryside.

By the mid-eighteenth century, England had transformed itself into a more or less capitalist economy in the countryside, towns, and cities. "Capitalism" is an economy in which a small group of people, known as capitalists, own all of the private business buildings and equipment. Capitalists also purchase the labor time of employees to produce goods and services. These products are sold at a profit in the market.

The new system of capitalist production had a strong incentive for innovation and growth. As a result, there were a large number of new inventions made and applied in the British economy. This stream of inventions and their applications to the English economy in the last half of the eighteenth century and beginning of the nineteenth century was called the Industrial Revolution.

By the end of the eighteenth century, England had a capitalist economy of trade, finance, and the beginnings of industry throughout the country. On this basis, the typical capitalist business cycle emerged. The first recorded modern type of business recession occurred in 1793 in England. This recession not only saw problems in trade and finance; it also saw industrial workers fired for lack of economic demand for their products.

Evolution of capitalism

Why do societies change and witness their economies evolving from one system to another? The above sections traced some of the major examples of evolution and revolution from one society to another. What lessons can be drawn?

In the period of transition from feudalism to capitalism in England in the sixteenth to eighteenth centuries, there was a major change in the economic relationships between the ruling elites and those who labored for them. Under feudalism, serfs had been forced to work a certain number of days per year through the threat of armed force. As their rights increased, they were able to exercise their freedom to change to an economic existence based on market exchange rather than feudal servitude. The increasing use of the market led to an increasing use of money and credit.

Each economic unit changed from self-sufficiency to production of commercial goods and services in order to make a profit in the market. The most prosperous farmers in the countryside, as well as the most prosperous merchants in the cities, soon employed large numbers of wage and salary employees to do the labor for them at certain rates of pay.

The power of the feudal lords declined during this transition because their serfs were able to leave them to become free farmers. The most successful lords managed to change from directors of feudal serfs to managing a collection of tenants on their land. The increasing strength of free farmers and merchants contrasted with the declining strength of the great feudal lords.

The feudal lords and the King made a last effort to protect their dominant status in the English Civil War from 1640 to 1651. The political revolution continued to develop in England until the new classes of farmers and merchants reached dominance by the last half of the eighteenth century.

Once the economic structure of capitalism and an appropriate political structure were in place, technological change was then strongly encouraged by the new system. As a result, the Industrial Revolution was born in England in the last half of the eighteenth century. Ever since then, vast changes have occurred whenever the capitalist system became dominant in a free country. In those countries with colonial rule, however, foreign capitalism brought destruction of native industry and slow growth.

There is no simple roadmap of social change that is made by a supernatural power and can be revealed by a profit. Rather, it is humans who make social change, though we make it under certain conditions of natural environment, technology, and given social, political, and economic institutions.

Often what happens is that advances in technology no longer fit our old, established political and economic institutions. The old institutions begin to cause problems such as extreme inequality and large-scale unemployment. Those who have made enormous profits and wealth from the old institutions try to preserve them. But millions of people become angry over this situation. Sometimes, those angry people are able to change the political and economic institutions to improve their lives. That is what happened, for example, in the 1640s in England or in the 1770s in America. Sometimes, change has resulted from a long, hard political struggle, but without violence and bloodshed.

A brief book presenting in simple language the details of the evolution of human society, including citations to a large number of other books on the subject, is *How Society Makes Itself* by Howard Sherman (2006a).

Three preconditions for business cycles and unemployment

Capitalism has three features that did not exist together in any previous economy. These are pervasive market exchange of all goods and services, use of money or credit in almost all exchanges, and the profit motive for production with the wage system for labor.

Remember that prehistoric clans had almost no market exchange, but only collective production and consumption for the whole clan. Under Greek and Roman slavery, there was long-distance trade with the use of money and credit, but about 95 percent of production was on plantations using slaves to produce every good and service needed on the plantation, with relatively small amounts of surplus sold to the cities. Similarly, feudalism in England produced about 95 percent of its goods and services on estates of the feudal lords. Almost all of the estate's production was consumed on the estate. There was little or no surplus, with only infrequent market fairs to sell a few items. The estate exchanged things among its members, but none of these transactions involved money. The estate seldom had any transaction with other estates.

Under modern capitalism, on the contrary, almost every agricultural and industrial enterprise produces goods and services for the market. Almost all exchange in modern capitalism is done with the use of paper money or credit in some kind of market. Money, such as pieces of paper guaranteed by the government, or credit, such as an IOU, is exchanged for goods and services at a given price.

Goods and services are seldom bartered from one person to another in this system. Rather, a price is set and money or credit is exchanged for goods or services. The economy works at full speed only if all of the goods and services on the market are bought for money or credit. If they are not bought, then production and investment decline.

Unlike a feudal estate that concentrates on survival by what it produces, a modern capitalist enterprise concentrates on production and exchange for money in order to make a profit. If there is insufficient money or credit offered for the goods and services of an enterprise, then the enterprise has less profit expectations for future sales of products. Therefore, it reduces its production and fires some employees. As less wages and salaries are paid, there is still less demand for goods and services. Thus begins every economic contraction under capitalism.

Use of market exchange, money, and the profit motive for production and hiring are the preconditions for the modern business cycle. These three preconditions explain why the cycle of boom and bust does not occur before capitalism, but does occur in every capitalist system.

Conclusions on the business cycle

Three of the main economic revolutions in human history were: the Neolithic Revolution that ended the prehistoric hunter-gather clans; the fall of the Roman Empire that ended the dominance of the slave system; and the English Revolution of the 1640s that ended feudalism and established capitalism in England. Each of these revolutions came as the result of long-run evolutionary trends in the society at that time. The resulting revolution ended the previous economic and political institutions and set up new ones. The present capitalist economic system ended feudal economic restrictions and set the stage for strong economic growth, but it also resulted in trends toward increased inequality as well as cycles of boom and bust.

Conclusions on inequality and capitalism

How did capitalism arise and why does it create inequality? Under slavery, workers are bought and sold. Under feudalism, they must work for a lord and are bound to the land. These societies had extremely unequal income. They had no incentives to work other than the threat of violence. Under feudalism, there were the beginnings of independent business, but there were heavy restrictions.

These conditions eventually led to a series of revolutions that produced capitalism. Capitalists do not buy and sell workers, nor are the workers tied to the land. Because of the lack of restrictions on labor and enterprise, capitalist economic growth was rapid.

The capitalist system, however, still maintains a high degree of inequality and a cycle of boom and bust. The inequality emerges due to relatively few people controlling all of the economy, while millions of people must accept whatever wages are offered. This extreme inequality leads to a lack of economic demand and large-scale unemployment in the form of recessions and depressions.

Appendix 1.1

Revolutions and democracy

The evolution from feudalism to capitalism did not take place peacefully. There was resistance by the feudal lords to the capitalist economic system and to the democratic political system. This chapter has explained the bumpy road to capitalism. It is also important, however, to see the role that violent revolutions played in obtaining political democracy.

Violent revolutions for democracy

Here are the most famous violent revolutions in favor of democracy: the English Revolution of 1640, the American Revolution of 1776, the French Revolution of 1789, the Russian Revolution of February 1917, and the Chinese Revolution of 1911. These revolutions were all necessary because the country was ruled by a king or a dictator who would not grant democracy without a struggle. Of course, the American Revolution was not only anti-monarchism, but was also anti-colonial rule of England.

Peaceful democratic revolutions

All of the above revolutions were violent attempts to change from kings or dictators to democracy. Where democracy exists, however, a peaceful revolution can drastically improve the quality of democracy, as well as the quality of economic life. In the United States, there has been a high level of democracy for a long time, but there have been grave limitations to democracy due to the power of accumulated wealth in the hands of a few.

In the Great Depression, during 1929 to 1938, there was a peaceful revolution by Franklin Roosevelt and the Democratic Party. It limited the power of the wealthy in many respects and helped the average person in many areas. For example, it established Social Security to give a minimum income to the elderly. It also established minimum wages for workers, as well as maximum hours of work. That revolutionary struggle helped to reduce inequality and helped the economy to recover from the Great Depression.

In 2016, Senator Sanders tried to make a revolution to reduce inequality, reduce unemployment, and create a country with far more equality and full employment. The evidence to be given in this book will support the thesis that a peaceful democratic revolution could help reduce economic inequality, reduce political inequality, and ensure full employment.

2

EVOLUTION OF INEQUALITY AND UNEMPLOYMENT IN AMERICA

This chapter is a brief walk through American history to explain how inequality and unemployment developed. Why focus on America? America is currently the largest and richest country in the global economy, so it has the largest single effect on the global economy.

Similarly, feudalism was examined only in England because English development had the greatest effect on early America. Why, however, not discuss the experience of other countries during each stage of their development, including the relation of inequality to unemployment in each sector of the economy? If all other countries, such as China, India, African countries, and Latin American countries, are included in this book in the issue raised in each chapter, then there would not be one book, but at least 19 or 20 large volumes.

To keep this book within bounds, each issue will be discussed only in terms of its relation to inequality and unemployment in America. Other scholars are encouraged to do similar volumes on all the other countries of the world, plus one on inequality and unemployment in the global economy as a whole. It is worth noting that Thomas Piketty (2015) did do some of this in one large volume on inequality.

Definitions

Here are some brief definitions, each of which will be discussed in depth in later chapters.

"Income" means the amount of money received in a given time period, such as a month or a year.

"Wealth" is the total money and other assets held by a person at a given time, such as January 1, 2016.

"Income inequality" represents the difference in average income between two groups.

"Wealth inequality" reflects the difference in average wealth between two groups.

"Conservative economics" is defined as: There is no such thing as economic evolution; capitalism has always existed in society and always will exist; a higher level of income inequality ensures a higher economic growth rate; capitalism never generates recessions, since all of them are caused by external shocks, such as government mistakes; and following the interests of the wealthiest 1 percent is in the economic interest of everyone.

"Progressive economics" is defined as: Socioeconomic evolution exists; capitalism evolved from the previous economic system and is likely to evolve into a new economic system; reducing inequality leads to higher economic growth; the institutions of capitalism cause recessions and unemployment; and following the interests of most of the people leads to the best economic outcome.

"Democratic revolution" is defined to mean a switch of power from the wealthiest 1 percent to the rest of the American people.

Economic growth in America

As capitalism slowly spread over Western Europe and then the rest of the world, the economic cycle of boom and bust also spread around the world. America began to have banking and trade problems on the East Coast by 1800. From 1800 to the Civil War in 1860 to 1865, British trade and industry was clearly dominant over American trade and industry. British finance was even more dominant over American finance. Before the 1870s, when Americans wanted a loan, they asked a London bank. When Americans wanted a piece of heavy equipment, they asked a British firm.

In the first half of the nineteenth century, there was no internal business cycle in America because most of the country was agricultural. East Coast cities had a small amount of trade and finance, but little industry until the 1850s. Therefore, the four or five downturns from 1800 to 1850 were mostly caused by downturns in the British economy, which led to a lack of markets for American goods that were usually sold overseas. There were also some monetary panics caused when weak and unregulated American banks failed. The biggest panic was in 1837, leading to a considerable economic downturn, mainly on the East Coast.

After the Civil War, American industry consolidated into larger and more powerful corporations. These large corporations spread all over the country, especially after the railroad and the telegraph managed to extend their lines all the way across the country in the 1870s. Since slavery had been defeated, the dominant capitalist system spread and developed its industry rapidly.

The American class relationships changed to a large degree from 1870 to 1900. Outside of the slave South, in 1800 over 90 percent of the people worked in agriculture. Most farms belonged to a single farm family. Most farms were self-sufficient. Often, the men hunted wild animals for meat, while the women did the farming, kept the house weatherproof, made the meals and minded the children, and also made all of the clothing.

By 1870, farmers were still at least 65 percent of the labor force. Their numbers, however, were falling rapidly as a share of the working population. Farmers were having a more difficult time earning a decent living because of increased competition due to technological progress. At the same time, as the cities grew, there were more interesting things to do there, so the children of farmers began to emigrate to the cities. As the prices of farm products fell, it also became more difficult for farmers to make their debt payments to the banks. Many of them therefore went to the cities and became factory workers. The result was that farmers dropped to 35 percent of the labor force by 1900.

In addition, immigration into America reached its highest yearly totals from 1870 to 1900. The largest part of the population by 1900 was now composed of industrial workers. Most were men, but about 20 percent of women had paid jobs.

In the late nineteenth century, American industry became larger than British industry. Accordingly, for some time after the Civil War, Great Britain and America each initiated business cycle downturns at various times. The business cycle of each country affected the other one. It was only after the First World War (1914 to 1918) that American industry became dominant. Then American economic ups and downs always started before British ups and downs.

The business cycle of boom and bust has remained a persistent feature of the American economy. From 1854 to 2009, there were 33 recessions in America, according to the National Bureau of Economic Research (NBER) (www.nber.org/cycles/cyclesmain.html).

Most of these recessions were fairly small, around 5 percent to 8 percent contractions. There were, however, four large depressions in American history: they began in 1873, 1893, 1929, and 2007. Each depression lasted several years, included a financial crisis, and had a weak recovery afterwards.

The era of the Great Depression

Business cycles in every era of American history since the 1850s have had the same basic pattern, since they all are based on the same fundamental institutions of industrial capitalism. Yet every era also has somewhat different characteristics. Our story begins after the First World War, in the period known as the interwar era, or the era of the Great Depression. In the Great Depression, the problem spread from country to country until the whole world was in depression, except for the centrally planned Soviet economy.

Then came the Second World War, which ended the Great Depression through enormous military spending by the American government. The next era, 1945 to 1970, was a time of American domination around the world and a Golden Age for the American economy in a number of ways. The last era, 1970 to 2009, was a time of increasing globalization, with a rapid improvement in transportation and communication in the global economy, but increasing problems in many national economies.

The 1920s, often called the roaring twenties to reflect all the luxury had by the elite, was mostly a period of economic growth, with only short and fairly mild recessions. Yet under that facade, there were growing problems. Income distribution became more and more unequal, and reached the highest point of inequality in 1929.

From 1927 to 1929, profits did well and the stock market went crazy with delight in a titanic bubble of irrationally high stock prices. Both consumers and firms borrowed more and more money to take advantage of the good times. The great increase in debt resulted in a more fragile financial system.

In mid-1929, aggregate profits began to decline. Then the stock market started to fall, and fell by 83 percent by early 1933. One-quarter of the labor force was totally unemployed at that time. Another 50 percent of workers were reduced to part-time jobs. The government refused to help the unemployed, and private charities soon ran out of money. More and more banks failed, until Franklin Roosevelt (in 1933) gave them all a holiday. In other words, he closed all the banks until they were certified to be safe. Only the strong ones were allowed to reopen under close supervision. The Glass-Steagall Act separated investment banks from depositor-based banks. In this way, the investment banks were allowed to take considerable risks, but the commercial banks were not allowed to take investment risks. The Federal Deposit Insurance Corporation (FDIC) was created to guarantee all deposits up to a certain amount.

The Democrats had a huge majority in Congress. They enacted many basic new laws. The Works Projects Administration (WPA) gave jobs to about 4 million people a year. The Roosevelt Administration and the Democrats in Congress enacted laws creating Social Security, Minimum Wages, Maximum Hours, and Unemployment Compensation.

In spite of some stimulus, recovery was slow, with unemployment finally dropping to 12 percent by 1937. Then Roosevelt was convinced by conservative economists to reduce government spending. The result was a new contraction in 1938, which took demand and production down and left 18 percent unemployed. The country was saved only by the all-out spending of the Second World War. Federal spending rose to 40 percent of the Gross Domestic Product (GDP) and unemployment fell to 1 percent.

The Golden Age of American capitalism, 1945 to 1970

America's economy dominated the world from 1945 to 1970. It was a Golden Age for American capitalism. It had the following 10 positive features:

1. The rate of growth per year of the real GDP from 1945 to 1970 was 4.4 percent.
2. America emerged from the Second World War as a victor and the only major industrial country that did not suffer from the war on its own territory. Therefore, in 1950, America actually produced more than the rest of the world combined.

3. In 1950, America also had the majority of all exports in the world. America had a surplus in foreign trade throughout the Golden Age.
4. With the increased income earned from abroad, American banks and corporations lent money to foreign banks and corporations. America thus became the world's largest creditor country.
5. Trade unions continued to gain as a percentage of the labor force until 1955. After that, they continued to increase in numbers, although their percentage of the labor force started to decline.
6. The distribution of income among all individuals in America grew more equal. Moreover, the percentage of national income going to employees, as opposed to capitalist owners, rose somewhat.
7. The business cycle contractions of this era were relatively brief and shallow.
8. The educational level rose throughout the entire era. There was a dramatic acceleration of both high school graduation rates and the attainment of bachelor's degrees from college. The higher education levels were clearly one reason for the increased economic growth. Another was the large influx of highly trained people from Europe during this era.
9. Real wages rose every year in spite of the mild cyclical contractions.
10. Profits had a moderate growth rate throughout this era. This is one reason that employers were willing to give reasonable wage increases, which reflected a considerable part of the increases in productivity.

The Age of Globalization, 1970 to the present (2017)

The third economic era is called the Age of Globalization. Globalization was greatly aided by the improvement in transportation and communication that is now often instantaneous around the globe.

Besides the technical advances, globalization also meant that the entire globe became a unified market in which all the giant corporations were able to make a profit. These new global corporations now owned subsidiaries in every major city around the world.

Many of the positive features of the American economy in the Golden Age of 1945 to 1970 ended. Some individual American corporations were greatly helped by globalization, but the country as a whole found that many of the favorable trends were reversed.

The following 10 points summarize the new trends in the Age of Globalization:

1. The economic growth rate of America was reduced from 4.4 percent in 1945 to 1970 down to 3.4 percent in 1970 to 2009. This rate of growth was measured in terms of real GDP per year.
2. In the period from 1970 to 2009, many countries grew faster than America. These were economies that had been devastated by the Second World War,

but had slowly recovered during the 1950s and then had accelerated growth in the 1960s. While America's economy continued to grow at a respectable rate of 3.4 percent per year, it became much weaker relative to other economies.

3. The foreign trade of those countries that were now growing rapidly and competing with America also had their exports grow more rapidly than America. Since America continued to buy a large amount of imports, but had lost some of its export markets to other countries, the trade position of America changed. In the Golden Age, it had a large trade surplus. America now had a growing trade deficit that became the largest in the world.

4. When America had to pay for its deficit, it borrowed money from abroad. All of that borrowing made America the largest debtor country in the world.

5. American trade unions had a decreasing percentage of the whole labor force during this period.

6. On some measures of inequality, the distribution of income among all individuals in America became more unequal from 1970 to the present. Moreover, the percentage of all national income going to employees fell after 1980, while the percentage of income going to all owners of capital and other property rose after 1980 to the present. Wealth from profits, interest, and rent rose dramatically in this period, while wages and salaries stagnated. Why did income from property (profit, interest, and rent) rise so dramatically after 1980? One important reason, especially in Europe, was the shift in assets from the public sector to the private sector, called privatization (see Piketty, 2014). Among the causes of this shift of assets was the Cold War. During the Cold War, there was a pervasive effort to convince the public and political leaders that all public ownership is bad and all private ownership is good.

7. The business cycle contractions of this era became somewhat longer and deeper than in the previous Golden Age. The end result of this trend was the devastating Great Recession of 2007 to 2009 and the financial crisis of 2008.

8. From the 1970s to the present, the price of a college education has risen enormously. Students are having more and more difficulty in financing their education. There is more of a need to borrow in the form of student loans, whose total has risen astronomically and whose interest rates are higher than the average interest rate in America. As a result, the percentage of people going to college has been dropping.

9. The real wages per worker increased to a peak in the 1970s. Since then, however, the real wage has stagnated in the entire era and is about the same as it was in the mid-1970s. Since wages and salaries have not risen over all, while production of consumer goods and services has risen since the 1970s, the result has been a lack of demand for aggregate consumer goods and services. This lack of demand has been partly met by a higher use of consumer credit, but there is still a gap between the long-run rise of production and the long-run rise of demand.

10. Although aggregate profits have risen somewhat in the long run during this era, the increase has been disrupted by the business cycle. In each expansion of this era, profits have risen rapidly, but in each contraction of this era profits have fallen rapidly. This rise and fall was spectacular during the Bush cycle of 2001 to 2009.

The effect of different eras on inequality

Up to this point, the chapter has explained the history of inequality and unemployment in America. It has focused on the major differences of the two eras, the Golden Age and the Age of Globalization, that will be discussed later in this book. With that information as the background, the chapter now turns to specific questions about inequality and unemployment in American history.

What has been the effect of different eras on inequality?

In the first half of the nineteenth century, most American families were farmers, many of whom were self-sufficient. Since few farm products were brought to the market, the less developed American economy generated no cycles, but was affected by British cycles. In that era, there were only a few rich bankers and merchants on the East Coast. Therefore, many European travelers commented on the high degree of equality in income and wealth in much of America.

In the last half of the nineteenth century, there was rapid growth of industry in America, producing a small class of rich capital owners, called the robber barons for their rapacious practices. There was a rapidly growing class of employees, most of whom were poorly paid. The numbers of independent farmers slowly decreased and fell as a percentage of the population. Therefore, even when slavery ended in the South, the degree of inequality in America grew rapidly.

In the tough times surrounding the deep depressions of the 1870s and the 1890s, there was strife between the employees and the elite robber barons in several industries, including the railroads and the mines. This conflict varied from large strikes to violent confrontations with the police and army. Both the police and army were highly influenced at this time by the robber barons.

By 1900, industrial workers were becoming the largest class, while independent farmers steadily declined in numbers. In the industrial sector, concentration of economic power continued to increase. Therefore, in the 1920s, income and wealth inequality continued to grow. Inequality hit a peak in 1929, followed by the Great Depression.

During the Great Depression, aggregate profits went below zero for a couple of years, so inequality of income decreased in percentage terms. Of course, if the income of a billionaire declined from $5 billion a year to $4 billion a year, the billionaire could still live at the same standard of living. If a worker's income declined from $50,000 a year to $40,000 a year, the living standard of that family would drastically decline.

In the Second World War, all wages and prices were controlled, so the degree of inequality was frozen by the government. In the 1950s and 1960s, the Golden

Age of American capitalism, there was an enormous increase in world demand for American products. This increased demand for products resulted in rising American wages and salaries. This led to declining inequality.

By 1970, the rest of the world began to catch up to America, and the Age of Globalization began. Wages and salaries stagnated, while profits soared. This was partly due to global competition, but also to weaker American unions facing stronger global corporations. Therefore, there has been rising inequality since the 1970s. Beyond the economic factors, the increased wealth was used to affect political power, resulting in policies that helped increase the wealth of the wealthiest 1 percent of individuals and the giant corporations.

What was the effect of the Golden Age on inequality?

It is impossible to overemphasize the importance of the structural shifts in the American economy that occurred in the 1970s from the old era, called the Golden Age, to the new era, called the Age of Globalization. The key to understanding the shift is the fact that the Golden Age from 1945 to 1970 resulted from unique historical circumstances. The Second World War devastated most of the major economies of the earth. America, however, emerged from the war stronger than ever before.

For a considerable time, the American economy was larger than the rest of the world economy combined, both in production and trade. This situation changed slowly. From 1945 to 1970, America was the largest creditor nation and also had the largest trade surplus in the world. Not surprisingly, this meant that America exerted political dominance over the rest of the world, except for the Soviet Union and its subordinate countries.

The political and economic dominance of America over much of the world created a flow of demand for American goods and services, a relatively high rate of economic growth, and weaker recessions.

The universities and government were dominated by a weak form of Keynesianism. It claimed that a small stimulus would always end unemployment and provide America with a perfectly functioning capitalist economy. That Keynesianism in government was supported by a strong trade union movement.

Trade unions had become strong during the Great Depression with the help of the progressive Roosevelt Administration. They continued to grow during the full employment of the Second World War. They continued to have a large degree of political power during the 1950s and 1960s.

The big corporations enjoyed good profits and production, yet their power was restricted by strong labor unions and a government that was friendly to labor. Tax rates on corporations and the wealthiest 1 percent remained high.

What made the Golden Age different from most of American history was that it was an age of peace, but also a time of unusual American dominance. It was that dominance that led to a prosperous economy with falling inequality.

The rising equality was seized by many conservative economists to prove that mature capitalism would now continue to have a higher degree of equality in the future. Instead of continuing high growth and more equality, what happened was more rapid globalization, which led to more recessions and greater inequality.

What was the effect of the Age of Globalization on inequality?

The 1970s proved to be a transitional period between the Golden Age of the 1950s and 1960s and the Age of Globalization from 1980 to the present. There were three major changes in the structure of American capitalism in the 1970s.

First, the whole globe, including America, became far more integrated. Second, this integration forced the previously dominant American economy to use every means against its competitors and against its own labor force, a type of warfare by the wealthiest 1 percent and the giant corporations, which can only be called class warfare. Third, these facts led to an ideological change from a weak Keynesian view and practice to a conservative view and practice as the dominant paradigm in both universities and government.

What exactly is meant by a process of strong integration in the global economy? What happened is that the giant corporations spread to every nook and cranny of the world economy. They were then able to control many aspects of each country's economy.

Capital can move anyplace in the global economy, but it is difficult for labor to move. This global integration has brought about more competition between labor and less power for labor, both in the poorer countries with lower wages and in the richer countries with falling wages. This weakness of labor is one of the direct causes of growing inequality of income and wealth.

As a result, the actual process of globalization has decreased the power of labor while greatly increasing the power of the largest capitalist corporations. This growing disparity is the most important factor underlying the continued increase of inequality in the Age of Globalization.

Growing inequality between labor and capital, as well as between rich and poor, has created ferocious class warfare in many countries. Extensive corporate power has affected the control of the media, bringing about pervasive biases in how the news is presented and reported. Another example of corporate influence is the funding of research projects in the universities with the goal of making a profit for some corporation.

One ideological fact of the 1970s was the undermining of the weak Keynesian view and its replacement in most universities and governments by conservative pro-corporate economics. Thus, the new institutions of global corporate capitalism in an integrated global economy are fully supported by most economists. They are using outdated views no longer applicable in the modern world, but this old theology is still helpful to the wealthy.

Approaches to the problem of rising economic inequality and instability

This book focuses on the rising inequality and rising instability of the American economy in the Age of Globalization from the 1970s to the present. The global economy will also enter into the picture, as will the devastating effects of the Great Recession and its financial crisis.

The background for the analysis relies heavily on the data of the Nobel laureate Joseph Stiglitz (2012, 2015a), as well as Thomas Piketty (2015). Most of the statistical analyses rely on the author's own data, in order to make concrete the points about inequality and instability in the Age of Globalization. It is impossible to name all of the progressive writers who have brought the facts about globalization into a unified theoretical explanation. The best book from the progressive view on the evolution of the American economic structure in recent decades is *Contours of Descent* by Robert Pollin (2003).

3

STORM OVER ECONOMICS

There is an ongoing war within the economics profession concerning inequality and unemployment. Most people in America have worked for stagnant wages or salaries for decades. They also live in fear of losing their jobs because the economy has suffered recurring cyclical unemployment. The rate of unemployment during the Great Recession and financial crisis of 2007 to 2009 was the highest since the Great Depression. This situation has not improved, with wages remaining stagnant, which has led to increasing anger among millions of Americans.

Economists have been at war since about 1800 over these basic problems. It is often said the politicians could easily solve the problem if they were just willing to make a reasonable compromise. One side of the argument reflects the interests of the wealthiest 1 percent, while the other side represents the interests of the other 99 percent of Americans. Therefore, there is no easy compromise.

Three related conflicts may now be introduced: inequality versus equality, cyclical unemployment versus full employment, and plutocracy versus democracy.

Inequality versus equality

"Inequality," as used here, means the unequal distribution of income and wealth among different groups in America. The wealthiest 1 percent holds 40 percent of all the wealth. The lower half on the income distribution ladder only holds 2 percent of all the wealth. The poorest 15 percent of the population live at or below the poverty line.

Rising inequality has been a major cause of every recession or depression since 1980. A recession is defined as a contraction of the economy. Every new recession has led to a rapid increase in inequality of income in the next expansion.

Most conservative economists believe that a high level of inequality is necessary for any well-functioning economy. Progressive economists believe that it is possible to eliminate all extreme inequality and continue to eliminate most inequality over time.

How can the American economy move toward far greater equality than at present? One cause of inequality is the enormous profits of many large corporations, such as the private health insurance companies. Universal public healthcare as a right of every American, therefore, would end one source of inequality. Expensive tuitions and high costs of education, which have led to onerous student debts, has been another source of inequality. This could be ended by free tuition at all educational levels. Another big source of inequality has been the huge profits and massive bailouts of the financial system.

Cyclical unemployment versus full employment

Cyclical unemployment arises from the business cycle of boom and bust in America. There have been 37 cycles of boom and bust in America since 1800. "The business cycle of boom and bust" is defined to mean an expansion of business in the capitalist economic system, followed by a contraction. The contraction is called a "recession" when it is of an average amplitude and duration; it is called a "depression" when there is a huge decline in production and employment over a considerable period.

Most conservative economists argue that inequality is necessary to give incentives for investment and work that makes the American capitalist system great. They also maintain that the business cycle of boom and bust is found in every economy because it results from outside forces, such as government mistakes. Therefore, nothing should be done by government about a high level of inequality during an expansion or a high level of unemployment in a recession. The best policy, according to the conservative view, is to cut back on all government spending for the economy because most of it is harmful and creates more inequality and recession.

The view of progressive economists is that inequality is created by the economic and political institutions of capitalism. They also argue that the business cycle of boom and bust is created by the same basic institutions of our present economic system. It follows that enough change in the economic institutions and political policies of the government can get rid of most inequality. In addition, enough institutional change can put an end to all unemployment (see Chapter 15).

Plutocracy versus democracy

This book will focus on the twin economic problems of inequality and unemployment, but one cannot understand economic problems without a clear understanding of political and class relationships. America today is undergoing a severe clash between the political power of the wealthiest 1 percent, known as the rule of the plutocracy, and the political power of all the people, known as democracy.

Increasing inequality is especially dangerous to a democracy because it allows a small group of wealthy people to exert enormous control over the government. What is needed is a democratic revolution that elects a President and Congress dedicated to ending extreme inequality and getting rid of involuntary unemployment. Such a revolution would still leave a mostly capitalist economy. It would, however, be a step forward toward an economy that is democratically run plus a political system where everyone has equal power.

Franklin Roosevelt's activist approach

The Great Depression was a period of immense human suffering, in which production in 1938 was less than it was in 1929. Because the issues were similar to today in many ways, the major themes of this book were stated by Franklin Roosevelt in his acceptance speech for the presidential nomination at the Democratic National Convention in 1932 (see Brands, 2008).

President-to-be Roosevelt pointed out how the increasing inequality of income and wealth in the 1920s led to the horrors of the Great Depression, including vast amounts of poverty and unemployed people. He explained how the Great Depression was characterized by a lack of demand in every area of the economy, from overflowing used car lots to mountains of potatoes that were eventually set on fire because they could not be sold.

The rising inequality, especially in the expansion of 1927 to 1929, meant that profits were zooming upward, but wages and salaries remained stagnant. Wages and salaries are the main component of consumer demand. This lack of expansion in wages and salaries led to restricted demand for automobiles, housing, or even pianos. Since employees could not purchase the rising flood of goods and services produced, business profits plunged. Therefore, companies fired millions and millions of employees who became an enormous army of the unemployed. It was an army with no income and very little money.

Roosevelt pointed out that there was no relief money for the unemployed because the Hoover Administration claimed it was bad policy for the government to give money to the unemployed as this made them dependent on the government. Therefore, over 25 percent of the American people who were unemployed simply had no money. If one has no money, then one cannot buy goods and services. As more workers were fired, demand dropped even further.

Among other policies, Roosevelt highlighted how government needed to provide productive jobs for the unemployed. He said if the government gave jobs to the unemployed, the Republicans would call it socialism, but something had to be done no matter what the Republicans would say. Any policy to do something was better than the Republican policy of doing nothing. The Republicans believed the economy would eventually recover by itself.

Roosevelt's speech sounds remarkably modern and somewhat applicable to the present American situation. Unfortunately, the reason why it sounds so up to date is that although the Roosevelt Administration did solve some of the problems of the Great Depression, some of the economy's most basic problems still remain. Roosevelt considered but was not able to enact national healthcare. Roosevelt changed a few institutions to make a future financial crisis less likely, but did not change any of the basic institutions that create financial crises, as well as recessions and depressions. The Roosevelt Administration and its program, called the New Deal, were successful to some degree in reducing the misery of Americans during the Great Depression.

Bernie Sanders' activist approach

Just as Franklin Roosevelt actively fought against unemployment in the 1930s, Senator Bernie Sanders spoke during the 2016 presidential campaign for revolutionary improvements in the economic system. Senator Sanders' major goals were:

1. Achieve a revolutionary reduction in the inequality of wealth and income.
2. A universal public healthcare system for everyone.
3. Free tuition for qualified students at public colleges and universities.
4. A large increase in the minimum wage.
5. Bring all the roads and bridges of America up to a reasonable level of safety—a project that would hire millions of people.
6. All financial and non-financial corporations that are "too large to fail," because their collapse would each cause the collapse of a considerable part of the economy, should be broken into a number of pieces.

Senator Sanders advocated a peaceful "political revolution" at the ballot box in order to overthrow the rule of the wealthiest 1 percent over the economy and the political sphere.

The long war in economics

In the nineteenth century, the classical economists considered that a large degree of inequality was necessary to provide incentives for the wealthy to invest in the economy. They also argued that lack of demand did not produce economic crises and unemployment, but that these were caused by outside forces, such as floods or droughts.

In the nineteenth century, on the other side, were the socialists, from the utopians to Karl Marx. They argued that increasing inequality is caused by the capitalist economic system. This extreme inequality causes not only long-run poverty for the poor and insecurity for the middle class, but also lower rates of economic growth and sometimes recessions or depressions. Therefore, the economy must be changed.

Mild socialists called for reforms to reduce some inequality and to help stabilize the system by stimulus to the economy. Economists with stronger socialist views argued that capitalism always produces extreme inequality and recessions or depressions. Therefore, it is necessary to end much of the capitalist system and replace it with a more democratic economy.

In the twentieth century, the same arguments were repeated with new twists and turns. Neoclassical economists convinced most people that government should do nothing about either extreme inequality or mass unemployment. On the other side, many progressive movements, including the socialists, the followers of Henry George, Thorstein Veblen, and the followers of John Maynard Keynes worked hard for reforms to reduce inequality and end recessions and depressions. Some of these economists also believed that the entire economic system needed to be replaced.

In the progressive view, the most important economist in the twentieth century was John Maynard Keynes. Before Keynes, the only economics taught in universities was that of individual economic decisions. Keynes invented a new kind of economics that deals with the whole economy. All universities now teach both types of economics.

Keynes wrote his most famous book, *The General Theory of Employment, Interest, and Money*, in 1936. He argued that the basic problem of the Great Depression was the lack of demand for all goods and services. Private enterprise could not solve the problem because if there is a lack of demand, they will not invest. Therefore, it was necessary to save the system by a large government stimulus, including vast public works projects.

From 1936 to 1946, there was intensive warfare between liberal Keynesians and conservative neoclassical economists. By 1946 in America, the Keynesians were dominant in both academia and the government. These were, however, weak Keynesians who wanted only a small amount of money to combat recessions, followed by a return to all of the assumptions and practices of neoclassical economics. For this reason, they were rejected by many left-wing economists, including an important follower of Keynes, the economist Joan Robinson, who called these weak Keynesians "bastard Keynesians."

The weak Keynesians ruled economics from 1945 to the 1970s in America. In the 1970s, conservative economists took advantage of the weakness of many of their arguments and took over the dominant position in economics up to the present. The conservative economists were strongly supported by the wealthiest 1 percent and the giant corporations. Trade unions tended to support the liberal Keynesian view, but their strength was being reduced relative to the giant corporations and their available money was always a tiny fraction of corporate money.

In the twenty-first century, conservative economists were shaken for a short time by the advent of the Great Recession and financial crisis of 2007 to 2009. In addition to progressive writers on the left, who had long been writing excellent studies on inequality and instability, new voices emerged from the mainstream economists.

Many new liberal Keynesians made themselves heard. Among these, Paul Krugman was successful with his book *End This Depression Now!* (2012) and his newspaper columns in attracting large numbers of people to a message that the aggregate demand in the economy needed government stimulus, and that conservatives' worry of the deficit and inflation were unfounded in the current economic situation.

There also emerged an excellent series of studies by Joseph Stiglitz (2012, 2015a, 2015b) on the inequality of income, wealth, and opportunity in America. His work is used as part of the base and framework for this book. What is added here is the cyclical pattern of inequality, which expands greatly the understanding of the inequality problem and the necessary cure.

There are also many other excellent, progressive economists who have produced outstanding related work in previous years. The strong Keynesian view is in the *Journal of Post Keynesian Economics*. The institutionalist view is in the *Journal of Economic Issues*. The Marxist, feminist, and other radical views are in the *Review of Radical Political Economics*.

Inequality not only plays a vital role in causing recessions in the short run, but it also results in long-term trends that lead to depressions. Economic inequality is an important source of human misery for most people. Some groups, such as the wealthiest 1 percent, gain from economic inequality.

One cannot fully understand the role of inequality without seeing it inside the framework of the cycles of boom and bust, and the cyclical unemployment that is created by it.

The basic difference

The theories and lives of the most famous economists are detailed in clear, well-written prose in *The History of Economic Thought* by E.K. Hunt (2015). A brief and most amusing book on the history of economic thought is *The Worldly Philosophers* by Robert Heilbroner (1953).

Using these two books, what are the views of conservative and progressive economist on the two issues of inequality and instability? Three great conservative economists are David Ricardo, Alfred Marshall, and Milton Friedman. They differ on many points, use different methods, and use different terminology. Nevertheless, they do agree on two important points.

First, these three conservative economists agree that economic inequality results from differences in the productivity of worker. The differences in productivity reflect the fact that some people are smarter than others and that they work harder than others; therefore, any inequality under the capitalist market system is a just reflection of ability. Second, they also agree that the capitalist economic system does not produce business cycle contractions; rather, all of the economic contractions under this system result from outside forces, such as bad weather or government mistakes.

The books by Hunt and Heilbroner describe, among others, three great progressive economists: Karl Marx, Thorstein Veblen, and John Maynard Keynes. These three have extremely different economic theories in certain respects. Nevertheless, they do agree on two important points.

First, these three progressive economists agree that economic inequality is a result of the economic system of capitalism. Second, they also agree that inequality is one cause of a lack of aggregate demand, and that the lack of aggregate demand is the basic cause of recessions and depressions.

These two issues constitute two of the basic differences between conservative and progressive economists.

4

INEQUALITY AND THE NORMAL OPERATION OF AMERICAN CAPITALISM

Before looking at inequality in America, one must understand the normal workings of American business.

The basic institutions of capitalism are no more and no less than human relationships. For example, economists speak of the relation between capital and labor, but labor is simply the millions of human beings who are employed, while capital refers to the ownership of buildings and equipment by a small number of people. At any given time, there is a certain degree of strength on either side, causing one group to have power over the other.

The wealthiest 1 percent get their political power from their wealth, most of which comes from profit. All other groups in the income pyramid have wages and salaries as the majority of their income. This relationship between employees and capitalist owners is the key dynamic in our economic system.

The resulting inequality of income leads to an even greater inequality of wealth. The reason is that only the wealthy have an excess of earnings beyond their consumption so that they can accumulate large amounts of wealth.

Besides the purely economic reasons given above, inequality of income and wealth also depends on certain types of discrimination embedded in capitalism. These include: discrimination against the poor in both the economic and justice system; discrimination based on gender, which produces lower wages or salaries and less wealth for women; discrimination by race and ethnicity, such as that used against African and Latino Americans; and discrimination by religion, such as the prejudice against Catholics, Jews, and Muslims.

In addition to the inequality of various groups of individuals, there is also inequality among businesses. There are millions of small, unincorporated businesses; hundreds of thousands of small corporations; many thousands of medium-size corporations; and a few giant corporations. In each industry, there are generally only three or four large corporations producing the majority of all sales. Moreover, these three or four corporations are usually owned by even bigger corporations. Only the largest corporations have extensive holdings around the world. The top 100 global corporations control the global economy.

The power relationships between human beings and between different sized businesses are expressed by economists as "supply" and "demand." For example, the demand for automobiles depends on how much money flows into wages and salaries. In this chapter, we are not dealing with the demand for individual products, such as bicycles or automobiles, but rather problems that afflict the entire economy. For example, why does the ratio of profits to wages and salaries in the whole American economy rise or fall? Why does the total, or aggregate, demand for all the products in America sometimes fall short of the flood of products coming into the market?

Effective demand

The term "effective demand" was developed by liberal Keynesians in the 1930s as a weapon in the war against conservative economists. The best single modern statement of this Keynesian view is in *End This Depression Now!* by Paul Krugman (2012), a clear and well-written book. Suppose two men are standing in an automobile sales room looking with desire at a Mercedes. The rich man is able to spend the money to buy the car. He drives away in a cloud of dust, leaving the poor man feeling sorry he cannot buy the car. Effective demand means there is both the desire and the money to buy the aggregate supply of all goods and services. Progressive economists argue that inequality leads to a lack of effective demand.

Two views of aggregate supply and demand

By 1800, capitalism was firmly established in England and was successful in producing the Industrial Revolution. Conservative economists believed the rapid growth of capitalist production would go on forever. In their view, capitalism ensured there would always be enough effective demand to buy the entire supply of goods and services. This assumes there is no government interference or destructive natural disaster.

Until the 1930s, almost all academic economists agreed that aggregate demand was not a problem. They believed various problems outside of the economy were causing the depression, such as the Dust Bowl in Oklahoma and mistakes made by the Federal Reserve. Only economists outside of the universities were saying that demand is important, such as Karl Marx and other socialists. In 1936, John Maynard Keynes wrote *The General Theory of Employment, Interest, and Money*, which swayed many economists. They then began to see the lack of demand as a real problem.

Yet there are those who still doubt the lack of aggregate demand is a problem. The lack of demand can be seen in several concrete ways: immense amounts of goods pile up and cannot be sold; large numbers of workers are idle because there is no demand for what they could produce; and vast amounts of raw materials pile up next to idle factories.

Chapter 1 showed that the business cycle did not exist in previous economic systems. It has existed only in capitalist economies, where it has exhibited somewhat the same pattern in every cycle in every capitalist country. The increase or decrease of inequality in the economy helps to cause expansions and contractions. Before trying to explain these changes, however, we need a clear framework of the whole aggregate economy.

Lack of demand and inequality

How are inequality and effective demand related to each other? Aggregate demand is not just a collection of desires by individuals, but instead is the total amount of spending on goods and services. Spending reflects demand from wages and salaries because they are the largest part of consumer demand.

The largest part of aggregate demand is consumer demand. The most dramatic example of the effects of lack of demand in an economic contraction may be seen in the Great Depression. There was a lack of demand in every major sector from automobiles to food at the time. One example is that huge stacks of potatoes were set on fire.

How is it possible for people to have a strong desire and need for a commodity, such as potatoes, yet there is no demand for it? Progressive economists in the Great Depression stressed the concept of effective demand, stating the need for both desire and money.

The lack of effective demand means that some goods and services cannot be sold. If goods and services cannot be sold, this leads to reduced production and a reduction or ending of investment. This causes a recession. Whenever this book refers to demand from now on, it means an effective demand backed by money, not an infective demand backed by nothing but desire.

The most famous economist to focus on the lack of demand in the 1930s was John Maynard Keynes. He began his progressive framework for understanding a modern capitalist economy with the observation that in a private capitalist economy, all economic growth results from the investment by individuals and corporations in new buildings and equipment. Why do people and corporations invest in an expansion of a business? The answer is that they expect to make a profit. Investment must therefore depend on the expectation of future profit from the purchase of buildings and equipment.

The expectation of profit is completely uncertain. It depends on many things that cannot be known at the present time. To approximate future profit, investors usually look at present profits and their change from the previous period. Thus, in reality, investment depends on what investors see happening with current and previous profits.

Profit can be defined as sales minus costs in the case of an individual business. What is profit in the aggregate for the whole economy?

In the case of the aggregate economy, the sales for all firms are the same amount of money as the aggregate spending in the economy. The four great rivers of spending are consumer spending, investment spending, government spending, and foreign spending.

Consumer spending means the total money spent by individual families on any type of goods or services, such as insurance or cell phones. Investment spending is the purchase of buildings and equipment by businesses. Government spending includes the purchase of goods and services needed for government activities, wages and salaries paid to all the employees, and payments required by law to individuals or organizations, such as Social Security payments. Foreign spending means the payments of money by foreigners to buy a country's exports of goods and services.

Aggregate cost of supply

In order to make a profit, a business must not only have demand for its goods and services; it must first produce them. The key to making a profit is to keep the flow of spending as high as possible, while the money spent on the cost of production must be kept as low as possible.

The main costs of production are: the cost of labor in the form of wages, salaries, and benefits; interest payments made by business; taxes on the business; and the costs of all imported goods and services used by the business.

Each of the elements of demand and each of the elements of costs is discussed later in separate chapters.

Profit

Business profits, including corporate profits, move approximately the same way in each business cycle. Aggregate profit of all firms tends to rise in every business expansion, but its growth per year usually begins to fall before the business peak, and then continues to fall during most of the contraction.

As profits go, so goes the economy. When profits rise in an expansion, most enterprises tend to expand as rapidly as possible. When profit is falling, most enterprises restrict their production and drastically lower their new investment. In this way, the expectation of profit determines the movement of the aggregate economy.

What makes aggregate profit rise and fall? To answer this question, one must begin by defining just what profit means. For the individual enterprise, profit is the difference between the revenue of the firm and the cost of its production. Aggregate profit uses the same definition, but notes that in the aggregate, the revenue of all business is exactly the same as the total spending in the economy.

The simple definition, that aggregate profit is defined as aggregate spending minus aggregate cost, is a powerful tool in aggregate or macroeconomics. Aggregate profit provides the key to understanding the movements of the whole economy.

Implications of this structure for inequality and recessions

Business owners spend a lot of time trying to hold down wages and salaries because they see them as the main costs of doing business. Yet the same business owners want employees of other businesses to make enough to purchase their particular product. Thus, every business owner has two conflicting desires: hold down wages and salaries for their own business while increasing wages and salaries in the rest of the economy. We will discuss these conflicting roles of wages and salaries in later chapters.

The struggle between wages and salaries versus profit-making determines the level of inequality in America and other capitalist countries. The ratio of profits to wages and salaries in the aggregate economy is a good indicator of inequality in the society.

Economic relations and the plan of the book

The next chapter completes the background by showing how the burden of recessions falls mainly on employees through unemployment and reduction of wages and salaries.

Chapter 6 shows how profit and investment are the key to the movement of the American economy. Since aggregate spending and aggregate cost determine aggregate profit, one chapter is devoted to each major element of spending and of cost. Thus, the reader will find description and explanation of the elements of demand: consumer spending, government spending, investment spending, and foreign spending. To understand how profit is affected by cost, there are chapters on wage and salary income, interest income, taxes, and spending on imports. Taken together, it becomes quite clear exactly how profit is determined in America. At the same time, each chapter shows how that particular element affects inequality and is affected by inequality.

At the end of this book, separate chapters examine the depression or Great Recession of 2007 to 2009 and the financial crisis of 2008 to 2009. Finally, the last chapter presents proposals for policies to achieve drastic reduction of inequality and unemployment.

5

UNEMPLOYMENT AND INEQUALITY

The poverty level describes an absolute level of income below which people have inadequate food, clothing, and housing. Since 1980, about 15 percent of the population has remained under the poverty level. When there is an economic boom, the number of people under the poverty level declines somewhat. For example, there was a significant decrease in poverty in the late 1990s under President Clinton.

In each recession, however, the number of people living under the poverty level increases. For example, during the Great Recession of 2007 to 2009, there was a sharp increase in the number of people living under the poverty level. This meant that many more individuals and their families were forced to choose between having enough food to eat or decent shelter to live in. In 2016, approximately 12 million children in America went to sleep hungry every night.

Inequality is defined in terms of the relationship of the income of one group versus another. For example, if there is a rise in the percentage of income going to the wealthiest 1 percent, this means that a smaller percentage of income is going to the bottom 99 percent.

The number of people living in poverty rises when there is more unemployment. Another cause of poverty, however, is the existence of discrimination against some groups. One group facing discrimination consists of women in the labor force, who are on average paid a lower amount of money than men. Poverty is also caused by racial discrimination against African Americans, Latino Americans, and other racial and ethnic groups.

The unemployment rate is defined as the percentage of people unemployed out of the entire active labor force. The active labor force is defined as those people who have a job or are actively seeking work. As each recession deepens, the unemployment rate rises. The higher unemployment rate includes millions of people who are then living only on their unemployment compensation.

Exactly how the unemployment rate is related to individual human misery is discussed in a later section.

The unemployment rate cited in the newspapers and on television understates the problem in at least two ways. First, a person is considered employed even if they work only one hour a week. All of those people who are involuntarily employed only part-time should not be included among the "employed."

The second reason is that many people cannot find jobs for a long time, so they are very discouraged and stop looking for jobs. Therefore, under the usual definition, they are not counted in the labor force. In fact, the number of people in the total population who are not employed in the economy has increased greatly in the last three decades.

In each economic recession or depression, millions of Americans suddenly lose their jobs through no fault of their own. Some are able to find low-paying part-time jobs, but for others no jobs of any kind are available. The system pushes them out to live on an excruciatingly small income of unemployment compensation, and this compensation usually only lasts six months.

When there is a severe recession and very large-scale unemployment, the discouragement effect on the unemployed tends to be very strong. For example, between November 2008 and April 2009, an average of 750,000 people were fired each month. The fortunate people began to get jobs in the coming year or two. Further reductions in unemployment were also achieved slowly over many years. Many workers, however, became permanently unemployed.

Millions of additional workers then joined people who had previously involuntarily left the labor force. Many of those people became so frustrated with the job market that they gave up looking for a job altogether.

Inequality and unemployment in a business expansion

How exactly is unemployment related to inequality? What happens to the inequality of income and wealth in the expansions?

During the expansion, production rises, so employment rises. Therefore, the unemployment rate eventually goes down. This may, however, take a considerable time after the economy starts to recover. So long as the unemployment rate remains high, millions of workers are readily available for employment at the prevailing wage.

In most expansions, including all of those since 1980, wages and salaries did not rise, or rose slowly, while profits soared. This produced growing inequality during these expansions.

Inequality and unemployment in economic contractions

During contractions, the unemployment rate rises as more and more people lose their jobs. The excess of available labor causes wages and salaries to fall. At the same time, during the contraction, profits fall even more rapidly than wages and salaries.

For example, in the Great Depression, wages and salaries declined about 30 percent, which caused enormous misery for many workers and their families. Nevertheless, profits declined much further in percentage terms. There were two years during the Great Depression, 1931 and 1932, when total corporate profits were negative.

As seen above, wages and salaries usually rise in an expansion, but inequality of income also rises because profits are going up even faster. In a contraction, wages and salaries normally fall less than profits, so income inequality falls.

The average worker has a much lower income and a more difficult lifestyle during a recession or depression. As noted above, the amount of profit falls even more than wages and salaries. Yet the rich are protected by their large reserves of wealth. They therefore can continue most of their luxurious lifestyle. Thus, the degree of inequality falls, yet the actual burden of the recession or depression is still mostly felt by the workers.

Most of the unemployment in American history has been due to the economic cycle of boom and bust. As shown in Chapter 1, the business cycle of boom and bust appears only under capitalism. It is, however, seen in every capitalist country in the global economy.

People in previous economic systems had plenty of problems, but these did not include the business cycle of boom and bust. Inequality under our present economic system is affected by the business cycle; moreover, inequality is a major cause of the business cycle.

The following chapters will show how inequality is also the major cause of recessions and large-scale unemployment.

Wesley Mitchell and the business cycle

Before Wesley Mitchell did his work, there were almost no reliable data on the cyclical movements of economic series. Most economists working on the business cycle simply made certain assumptions from their casual knowledge of the cycle. Mitchell spent most of his life working on the acquisition of carefully documented data. These data helped reveal the exact path of each economic series over the cycle. He worked on many books and reports on the business cycle from 1913 until his death in 1948; the last report was published after his death in 1951.

In order to study the business cycle, Mitchell founded the National Bureau of Economic Research (NBER) in 1920. He was Director of Research there until 1945.

Mitchell was not an ordinary classical or neoclassical economist. His most important teacher was Thorstein Veblen, the greatest radical economist in American history up to that time. Veblen was known as an institutionalist because he focused on basic economic institutions, such as the rules regarding the relations between capital and labor. Under the influence of Veblen, Mitchell used the enormous amount of data he collected to study the basic economic institutions of capitalism.

He found a repetition of the cycle of boom and bust in every capitalist country, beginning with England in 1793. For his last work published in 1951, *What Happens During Business Cycles*, Mitchell had collected and calculated the cyclical behavior of 958 economic series.

The NBER has found that there were 33 economic cycles in America since 1850. Mitchell also found that there were no business cycles of the modern type under slavery or feudalism.

Using Mitchell's method of calculation, this chapter finds the following conclusions. First, the total or aggregate employment of America continues to rise in the long run from cycle to cycle. Unfortunately, the growth rate of employment has been lower than the growth rate of the population, leaving an increasing number of non-workers in the population.

Second, total employment has not continued upward in a straight line. For example, in the Great Depression of the 1930s, employment fell by 30 percent. In the Great Recession of 2007 to 2009, employment fell by 6 percent.

Cycle peaks and troughs

The first task in understanding the behavior of employment, or any other variable, is to set up a series of dates showing the peaks and troughs of the business cycles. A "cycle trough" is when aggregate business activity reaches its lowest point in the cycle. A "cycle peak" is when aggregate business activity reaches its highest point in the cycle.

According to the NBER, the correct dates for cycle peaks and troughs are those given in Table 5.1.

TABLE 5.1 Troughs and peaks of the business cycle

Initial trough	Peak	Final trough
Interwar (Great Depression) era		
1921.3	1923.2	1924.3
1924.3	1926.3	1927.4
1927.4	1929.3	1933.1
1933.1	1937.2	1938.2
Golden Age		
1949.4	1953.2	1954.2
1954.2	1957.3	1958.2
1958.2	1960.2	1961.1
1961.1	1969.4	1970.4
Age of Globalization		
1970.4	1973.4	1975.1
1975.1	1980.1	1980.3
1980.3	1981.3	1982.4
1982.4	1990.3	1991.1
1991.1	2001.1	2001.4
2001.4	2007.4	2009.2

Definition: Dates in year and month.

Source: National Bureau of Economic Research, www.nber.org/cycles/cyclesmain.html.

The NBER has all the dates for the peaks and troughs for all cycles going back to 1800. This table, however, only lists the dates from the three most important periods in the last 100 years of American history. The first part of the table shows the peaks and troughs for the four cycles from 1921 to 1938. These are especially important because they contain the two cycles leading up to the Great Depression and the two cycles that were in the Great Depression. The second part of the table shows the four cycles from 1949 to 1970 of the Golden Age. The third part of the table shows the six cycles from 1970 to 2009 of the Age of Globalization.

The cycle base

Employment is used here to mean the total number of people who have jobs in the American economy. It includes rich executives and poor fast-food workers, people of all races and religions, and working women and men.

The "cycle base" is defined to mean the average of the variable for that cycle. For example, the cycle base of employment is the average employment for the cycle. In Table 5.2, each number is the cycle base of one cycle. In this case, the variable is total employment, given in millions of people working.

The cycle base seems to rise smoothly. That is because it is an average that leaves out all of the ups and downs in the cycle. Moreover, employment has been rising more slowly than population, so more and more people are not employed.

The cycle base is important for describing any long-run series. The cycle base does not include any economic booms and busts, but shows only the long-run movements as given by the average from each cycle. Cycle bases hide these details because each point is just an average of one whole cycle.

The nine stages of the cycle

Mitchell is famous for dividing the business cycle into nine stages for purposes of analysis. Each stage is calculated in terms of the number of quarters in it. Stage 1 is the initial trough and one quarter long. Stage 5 is the cycle peak and also one

TABLE 5.2 Total employment, cycle bases, Age of Globalization, six cycles, 1970–2009

Cycle	Total employment cycle base
1970–1975	83.2
1975–1980	93.2
1980–1982	99.8
1982–1991	110.8
1991–2001	127.4
2001–2009	141.4

Note: Total employment means the employment level, in millions of people in the actve labor force, 16 years and older, seasonally adjusted quarterly data.

quarter long. In order to find the length of Stages 2, 3, and 4, the total number of quarters in the business expansion between the trough and the peak are divided by three. Thus, Stages, 2, 3, and 4 are each one-third of the expansion. Stage 9 is the final trough and is one quarter long. Stages 6, 7, and 8 constitute the business contraction, and each is one-third of the contraction between Stage 5 and Stage 9.

The rise and fall of employment

The economic series used here as an example is the cyclical behavior in the Bush cycle. The expansion and contraction of total employment for the cycle of 2001 to 2009 is shown in Figure 5.1.

Figure 5.1 shows clearly that employment in the aggregate economy rose during the expansion of the Bush economy, then fell drastically during the contraction of the Bush economy, usually called the Great Recession. Now let us examine some of the details. These same details will be found in each cycle chart, so they are worth some attention.

In the middle of the graph, the dotted horizontal line is the cycle base (or average). Along the bottom, the numbers are for the nine stages of the cycle. Notice that the average expansion in this whole era was longer than the average contraction, so the stages are much smaller during the contraction.

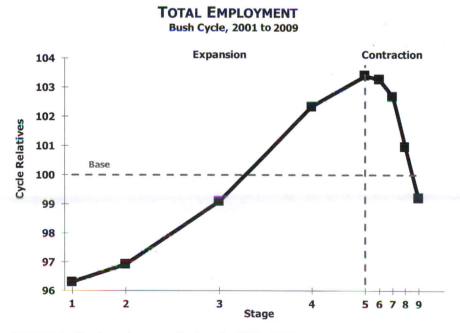

FIGURE 5.1   Total employment, Bush cycle, 2001–2009

The vertical axis measures the percentage of employment at each stage above or below the cycle base. Thus, if employment is at 80, that means that its value at that stage of the cycle is 80 percent of the cycle base. Since each of these percentages is relative to the cycle base, each one is called a "cycle relative." Just remember that cycle relatives are not your relatives, like your aunts or uncles, but are just percentages relative to the cycle base (see Appendix 5.1 for exact definition).

Unemployment in the two eras

How did the unemployment rate behave in these two eras? Remember that the unemployment rate is important because the amount of human misery is reflected in the unemployment rate. Using the official unemployment rate, Figure 5.2 reveals how unemployment behaved in the two historical eras under examination.

Figure 5.2 reveals that the basic pattern of the unemployment rate was similar in both the four cycles of the Golden Age and the six cycles of the Age of Globalization. In both eras, the unemployment rate fell in every expansion, but it rose in every contraction.

One important difference between the two eras is that in the four cycles of the Golden Age, the unemployment rate continues to decline throughout the expansion, all the way to the cycle peak in Stage 5.

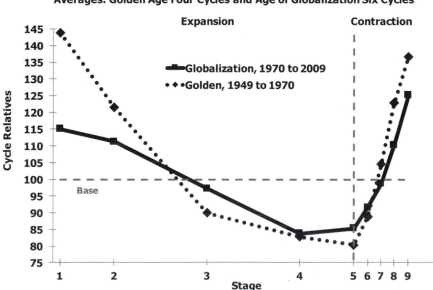

FIGURE 5.2 Unemployment rate, cycle averages, Golden Age, 1949–1970, and Age of Globalization, 1970–2009

In the six cycles of the Age of Globalization, the economy grew weaker in some respects during the stage before the peak of the cycle. Therefore, the unemployment rate actually started to rise slightly from Stage 4 to Stage 5.

The graph shows that the unemployment rate rose and harmed millions of people in the contraction phase. Exactly what human misery was caused by this unemployment? On the individual level, many studies show how the cities with the highest unemployment also have the highest indicators of human misery (Sherman and Meeropol, 2013, Chapter 1). The indicators of human misery caused by unemployment include higher rates of the following: mental depression, divorce, all physical diseases connected with tension, suicide, and child abuse.

In addition to all of the individual misery, the economy also suffers. Every unemployed worker means less income, so it leads to less consumer demand. Lower consumer demand leads to less production. Less production causes more unemployment. More unemployment leads to less consumer demand. Thus, there is a vicious circle leading downward.

Furthermore, the more people unemployed, the lower the production capacity of an economy. When America has increased unemployment, it usually has both less production of consumer goods and less production of both buildings and equipment for investment purposes. If fewer workers are employed to produce buildings and equipment, then the starting point for production for the next year has been lowered. This lower starting point means a certain amount of production is lost forever.

It has sometimes been argued that unemployment rather than business activity should be the basis for determining the dates of the economic cycle of boom and bust. It would better reflect the level of human misery and would demonstrate that recessions have generally been longer than under the present definition (see Sherman and Sherman, 2012). This book will use the usual business cycle dates given by the NBER.

Appendix 5.1

The terminology of Wesley Mitchell

Mitchell finds that the American economy is always in the business cycle. The economy is either in an expansion or contraction. Every cycle begins with an initial trough in Stage 1, a peak in Stage 5, and the final trough in Stage 9.

Each cycle is measured by duration and amplitude. The duration is the number of quarters in the cycle. The expansion amplitude is the percentage rise from the initial trough to the peak as a percentage of the cycle base. The contraction amplitude means the percentage decline from the peak to the trough. A cycle relative is the amount of the variable at each stage of the cycle, divided by the cycle base, then multiplied by 100 to become a percentage.

Further reading

The two cycle figures in this chapter, and all cycle figures in the rest of the book, are based on Mitchell's approach. This method of describing business cycles was developed by Arthur Burns and Wesley Mitchell at the NBER, so it is sometimes called the NBER method (see Burns and Mitchell, 1946).

A simple spreadsheet program that can be viewed and used for free can be accessed at the following website: www.routledgetextbooks.com/textbooks/ 9780765636119/student.php

The program measures the cycle bases and the cycle relatives of every cycle for any variable that is inserted.

The NBER method is applied to 958 economic series in Mitchell (1951). A discussion of Mitchell's role in business cycle theory may be found in Sherman (2001), while his view of capitalist institutions in the business cycle may be found in Sherman (2003). The model is further explained in a treatise on the business cycle by Sherman (1991).

6

PROFIT, INVESTMENT, AND INEQUALITY

In a book that focuses mostly on inequality and the harm it does to people, why detour to look at profit and investment? Aren't the topics of profit and investment the primary concerns of wealthy men sitting around in corporate headquarters? The reality, however, is that the American economy is moved by the changes in business profits, not by the harm done to most of the population. Therefore, to understand economic inequality, it is necessary to understand how profits cause the economy to go through a cycle of boom and bust.

Investment and inequality

Investment is defined as the purchase of buildings and equipment by business in order to expand production of goods and services. When there is investment, there is an increase in production. That production is created by workers so there must be an increase in employment. The workers are paid, so there must be an increase in wages and salaries.

A majority of the income of the wealthiest 1 percent is profits. All other groups receive a majority of their income as wages and salaries. Aggregate profit rises in each expansion much faster than employee income, so inequality of income and wealth tends to increase in every expansion in every capitalist country (see Chapter 7).

When investment declines in a contraction, wages and salaries decline slowly, while profits decline more rapidly. Therefore, the fact that profits decline more rapidly than wages and salaries causes inequality to decrease in each contraction. This decline in inequality is no comfort to either employed workers with lower wages or unemployed workers because their standard of living also falls considerably.

On average, contractions are much shorter than expansions. In the longer expansion, inequality increases a great deal. In the much shorter contraction, there is time for only a small decrease in inequality. Therefore, when you add them together, the result for the whole cycle is an increase in inequality.

Profit leads, investment follows

Aggregate profit reaches a peak and then turns downward, usually six to nine months before the peak of the business cycle. The only reason for investment in our capitalist economy is to make profits. When expected future profits begin to look dismal, business investment will soon decline.

Investment behavior

Investment follows the same basic path in every cycle for which there are data. There are differences, however, when long-run trends change the nature of the cycle to some degree. Figure 6.1 shows how the pattern of investment in the Golden Age, 1949 to 1970, differs from the pattern that emerged for investment in the Age of Globalization, 1970 to 2009. The picture in Figure 6.1 reveals the differences.

Both eras have the same basic features. In each era, the good news is that investment rises considerably during the economic expansion. The bad news is that investment declines during the economic contraction.

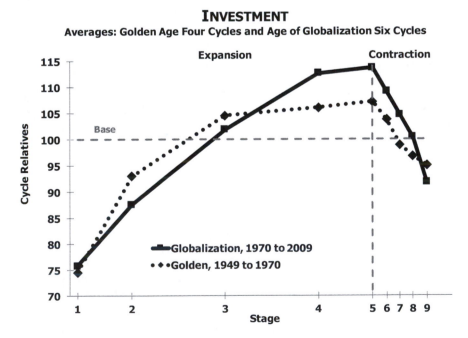

FIGURE 6.1 Investment, Golden Age, 1949–1970, and Age of Globalization, 1970–2009

The main difference between these two ages of capitalism, the Golden Age and the Age of Globalization, is that in the Golden Age, the rise in investment during the expansion as well as the fall in investment during the contraction are both relatively mild. The graph shows that investment during the Golden Age rises and falls more slowly than during the Age of Globalization.

In the six cycles from 1970 to 2009, private investment has continued to rise in expansions, but it declines very rapidly in contractions. Private investors in the stock market know enough to be more worried and less confident than in the Golden Age. The result is that the swings in the stock market have become even more pronounced and exaggerated in the Age of Globalization.

What causes investment?

When there is a rise in the profits from sales of its goods and services, a corporation will then assume that it will make more profits in the future. This optimistic view leads them to make more investments. When profits rise in the aggregate economy, then all corporations tend to increase their investments.

When a single corporation's profits fall, the corporation reduces the amount of new investment. As soon as aggregate profits decline, aggregate investment always declines, but sometimes six to nine months later. In some economic situations, the time lag could be even longer.

The economy is pulled upward by expectations of future profits. The economy is pulled downward by expectations of business losses. Profit is king. The history of profit behavior is presented here in three different eras.

Profit in the Great Depression

The interwar era witnessed four cycles in the years 1921 to 1938. The behavior of these cycles was dominated by the downturn of 1929 to 1933 at the beginning of the Great Depression.

The cyclical movements of the economy during the Great Depression can be traced to the behavior of capitalist investment. In the average of the four cycle expansions from 1921 to 1938, investment rose by 55 percent. Investment collapsed, however, by 43 percent in the average contraction.

The investment behavior was due to the fact that corporate profit was on a roller coaster; it went way up in expansions and way down in contractions. Corporate profit rose 169 percent in the average of the four cycle expansions. Then, corporate profit went down 175 percent in the average contraction of the four cycles (all data in this section are from Mitchell, 1951).

Profit after the Great Depression

At the end of the Great Depression in 1938, the unemployment rate was 18 percent. By 1939, however, the Roosevelt Administration began to spend money for military preparedness as war loomed over the horizon. The dramatic increase in military spending by 1942 led to an unemployment rate of only 1.5 percent. Profits climbed to a high level during the Second World War because there was full employment and practically unlimited demand. Wages also rose somewhat, but they were held down by price regulations.

Following the Second World War, the rest of the world lay in ruins, so America produced an increasing amount of goods and services to meet the resurgent global demand. Profits therefore rose steadily. Thanks to strong trade unions, the flow of national income in America was shared with employees in steadily rising wages and salaries. Since wages and salaries actually rose a little faster than profits, inequality declined. Because demand remained at high levels due to rising wages and salaries, business cycle recessions were fairly short and mild.

By the end of the 1960s, there was strong competition in the global market from other countries' exports. Moreover, as trade union membership declined as a percentage of the labor force, the growth of wages and salaries slowed and then stagnated. This stagnation of wages and salaries has lasted all the way to the present. American corporations, however, have become much stronger economically and increased their political influence.

The combination of stagnant employee income and competition by foreign business has led to a weaker economy, so that the rate of growth was far less in the Age of Globalization than it had been in the Golden Age. The rising level of inequality was a limitation on consumer demand, so uncertainty led to an increasingly volatile economy. There were booms in profits, but there were also busts in profits, concluding in the disaster of the Great Recession in 2007 to 2009.

Profit in the Golden Age and the Age of Globalization

In the four business cycles during the Golden Age of American capitalism, 1949 to 1970, profit continued to move up and down, but far more gently. In the average expansion, investment rose 33 percent, but only fell 12 percent in the average contraction. In the Golden Age, there was net growth of investment in each of the four cycles.

The cyclical behavior of profits in the Golden Age and in the Age of Globalization may be seen in Figure 6.2.

The investment behavior in the Golden Age was the result of the profit behavior revealed in Figure 6.2. In the average expansion of the four cycles, 1949 to 1970, profit grew by 17 percent. Profit then had a fall of 6.8 percent in the contractions of the same four cycles. Unlike the Great Depression, the aggregate profit had a net rise in the average of the four cycles. All of the data in this section are from the source given in the caption of Figure 6.2.

As pictured in Figure 6.2, aggregate profit rose in every expansion of this era, and then fell more mildly in every contraction. As a result, aggregate investments rose in every expansion, and then declined somewhat less in the contraction.

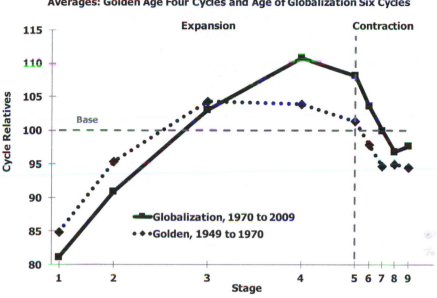

FIGURE 6.2   Business profit, Golden Age, 1949–1970, and Age of Globalization, 1970–2009

Source: U.S. Department of Commerce, Bureau of Economic Analysis, NIPA, Table 1.1.6, line 7, at www.bea.gov; U.S. Department of Commerce, Bureau of Economic Analysis, NIPA, Table 1.12, lines 9 and 13; source for implicit price deflator: U.S. Department of Commerce, Bureau of Economic Analysis, NIPA, Table 1.1.9, line 1, at www.bea.gov.

The small declines and long-run growth of profits and investment made this a truly Golden Age for American capitalism.

What happened in the Age of Globalization? In the six business cycles from 1970 to 2009, the average expansion investment rose by 38 percent. In the average contraction of those six cycles, investment had a fall of 22 percent.

In this case, the investment behavior was again caused by similar movements of profits. During the average expansion from 1970 to 2009, aggregate profit rose by 27 percent. During the average contraction of the six cycles, aggregate profits had a fall of 11 percent.

Figure 6.2 thus shows that investment and profit declines were fairly mild in the Golden Age, but became considerably stronger in the Age of Globalization.

Specific and reference cycles

The National Bureau of Economic Research (NBER) provides the dates at which most economic series reach their peak and the dates they reach their trough (see Table 5.1). These dates are usually used by the American government and almost all economists.

These dates are called the reference cycle peaks and the reference cycle troughs. The peaks are the times when the NBER finds the most business activity in the whole economy. The troughs are the times when the NBER finds the least business activity in the economy. Over 90 percent of all economic series reach their peaks and troughs at the reference cycle peaks and troughs. Thus, they are the reference points for all cycles.

Yet some economic series reach their peaks and troughs at times other than the reference cycle points. If one measures the amplitude of these economic series according to the reference cycle points, then the measurements will be incorrect. Therefore, the NBER also considers specific cycles. A "specific cycle" is simply the cycle of one individual economic series according to its own peaks and troughs.

Economic indicators

Those economic series that always have their peaks and troughs at the same time as the reference cycle peaks and troughs are called "coincident" indicators. These include GDP, national income, aggregate consumption, and aggregate investment.

Those economic series that have their peaks and troughs before the reference peaks and troughs are called "leading indicators." They are measured correctly only by calculating their rise and fall according to their own peaks and troughs.

If over 90 percent of all economic series are coincident with the reference cycle, then why bother with specific cycle measurements for leading indicators? The simple answer is that the leading indicators may be few in number, but many are extremely important.

For example, stocks are a leading indicator. There are nine stages in the business cycle. These include the initial trough at Stage 1, the peak at Stage 5, and the final trough at Stage 9. If someone wants to invest in the stock market, they had better remember that it is a leading indicator, which usually peaks in Stage 4 and reaches a trough in Stage 8. Stocks are discussed in Chapter 9.

The aggregate profit of all businesses is also a leading indicator. It also reaches a peak at Stage 4 and reaches its trough at Stage 8. The usual lead time for most leading indicators, including profits, is six to nine months.

Income inequality, as represented in the Inequality Ratio, also peaks in Stage 4 and reaches a trough in Stage 8. Behavior of the Inequality Ratio is discussed in Chapter 7.

Finally, there are some economic series, such as some interest rates, that usually reach a peak in Stage 6 after the reference cycle peak, and also reach a trough after Stage 9, so the trough is in the next cycle. These are called "lagging indicators." Why some interest rates are a lagging indicator is discussed in Chapter 9.

Profit and investment in the Age of Globalization

Specific cycle amplitudes of profit and investment in the average of the six cycles of the Age of Globalization are shown in Table 6.1.

TABLE 6.1 Profit and investment, average amplitudes for specific profit peak at Stage 4 and specific profit trough at Stage 8, Age of Globalization, average of six cycles, 1970–2009

Economic series	Expansion amplitude	Contraction amplitude
Business profit	29.4	−13.8
Investment	37.06	−12.8

Source: Business profit: Department of Commerce, Bureau of Economic Analysis, National Income and Product Account (NIPA), Table 1.12, lines 9 and 13. Investment: Department of Commerce, Bureau of Economic Analysis, National Income and Product Accounts, Table 1.1.6, line 7.

Note: Expansion amplitude is Stage 4 minus Stage 1. Contraction amplitude is Stage 8 minus Stage 4. In stating the amplitudes, if the variable has declined, then a minus sign is used. If the variable has risen, then no sign is used. Business profit means all corporate profit plus all non-corporate profit, including proprietors' income. Data are quarterly, seasonally adjusted, and adjusted for inflation by the U.S. government. Investment means Gross Private Domestic Investment.

Table 6.1 provides the average specific expansion amplitude and specific contraction amplitude for both investment and profit. The expansion amplitudes of both investment and profit are calculated from the initial cycle trough (Stage 1) to the profit peak (Stage 4). Both investment and profit are calculated for the contraction amplitude from the profit peak (Stage 4) to the profit trough (Stage 8). In the rest of this book, all of the cycle amplitudes will be calculated using the specific profit peak and the specific profit trough.

The reason that all amplitudes will be calculated for the specific cycle peaks and troughs of profit is that profit determines the peaks and troughs of the reference cycle. Once profit reaches its specific cycle peak in Stage 4, the reference cycle peak follows in Stage 5. Once profit reaches its specific cycle trough in Stage 8, the reference cycle trough will be reached in Stage 9. This point was made in detail so as to avoid confusion in the rest of the book.

Table 6.1 reveals that investment and profit both have fairly large amplitudes compared with most other variables. Investment and profit both decline together at about the same rate because profit determines investment. In the business expansion, however, businesses are almost always overly optimistic. Therefore, it is common for investment to rise considerably faster than profits in an expansion based solely on overoptimistic expectations of future profit. As discussed below, profit usually leads and investment follows.

Why is profit a leading indicator?

Figure 6.2 provides us with a picture of the cyclical behavior of profit both in the Golden Age and in the Age of Globalization. The figure shows that profits rise and fall somewhat less in the Golden Age than in the later Age of Globalization.

During the Golden Age, the picture also shows that profit reaches its peak a little after the mid-expansion in Stage 3. Profits then have a relatively mild decline until the cycle peak is reached. On the other hand, profits in the Age of Globalization rise to a much higher point and continue to rise until Stage 4. It then falls significantly down to the cycle trough.

In either case, the decline of profit eventually led to a decline of investment and a recession or depression. The milder oscillation of profit in the Golden Age, however, led to a milder recession. The greater oscillation of profit in the Age of Globalization led to a stronger recession or depression.

Why does profit lead investment?

Profit has been a leading indicator in every business cycle expansion since the Second World War. Investment has usually been a coincident indicator, which means that investment usually reaches a peak at the exact cycle peak and usually reaches a trough at the exact cycle trough. Thus, investment and GDP are the major markers of the business cycle.

So why does profit lead investment and also the business cycle in almost every case? The reasons are simple and straightforward. In the first place, when aggregate profits turns down, it usually takes at least one quarter before that fact appears in the government statistics. Second, if a corporation sees that aggregate profits are declining, it may still believe that its own profits will continue rising. So there is often a time lag until it is convinced that its own profit is going to decline.

Third, suppose a corporation is convinced that there is going to be a recession; it still takes some time to cut back on its production of various goods and services in a way that does the least harm. Fourth, if there is a rise in aggregate profits from the lowest point of the recession, it still takes the corporation time to discover that aggregate profits have risen and to decide that its own profits are likely to rise.

Fifth, once a corporation has decided that profits are likely to rise, it then has to make a decision to go ahead and expand by making new investment. Having made that decision, there are many kinds of planning that still need to be done. For example, there is engineering planning to decide what kind of equipment to buy, plus architectural planning to decide what type of building to construct.

Sixth, if a corporation decides to invest, it must also find the money to borrow for that investment. Seventh, it must get permission to make new investment from various governments at the city, state, and federal levels. Finally, it takes more time to actually spend the investment money.

The only partial exception to the rule that there is always a time lag from a change in profit to a change in investment came just before the Great Recession. In Stage 4 of the expansion, the economy was already so weak that investors reduced their spending at the same time that profit started to fall.

Profit and investment interactions in the Golden Age

The Golden Age was an era of fairly consistent growth and mild cycles. The comparison of profit movements and investment during the Golden Age may be seen in Figure 6.3.

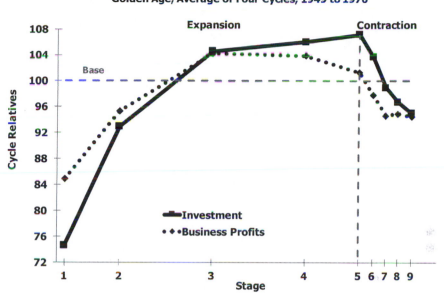

FIGURE 6.3 Investment and profit, Golden Age, 1949–1970

Figure 6.3 reveals that profits and investment mostly moved together in this era. In the first half of the expansion, both profits and investment grew rapidly. In the second half of the expansion, however, growth was slow. Investment continued growing, but at a slower pace all the way to the cycle peak.

Aggregate profit, however, leveled off in the last half of the expansion, with a slight decline at first, then a considerable decline from Stage 4 to the cycle peak. As explained above, profit has usually been a leading indicator, so investment normally lags by one stage behind profit.

In the recessions of the Golden Age, both profit and investment declined, but only at a moderate pace for a fairly short time.

Investment and profit in the Age of Globalization

The Age of Globalization is characterized by lower economic growth and sharper business cycles. The picture of profit and investment in the six cycles of the Age of Globalization may be seen in Figure 6.4.

Figure 6.4 examines the six-cycle average from 1970 to 2009. During that period, investment and profits tend to move fairly closely in the same direction.

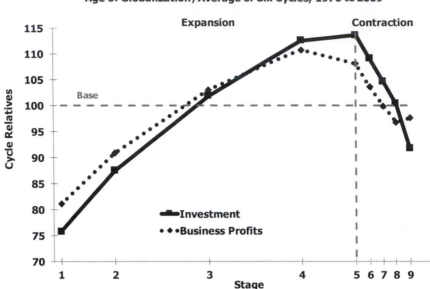

FIGURE 6.4 Investment and profit, Age of Globalization, 1970–2009

Conclusions

Investment is considered the key variable in the business cycle because its increase leads to an expansion of production. The decrease in investment also leads to less production.

The key to investment, however, is expected profit. Expectations of profit depend on the movements of profit in the recent past. Profit begins to decline just before the end of the expansion when the rate of growth of demand slows.

Inequality also plays a major role in the reduction of demand. While inequality plays the greatest role in ending the rise of profits in the expansion, in the contraction the decline of inequality sets up conditions for a new economic expansion. This will be shown in detail in later chapters.

Appendix 6.1

Four phases of profit and investment

How investment and profit are interlinked can be depicted most clearly in the four phases of the business cycle. The four phases are: Recovery, Prosperity, Crisis, and Recession. The concept and most of the terminology comes from Wesley Mitchell (e.g. see Mitchell, 1951). Figure 6.5 shows how profit and investment are related at each phase of the cycle during the present Age of Globalization.

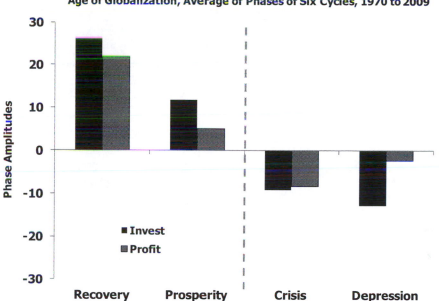

INVESTMENT AND PROFIT
Age of Globalization, Average of Phases of Six Cycles, 1970 to 2009

FIGURE 6.5 Phases of investment and profit, Age of Globalization, 1970–2009

In the Recovery phase, Stages 1 to 3, profit rises rapidly, but investment rises even more rapidly. Although investment is determined by profit and expectations of profit, the expectations are usually irrationally exaggerated. For example, actual investment rises more rapidly than actual profit.

In the Recovery phase, the inequality reflected in stagnant wages and salaries with soaring profits drives the expansion forward rapidly because of exaggerated expectations by capitalist owners. Problems arise only in the Prosperity phase.

In the Prosperity phase, Stages 3 to 5, profit initially continues to rise, although more slowly than in the Recovery phase. Investment also continues to rise more slowly than it did in the Recovery phase. Investment always rises faster than profits. Again, the greater rise of investment is due to irrational optimistic profit expectations.

By Stage 4, however, the rising inequality between profits and employee income turns into a major problem, causing inadequate demand (discussed in Chapter 8). Thus, inequality eventually leads to an economic crisis. The inadequate demand, caused by low wages and salaries, is delayed for a while by massive consumer credit, but even that eventually is insufficient for the required demand (see Chapter 9).

In the Crisis phase, Stages 5 to 7, profit falls, but investment falls even faster. The fall of investment is based on profit movements plus an irrational pessimistic view of profit in the future.

In the Recession phase, Stages 7 to 9, profit continues to fall, but more slowly than it did in the crisis. As a result, investment falls an even greater amount, reflecting the actual fall of profit plus further pessimistic views.

In the Crisis and Recession phases, with falling wages and salaries, it at first seems odd that aggregate inequality declines (see Chapter 7), but the reason for the declining inequality is simply that profits fall much faster than wages and salaries.

What determines the profit movements in each of these four phases? Profits are based on sales and costs. Sales reflect demand. The four elements of demand are consumer spending, investment spending, government spending, and foreign spending for U.S. exports. The four main elements of costs are: labor costs, interest costs, import costs, and taxes. The effect each has on profit and inequality will be dealt with in separate chapters: wages and salaries in Chapter 7, consumption in Chapter 8, credit and interest in Chapter 9, government spending and taxes in Chapter 10, and international relations in Chapter 11.

7

HOW INEQUALITY IS AFFECTED BY BOOM AND BUST

This chapter will show that the overall trend of inequality has been increasing since 1980. It will also show a sometimes-neglected point: that increasing inequality in each business expansion is the most important factor leading to recessions and unemployment. These findings show the need for a policy to reduce inequality, which is detailed in Chapter 15.

Inequality means millions of poor women and men trying to feed children on a poverty-level income in old kitchens in small apartments. In America, the wealthiest of all capitalist countries, 22 percent of all children lived in poverty in 2015!

Inequality also means a small number of billionaires live in luxury, spending vast sums of money and never having to worry about covering the essentials of life. To explain how these conditions were created, however, one must unearth and explain a statistical portrait of inequality.

This chapter will demonstrate that the level of inequality in America is extremely high. Inequality rises during each business expansion because the rapid rise of profits contrasts with the tiny increase in wages and salaries. The next chapter will show how this increasing inequality in the expansion is a major cause of the following recession or depression.

The causes of inequality in capitalism have been debated since the beginnings of capitalism. The following sections will show how conservatives see inequality as a result of unchangeable differences among people, while progressives see inequality as the result of capitalist institutions, which can be changed.

The conservative view

Conservative economists argue that demand is not a major cause of recessions or depressions. They also argue that inequality is not as high as progressives claim. Moreover, they say that inequality is a necessary incentive to get people to work as hard as possible. If there is no inequality, there are no incentives, so there is no economic growth.

Conservatives believe that money given to the poor or the unemployed, such as unemployment compensation or food stamps, causes a lack of incentive to work because one can live on those handouts without having to work. Yet every direct interview finds that the unemployed are struggling on their small compensation. When any job is offered in a recession or depression, there are always four or five times as many people applying as there are jobs. It is general unemployment that prevents people from working, not lack of incentive.

Conservatives have argued since 1800 that the lack of demand is at most small and temporary. They believe the lack of demand can always be traced to some external cause, not to the capitalist economy itself. According to their view, every sale of goods and services provides new income. If all that income is added together, then there is always enough aggregate demand as soon as any external obstacles are removed. Therefore, private enterprise can always recover from any recession without government intervention. In fact, government intervention is always bad for the economy.

The progressive view

Progressive economists have been discussing inequality and its causes in great detail ever since the conservative view was first presented in the nineteenth century. For details of the evolution of the conservative and progressive view, see Hunt (2015). Since the Great Recession of 2007 to 2009, progressive economists have been joined by the powerful contributions of the Nobel Prize winner Joseph Stiglitz (2012, 2015a, 2015b).

Stiglitz (2012) shows in persuasive detail exactly how much poverty and inequality there is in America. He also reveals that this inequality has been increasing since 1980. He describes how extremely difficult it is to rise from the lowest income level to become a member of the middle class. There is even less possibility of moving up from the middle class to the wealthiest 1 percent. The role of inequality in lowering economic growth is clearly and eloquently stated in Stiglitz (2012), with further evidence in Stiglitz (2015a, 2015b).

The same type of data on inequality are further expanded to the whole world and the last few centuries by Piketty (2014). From the data used by Stiglitz, as well as the data published by Piketty, we have a full picture of the whole process.

A portion of the data from these two books makes the picture of inequality concrete and dramatic. This picture of inequality in America is presented in Figure 7.1.

In Figure 7.1, people are represented by small images of people. Wealth is represented by dollar signs. The data as examined below show that each small figure of a person is roughly 5 percent of all the people. Each dollar sign represents about 10 percent of all the wealth.

When people are listed by their wealth, they can be divided into 100 groups. These groups can be added together into larger groups according to which ones are similar in wealth. The picture presented here consists of just three larger

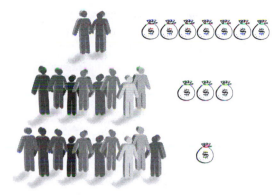

FIGURE 7.1   People and wealth

groups, arbitrarily called High, Middle, and Low. This picture roughly follows the data presented in Stiglitz (2012). We see in it two pyramids. One pyramid consists of people. In that pyramid, the largest group of people are those at the base with relatively low wealth. The next layer up the pyramid consists of somewhat fewer people who have the median wealth. Finally, at the top of the pyramid are the few people with a relatively high amount of wealth.

The pyramid of dollar signs is inverted. In this pyramid, dollar signs represent wealth. It shows that even if we combine all the wealth of the lower-income group of people, they have a small total amount of wealth. The next layer shows that the people in the middle of the pyramid have a considerably higher percentage of the total wealth. Finally, the few people at the top have an enormous amount of wealth.

Let us now translate these general statements into specific ones, using the data made available by Stiglitz. Here, the story begins with the top 10 percent of Americans by wealth, which is called the high wealth group. It is shown in Figure 7.1 as the images of two little people at the top of the pyramid. Who is in this group? It includes a wide range of professionals and business people, up to and including the wealthiest people in America.

The group in the 100th percentile is the wealthiest 1 percent of the people in America. On the other hand, those who are only at the 91st percentile of wealth are mostly well-paid professionals and various people in business. This whole group constitutes 10 percent of the economically active population, but it holds 70 percent of the wealth, a fact showing great inequality in America (Stiglitz, 2012). These data come from 2011, and inequality has grown rapidly since then.

The second group is called the middle wealth-holding group. This 40 percent of the people, from the 51st to the 90th percentile, holds only 28 percent of all the wealth (Stiglitz, 2012). This group does not hold a share of wealth equal to their percentage of the population. Complete economic equality means that the percentage of wealth held by each group equals the percentage of the whole population in that wealth group. That is, there is economic inequality whenever the percentage of wealth is lower than the percentage of population in that group.

This middle wealth-holding group represents a wide range of positions held by individuals in the society. Some of them at the 51st percentile level simply are average employees. This average American has considerably less wealth than those at the top of this wealth group. At the upper end of the wealth group, at the 90th percentile, there are a large number of well-off individuals, including well-paid professionals and small business people. This slice of Middle America is far better off than the poor, but it is still suffering from inequality caused by the fact that so much income is in the hands of rich people in the high wealth group. For example, the average wage and salary has not increased since 1980.

The third group depicts that the entire bottom half of the wealth pyramid gets only 2 percent of all the wealth (Stiglitz, 2012). That wealth is not spread equally among the bottom half. The bottom 15 percent of the population lives in poverty, usually with large amounts of debt. Those near the middle of the wealth spread, from the 40th percentile to the 50th percentile, usually, though not always, make just enough income to sustain the average American requirements for food, clothing, shelter, and recreation. Some of them even save a little each year, which accounts for the 2 percent of wealth that is found in the whole bottom half of the population. Most of the bottom income half of Americans are hard-working, full-time employees. Some, who are at the poverty level or lower, can only get part-time jobs that pay an average of half of a full-time salary—hardly a living wage. Finally, among this group are the unemployed, who live on an extremely low level of compensation from the government.

Long-run trend of inequality

Thomas Piketty (2014) showed that capitalism has generally resulted in an increase in inequality over time. Thus, he found that Karl Marx was correct in his statement that inequality had increased under capitalism in the first two-thirds of the nineteenth century in Great Britain. Piketty found, however, that the trend Marx predicted did not continue in any simple way. Wages and salaries had been stagnant throughout the nineteenth century until about the time that Marx published Volume 1 of *Capital* in 1867. In the last third of the nineteenth century in Great Britain, however, wages and salaries did begin to increase somewhat, so the trend toward inequality was slightly reversed for a while.

Piketty found inequality increased in America from the First World War to 1928, just before the Great Depression. He also reported that inequality declined from the end of the Second World War until 1980. He then found that inequality has been increasing significantly from 1980 to the present. Both Stiglitz (2012) and Piketty (2014) found that long-run inequality fell between 1945 and 1980. From 1980 until 2007, inequality rose strongly. Profits on capital rose rapidly, but wages and salaries remained largely stagnant. In spite of the long-run increase in productivity and in profits, the median income of all full-time employees actually declined from 1980 to the present.

Our own business cycle data support the long-run conclusions to a large degree, but they add some additional insights. Our data show that inequality in the aggregate economy did show a long-run decline from 1949 to about 1980. After 1980, inequality rose to the present. They also show, however, that increasing inequality during each economic expansion from 1980 to the present played a major role in causing each cyclical contraction, including the Great Recession.

The Inequality Ratio

To see clearly what is going on with inequality during the business cycle, the clearest indicator is the "Inequality Ratio." The Inequality Ratio is defined to mean the ratio of profit income to employee income.

Profit is defined here to mean all business profit, including that of corporations, individuals, or partners. Employee income consists of wages, salaries, and benefits. Therefore, the ratio of profit income to employee income directly reflects the economic strengths of those who receive profits and those who sell their labor.

The Inequality Ratio reflects the inequality of income. This is because profit income is concentrated among the wealthy, whereas wage and salary income is received by the middle class and the poor. Specifically, most of the income received by the wealthiest 1 percent is profit from capital ownership. Moreover, a majority of the income in each of the 99 percentile groups below the wealthiest 1 percent is wages and salaries.

Inequality in the long run

Table 7.1 reveals the rise and fall of the Inequality Ratio in the long run; the long run here is defined to mean from cycle to cycle.

TABLE 7.1 Inequality Ratio, cycle bases, ten cycles, 1949–2009

Cycle	Cycle base Inequality Ratio
1949–1954	42.7
1954–1958	38.5
1958–1961	35.9
1961–1970	34.0
1970–1975	27.5
1975–1980	27.1
1980–1982	21.4
1982–1991	23.9
1991–2001	28.5
2001–2009	32.0

Note: Inequality Ratio is business profit divided by employee income ratio. Business profit is corporate profit plus proprietors' income. Employee income is all wages, salaries, and benefits.

Table 7.1 shows the cycle base of the Inequality Ratio in every cycle from 1949 to 2009. It thus traces the long-run growth or decline of the Inequality Ratio. It finds that the Inequality Ratio fell in the Golden Age from the cycle of 1949 to 1954 until the cycle of 1961 to 1970. Then, in the Age of Globalization, it continued to fall, though more slowly, until the cycle of 1980 to 1982. After the 1980 to 1982 cycle, the Inequality Ratio rose in every cycle to the end of the data in the cycle of 2001 to 2009.

Joseph Stiglitz and Thomas Piketty, in their books mentioned above, find in the annual data that long-run inequality falls until 1980, and then rises to the present. The data above show approximately the same thing. Since our data are composed of cycles rather than individual years, the closest thing to 1980 is the 1980 to 1982 cycle. Therefore, their finding that 1980 begins the rise of inequality is supported by the data above as closely as is possible.

Since the data here begin in 1949 (the first year of quarterly data issued by the government), the long-run decline of the Inequality Ratio lasted 31 years until 1980. Since then, in the long run, there have been 36 years of increased inequality since it began to rise in 1980.

Why did the Inequality Ratio decline until 1980?

In Chapter 4, the Golden Age was defined to be from about 1950 to 1970. This was the age of America's total dominance of the global economy. During the Golden Age, it was noted that American production was by far the largest in the world; American banks were dominant and it was the largest creditor nation; American trade was dominant and it had a large trade surplus; and American trade unions were strong with a rising wage level year by year. Under these conditions, there was plentiful demand for all-American goods as well as a rapidly expanding amount of production.

Since unions were strong, corporations were much weaker than they became in the Age of Globalization. The government was not actively anti-union during the Golden Age. Wage gains were made by the average worker every year. As wages and salaries rose faster than profits, the Inequality Ratio fell.

In the 1970s, there were a large number of basic changes in the American economy, revealing the end of its total dominance. Among these were a rising trade deficit, rising debt to the rest of the world, a higher unemployment rate, a lower economic growth rate, and deeper recessions.

In spite of all these changes, the Inequality Ratio continued to decline until 1980. The decline slowed somewhat, but it did continue because the dominant position of America continued in the 1970s, though it was not as strong relative to other countries as it had been.

These drastic changes in the American economy, as well as several others, are good reasons to support the definition of the Age of Globalization beginning in 1970. Yet decreasing inequality continued until 1980. That seems somewhat contradictory.

The answer is clear and will be documented below. It will show that the 1970s was a transitional era, with slowly declining long-run inequality, but with a changed picture in the business cycle.

Why did inequality rise since 1980?

The previous section showed the sources of strength and weakness that determine the percentage of income going to the aggregate capitalist class and the aggregate employee class. Starting in the 1970s, and accelerating in the 1980s, there was a shift in the relative strengths of these major classes. As a percentage of the whole labor force, trade unions strength reached its peak in the mid-1950s. Although union membership continued to rise, its relative strength has declined ever since. Some of the reasons for this relative union decline include strife within the union movement, harsh laws against unions from Congress, and a shift in the labor from large industrial plants to large numbers of small offices, making it more difficult to organize.

Beginning in the 1970s, on the other hand, corporations have grown far larger at a rapid pace. Their economic influence has also greatly increased. This increase in the economic power and wealth of the largest corporations is reflected in a stronger influence on politics: through Congress, through subsidies for political parties, through subsidies for individual candidates, through pressure exerted by conservative religious organizations, through pressure exerted in the media, and through pressure exerted in the educational system.

All of these factors reduced the strengths of labor and increased the strengths of those owning capital. The direct effect was the lowering of relative increases in wages and salaries, while allowing private wealth to increase rapidly. As those owning capital gained strength throughout politics and society, there was a vicious cycle. This cycle of events led to more economic wealth, which then led to still more political influence by the wealthiest 1 percent, and less and less influence by labor. This led to a smaller and smaller percentage of employee income in the economy. How did these long-run developments affect the cyclical behavior of inequality?

Class and inequality

In America, there is inequality according to the amount of income received, as well as inequality according to the amount of wealth that is held. In addition, the concept of an economic class is affected by the type of income that is received. Most of the bottom 99 percent of income receivers earns mainly labor income. Labor income means wages, salaries, and benefits. The other main type of income is income from capital, including profits from corporate stock or individual business, rent from land or mineral rights, and interest from financial instruments. People who have a majority of their income from profit, rent, and interest are called capitalists. Those whose income comes primarily from wages, salaries, and benefits are called employees.

This description applies pretty well to almost everybody at present in the active labor force. In American history, however, there have been other large and significant classes.

Around 1800, perhaps 80 percent of all families were engaged in self-sufficient agriculture and hunting. Most of them did not sell their produce in the market, but rather used it only for their own family. Most did not hire other workers. This class of independent farmers has largely disappeared. Agriculture has declined to a small part of the whole GDP, while corporate farming has replaced many independent farmers.

From the Declaration of Independence to the Civil War, there was a class of plantation owners in the Southern United States who made their profits by using slave labor. The Civil War, at the cost of 600,000 human lives, ended both the small, rich class of slave owners, as well as eliminating the class of slaves. Nevertheless, the South remained divided along lines of race and income inequality for a century or more.

From 1800 to the Civil War, there was also a large class of shopkeepers in the cities. They have remained to this day. Their numbers, their profits, and their influence have steadily declined as a percentage of the population since the beginning of the Age of Globalization.

There are also differences within the present capitalist class. Only the top 1 percent of income receivers has most of their income from capital. Others in the top 1 percent of income receivers take most of their income in the form of salary for corporate executive officers. Most of this is actually profit, not labor income. It is called labor income when it is reported to the government because everything called labor income can be subtracted from corporate income before taxes.

The most important point about class is to remember that each class has a separate and distinct interest, mostly contrary to the interests of other classes. For example, the top 1 percent of the wealth pyramid has 40 percent of all the wealth. Most of that wealth comes from capital ownership, whether corporate stock, real estate, or lending of money. Their common class interest is to have taxes on capital returns as low as possible, plus low wages and salaries for most people, as well as high taxes on labor income.

The bottom 90 percent in the wealth pyramid has only 30 percent of all the wealth, as shown earlier. Most of the income of the bottom 90 percent of Americans comes from some form of labor income, wages, or benefits. It follows that it is in the interest of the bottom 90 percent of the income pyramid to have higher wages and salaries. They therefore have a class interest in having taxes as low as possible on the average employee.

In the American economy, class warfare has been initiated by members of the wealthiest 1 percent and by their conservative representatives in Congress. Only when their real wages are lowered significantly do most employees oppose the class interests of the corporate executive officers, bankers, and other members of the capitalist class.

Because it has less economic and political power, the employee class is forced to react defensively. Crusaders for each side fight in Congress for the class interests of the class that they represent. There are also daily class battles over the amount of wages and salaries.

In brief, the greater strength of those who hold capital and receive profit has enabled them since 1980 to increase profit while maintaining stagnant wages and salaries.

The Inequality Ratio over the business cycle

With this long-run background, it is now possible to look at the cyclical behavior of the Inequality Ratio. This cyclical behavior is shown both for the Golden Age and the Age of Globalization in Figure 7.2.

Figure 7.2, which shows the behavior of the Inequality Ratio in the Golden Age and Age of Globalization, is the key figure for this entire book. It is a treasure trove of facts that will be slowly sifted and explained. Here, we begin by briefly mentioning again the meaning of the Inequality Ratio and the meaning of the Golden Age and Age of Globalization in this context.

To make sure that the following arguments are presented logically, the reader is reminded of three points made earlier in this chapter. First, the Inequality Ratio is profits divided by wages and salaries. Second, the Golden Age, approximately from 1949 to 1970, witnessed a decline in inequality mainly because of the unique circumstances after the Second World War. Third, the Age of Globalization is defined here to be from 1970 to the present. In the transitional period of the 1970s, the Inequality Ratio continued a slow decline, but a great many of the basic institutions of American capitalism had enormous changes. These changes led to the rise in the Inequality Ratio all the way from 1980 to the present.

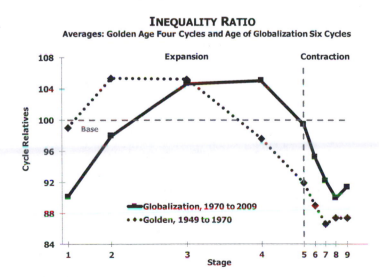

FIGURE 7.2   Inequality Ratio, cycles, Golden Age, 1949–1970, and Age of Globalization, 1970–2009

Inequality Ratio in the cycles of the Golden Age

In the Golden Age, there was a long-run decline of the Inequality Ratio, as shown in Table 7.1. Figure 7.2 adds important information to that point. The Inequality Ratio for the Golden Age is shown in Figure 7.2 by a dotted line. In this figure, during the average cycle for all four cycles of the Golden Age, the reader may be startled to find that the Inequality Ratio declined all the way from Stage 2 to Stage 8. Thus, Figure 7.2 supports the conclusion that there was a long-run decline in the Inequality Ratio during this age.

Furthermore, Figure 7.2 clearly shows that in the average expansion of the Golden Age, there was a brief increase in the Inequality Ratio followed by a long decline in the rest of the expansion. In Chapter 6, it was shown that all profits—including corporate profits—reach their peak in Stage 4, leading the cycle by one stage. Since the Inequality Ratio in the Golden Age declined all the way from Stage 2 to the end of the expansion, it clearly was not the main factor causing a cyclical contraction. In this age, inequality played only a secondary role in the business cycle, not the most important role.

This condition was due to the uniqueness of that age in American history, as stressed in the introductory material stated above. The cause was the unusual long-run conditions while America was the dominant power in the global economy after the Second World War. This dominance provided such a strong flow of income into America that it was possible to raise profits, but also possible to raise wages and salaries even more.

Inequality Ratio in the cycles of the Age of Globalization

The average data for the six cycles of the Age of Globalization, 1970 to 2009, is shown by a solid line. The solid line in Figure 7.2 shows the opposite of the Golden Age. During the Age of Globalization, from 1980 to the present, the Inequality Ratio has risen from cycle to cycle. This long-run effect has caused rising political inequality along with rising anger by the great majority whose real income has stagnated.

In addition to the long-run rise of inequality since 1980, Figure 7.2 also reveals that inequality rose in every cyclical expansion of the Age of Globalization. The Inequality Ratio fell in every expansion of the Golden Age, but rose in every expansion of the Age of Globalization.

In the average cyclical expansion of the Age of Globalization, the Inequality Ratio rose from Stage 1 to Stage 4 by over 15 percent. In other words, inequality of income rose during the average expansion during the Age of Globalization all the way from the initial trough to the profit peak in Stage 4.

Altogether, Table 7.1 and Figure 7.2 say emphatically that inequality has been rising since about 1980, from cycle to cycle, and that something must be done to move toward more equality in income, wealth, and opportunity. Extreme inequality must be reversed because it has led to widespread human misery at the bottom of the income scale. Increasing inequality in each expansion is the main factor leading to recessions and unemployment (see below). Because the high level of inequality has led to enormous political influence by the wealthiest 1 percent, this has undermined democracy.

The transitional period of the 1970s

The 1970s was a transitional period in the sense that long-run inequality continued to fall slightly, but the Inequality Ratio did rise from the beginning of the cycle up to the profit peak. All of the major changes in the economy occurred during this transition. The American economy changed in the 1970s from a trade surplus to a trade deficit, from rising trade union strength to falling trade union strength, from a fairly smooth rise of GDP in the long run to significant GDP declines in each cycle, and from falling inequality in expansions to rising inequality in expansions. It is included in the Age of Globalization because it initiates all of these changes. Finally, it is similar to the rest of the Age of Globalization in that inequality rises in expansions, which then lead to recessions.

How was it possible during the 1970s for the Inequality Ratio to rise in expansions, but to fall in the long run? The answer is that the Inequality Ratio did rise from Stage 1 to Stage 4 of the cycle, but it fell even more in the cyclical contraction during this transitional period.

Inequality in expansions during the Age of Globalization

In the transitional period from 1970 to 1982, the Inequality Ratio did rise in the cyclical expansions from Stage 1 to the profit peak in Stage 4. The increases are substantial, but not rapid. The Inequality Ratio rose by 10 percent in the average expansion from 1970 to 1982.

In the three cycles in the Age of Globalization since 1982—consisting of the Reagan cycle of 1982 to 1991, the Clinton cycle of 1991 to 2001, and the Bush cycle of 2001 to 2009—the Inequality Ratio rose much faster. The average increase in those three cycles was an unprecedented 22 percent rise in the Inequality Ratio.

The Bush expansion that led to the Great Recession had the strongest increase of inequality of any of the cycles since the Great Depression. The Inequality Ratio, which is aggregate profit to aggregate wages and salaries, rose by 25 percent in that cyclical expansion from the beginning trough to the profit peak.

Why did inequality increase in expansions from 1980 to 2007?

The long-run changes that helped account for the rise of the Inequality Ratio in expansions includes increasing weakness in unions, rapid rise in the size and power of corporations, and the rise in power of political forces representing the wealthy and corporations.

What are the usual reasons that the ratio of profits to employee income rises to some extent in every expansion? Under capitalist institutions, employees are tied to a given wage or salary rate by contract. Therefore, wages and salaries do not automatically rise with the growth of productivity or sales. Every growth in productivity, however, automatically increases profits if there is no similar growth in wages and salaries. Therefore, employees are always playing catch-up.

There are additional reasons profits rise faster than wages and salaries. First, there are various government regulations making strikes difficult, so unions always have a somewhat weak bargaining position. Workers are even weaker when they are bargaining as individuals without unions against giant corporations.

Second, there is always some inflation in the price of goods and services in an expansion. So even if the employee's salary or wage is raised, they may still have the same or lower purchasing power as before the raise. Since it appears that wages are rising, employees do not feel a strong urge to fight as hard as possible for wage and salary increases. The same factor of monetary wage increase tends to reduce public support for any strike.

Third, the media are controlled by the same giant corporations who wish to defend profits against any increase in employee income. Although there are exceptions in the media today, most of the media focus is on the trouble given to citizens by any strike. They seldom notice the actual hardships of employees who feel they are forced to go on strike to defend their living standards.

Impact of increasing inequality in expansions

What was the impact of the increase in inequality during each of the cyclical expansions from 1980 through 2007? The increase in inequality has two major effects on the business cycle. One is through the change in political power. The other is through changes in profits.

The increase in political power by the wealthy and large corporations is a slow, long-run effect. The increase of inequality in each cyclical expansion merely adds to the already existing political power exerted by the wealthy and giant corporations. That power is used to prevent any government spending on public services for the middle class and the poor. The wealthy believe that any increase in government spending will also increase their taxes (for more detail, see Stiglitz, 2012, 2015b). One major area of government spending strongly supported by the wealthy, however, is military expenditure because they receive extremely high profits from military production.

This increasing inequality in expansions, due to stagnant wages and salaries, is also a major cause of the lack of effective demand, which leads to economic contractions. This argument has been strongly attacked by conservative economists and has often been ignored by progressive economists.

The argument that inequality leads to recession has two steps. The first step is to show strong evidence that inequality does increase during cyclical expansions.

This argument was documented in this chapter. The second part of the argument is to show that the increasing inequality in the expansion has a strong negative effect on consumer demand. That impact on consumer demand will be shown in the next chapter.

The increase in inequality is not ancient history. On November 7, 2014, the Economic Cycle Research Institute (ECRI), a group of business cycle experts that publishes a series on the leading indicators, stated in a note entitled "The agony and the ecstasy" that the "incredible decline in the employee compensation share of national income is gutting middle class income" (ECRI, 2014). In other words, greater inequality was showing up as stagnant wages and salaries. Yet it is those wages and salaries that are the main source of consumer spending, as revealed in the next chapter.

Conclusions

During the 1920s, inequality rose in each expansion, and it also rose from one cycle to the next. Inequality reached its highest point in 1928, when it was a major cause leading to the Great Depression.

In the Golden Age of American capitalism, 1949 to 1970 in our data, the Inequality Ratio fell in every expansion. The Inequality Ratio also fell from cycle to cycle. In the long-run trend measured from cycle to cycle, the Inequality Ratio continued to fall until 1980. The falling Inequality Ratio in the long run led to a fairly high rate of economic growth in the Golden Age.

During the Age of Globalization, the Inequality Ratio rose in every business cycle expansion from 1970 until 2007. From 1980 until 2009, the Inequality Ratio rose from cycle to cycle. The rising long-run Inequality Ratio led to a declining rate of economic growth during the Age of Globalization. Long-run and cyclical Inequality Ratios both reached a peak in 2007. The Great Recession began at the end of 2007.

During the Age of Globalization, the Inequality Ratio rose in every cyclical expansion, but it fell in every cyclical contraction. Furthermore, business expansions have been much longer than contractions. Therefore, the Inequality Ratio had to rise from the beginning to the end of every cycle. The long-run effect has been to increase the level of inequality from cycle to cycle.

During the Golden Age, because inequality played only a small role, cyclical recessions were relatively mild and the growth rate high. In the Age of Globalization, the rise in inequality during each expansion eventually led to a recession or depression.

As a general conclusion, the major change in the behavior of inequality from the Golden Age to the Age of Globalization explains the more powerful recessions occurring in the Age of Globalization. The detailed process by which a rise in inequality to the profit peak causes profits to decline and a recession to follow is spelled out in the next chapter.

8

HOW INEQUALITY AFFECTS CONSUMER DEMAND

Consumption is about 70 percent of the Gross Domestic Product. It is a fact of life for every individual in the economy. In a recession, a decline in consumption means that someone in the wealthiest 1 percent may decide to postpone buying another yacht until the next year, a woman in the middle-income group must decide how to feed her children on a lower income, and a woman whose income is pushed below the poverty level may decide to postpone her healthcare in order to provide a sufficient meal to her children.

Before turning to the question of how inequality of income and wealth affects consumer demand, it is useful to begin by looking at the atmosphere in which consumer spending occurs within America and most of the capitalist world.

Consumerism and alienation

Consumerism is when people focus exclusively on the goal of having more and more consumer goods and services to the exclusion of almost every other goal. An addiction to consumerism prevents people from worrying about other social goals, such as the general happiness of the society. Consumer goods and services must be piled up, especially to show one is able to spend more than one's neighbors. Thus, an individual man with a lot of money to spend may get his wife a fur coat even though they live in the sunshine of Florida.

The desire for more and more consumer goods and services becomes stronger than any religion or solidarity for the whole community. Many examples of consumerist spending patterns by Americans may be seen in the classic book *The Theory of the Leisure Class* by Thorstein Veblen (1899). It would be interesting to hear what Veblen would have had to say about the five mansions owned by Mitt Romney, the Republican candidate for president in 2012, or what Veblen would have said about the extremely ostentatious consumption patterns of President Donald J. Trump.

The single-minded pursuit of consumer goods and services is one of the factors leading to alienation in America. "Alienation" means the feeling that one is alone and separate from anyone else in the society, often including the feeling that the whole society is unfairly attacking the individual. The attitude expressed by many Americans is that one should act solely for oneself, with no compassion for others.

In the 1930s, when most people had few consumer goods and services, often not even enough to sustain their families, people nevertheless were transformed by the Great Depression to believe they must work unselfishly with others to correct the situation. The most popular songs among the labor movement expressed the opposite of alienation. For example, the song called "Solidarity Forever" begins with the words: "When the union's inspiration through the worker's blood shall run, there can be no power greater anywhere beneath the sun." A great many Americans today would sneer at this sentiment as idealistic nonsense. Those who sneer at it would say that one must attend solely to making one's own fortune or else the world will eat you alive.

Extreme inequality also causes alienation between large numbers of poor employees and a few wealthy owners. One type of alienation expressed by employees is the feeling that all their hard work in production is done solely to make profits for the capitalist owners, while they themselves are cheated of much of the fruits of their labor. This sentiment was strongest in the mass production industries of the 1930s. It is weakest in small offices in good economic times. This type of alienation from the society and the elite who control it is strongest today among Latino and African-American groups because of the discrimination against them. Alienation is least among professionals and other highly paid employees.

The anger and alienation of large numbers of people makes it easier for bigots to convince one group that it is poor or unemployed simply because of another group. Alienation makes it easier, for example, to convince some voters of the fallacy that they would have more jobs and higher wages if only a mile-high fence would keep out everyone to the south of the American border.

Effective demand for consumer goods and services

During the Great Depression, President Franklin Roosevelt observed that a large percentage of the population did not have enough food to eat, clothing to wear, or housing and shelter. Under these circumstances, a rational society would always attempt to keep producing more consumer goods until everyone has enough for at least the minimum of food, clothing, and shelter. Yet during the Great Depression, the production of consumer goods in the form of food, clothing, and shelter all declined by a large percentage.

Why should the production of food, clothing, and shelter ever decline when people are in need of them? Of course, the production capacity might be destroyed by war or a natural or man-made disaster. The demand might also be reduced if the population declines. None of those things was true in the Great Depression. This chapter will try to explain the reason why such seemingly irrational declines in the production of food, clothing, and shelter actually do take place in our society.

This strange phenomenon is not just ancient history. Since the end of the Second World War, there have been 10 recessions in which the production of food, clothing, and shelter all declined. In every one of these cases, there was no war devastation and no population decline. Instead, there was continued poverty and millions of people without enough to meet the minimum standards for food, clothing, and shelter. Most of these declines were by a small percentage, but it will be shown that the percentage decline in the production of consumer goods and services was considerable in the Great Recession of 2007 to 2009.

In the modern capitalist economy of America, goods and services are produced only if there is a demand for them with the money to pay for it. The problem in each of those 10 recessions has been the lack of aggregate demand in the economy. Consumer demand is larger than all other types of demand combined. Therefore, the explanation for the lack of demand begins in this chapter with the lack of consumer demand.

Consumer demand in America is affected by three main factors. First, the aggregate demand for consumer goods and services is obviously affected by the aggregate amount of income received by all Americans. Second, net income may be increased beyond the amount that is earned by the use of borrowed credit. This use of credit will be discussed at length in the next chapter, so it is temporarily ignored. Third, the degree of inequality will determine how much of the national income goes to wage and salary earners, who spend most of their income on consumer goods. Suppose, for example, that one person, such as a powerful ruler, has 99 percent of all income, while everyone else has an equal amount of the remaining 1 percent of national income. In that case, the 99 percent of the people will spend all of their small incomes on consumer goods and services, thus using up their total of 1 percent of the national income. The ruler may use 10 percent of the national income to satisfy his most imaginative desires for consumer goods and services. That will still leave 89 percent of all national income that is not used for consumer goods and services.

On the contrary, if every person has an exactly equal share of the national income, then each will spend a sizable share of their income on consumer goods and services. The result is an aggregate consumer demand that is many times as great as when one person has almost all the national income.

The degree of inequality in the society measures how the national income is distributed. As was seen in the previous chapter, every institution of capitalism in America and around the world will influence the degree of inequality. For example, it was shown that the labor market is an institution in which the strengths of the opposing parties of capital and labor determine the level of wages and salaries. Thus, it is no exaggeration to say that the institutions of capitalism in each country, as well as the global institutions of capitalism, together determine the demand for consumer goods and services under the capitalist economic system.

Each person has a certain set of preferences among goods and services. The aggregate amount of consumer goods and services sold, however, depends on the aggregate national income and the degree of inequality in the distribution of that income. The demand for goods and services is determined not only by the preferences of people, but by the aggregate income and its distribution.

The previous chapter tracked the behavior of income inequality over the business cycle. In order to solve the mystery of the lack of consumption, this chapter will examine the behavior of consumer spending over the cycle. It will then examine the relationship of consumer spending to national income and to income inequality over the business cycle.

Consumer spending in the Great Depression

What happens in times of great volatility and depression? What happened in the average of the four cycles from 1921 to 1938? Those were the cycles of the interwar era, which included the Great Depression. In those cycles, personal consumption rose in the average expansion by 15 percent. In the four cyclical contractions of that volatile time, on average, aggregate personal consumption spending fell by 10 percent. Thus, even life-giving consumer spending declined considerably during the Great Depression. The desire for necessities was still there, but the money was not.

Consumer spending in the Golden Age

How does consumer spending rise and fall during the average business cycle? Figure 8.1 shows this behavior for the Golden Age, 1949 to 1970, and for the Age of Globalization, 1970 to 2009.

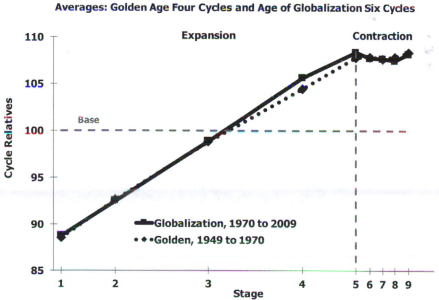

FIGURE 8.1   Consumer spending, Golden Age, 1949–1970, and Age of Globalization, 1970–2009

Figure 8.1 reveals that consumer spending during the average expansion of the Golden Age rose in almost a straight line in the first half of the expansion, then rose at a slower pace during the last half of the average expansion. During the average contraction of the Golden Age, consumer spending fell a little, and then rose again to the final cycle trough date. In the Golden Age, every contraction was much shorter than the average expansion. Therefore, the average amount of consumption rose considerably from one cycle to the next.

During the Golden Age, aggregate personal consumption spending rose by 19.3 percent in the average expansion. In the average contraction of the Golden Age, however, the aggregate personal consumption spending actually rose by half a percent. Consumer spending actually had a brief decline in the early part of the contraction, but then continued to rise in the rest of the contraction. In other words, in the Golden Age, consumption rose during the whole expansion, then rose more slowly during most of the contraction.

Consumer spending in the Age of Globalization

According to Figure 8.1, in the average of the six cyclical expansions of the Age of Globalization, aggregate consumer spending rose by 19.5 percent. In the average contraction, personal consumer spending fell by half a percent.

Thus, while consumption in the average contraction of the Golden Age actually rose a half percent, consumption in the average contraction of the Age of Globalization fell by a half percent. The average mild contraction of the Golden Age gave way to a stronger contraction in the Age of Globalization.

Consumer share

The "consumer share" is defined as aggregate personal consumer spending as a percentage of national income. When they discuss the relationship of consumer spending to the income of an individual consumer, most economists call this percentage the average propensity to consume. A propensity calls to mind some kind of psychological preference. That may make some sense for those consumers who have enough income and wealth to make choices between consumption and saving. Most consumers, however, only have enough income for their basic consumer requirements. Some consumers have even less than is needed for the basic requirements, so they must go into debt in order to meet their minimum needs.

When considering aggregate consumption, it is not a personal psychological preference, but the distribution of income among all possible consumers, that is the most important issue. Lower-income individuals spend every dime they get because they need that much and more to purchase a subsistence amount of food. Therefore, at least in terms of aggregate behavior, the notion of a consumer share of national income is a more useful concept than the somewhat misleading propensity to consume.

How does the consumer share behave over the business cycle? This question is answered in Figure 8.2.

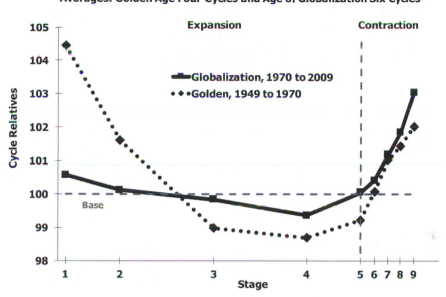

FIGURE 8.2   Consumer share, Golden Age, 1949–1970, and Age of Globalization, 1970–2009

Figure 8.2 tells us that in the average cyclical expansion of both the Golden Age and the Age of Globalization, the consumer share declines during the expansion from Stage 1 until Stage 4.

The consumer share then rises, in both the Golden Age and the Age of Globalization, from Stage 4 until the end of the contraction in Stage 9. This behavior was approximately the same in both the Golden Age and the Age of Globalization.

Thus, during most of the expansion, the aggregate consumer spending rises, but national income rises faster, so the consumer share of national income falls. Similarly, in the economic contraction, aggregate consumer spending tends to fall a little, but the consumer share of national income actually rises.

Employee share in the interwar era, 1921 to 1938

The interwar era, including the Great Depression, covers four cycles from 1921 to 1938. The two cycles of the 1920s contain the evolution toward the Great Depression, while the two cycles of the 1930s constitute the Great Depression.

In order to understand economic contractions such as the Great Depression, one must focus on the expansion that came before it. It is during the expansion that inequality increases. This rising inequality and other economic problems result in the end of the expansion and the beginning of the contraction.

In the average expansion of these four cycles, employee income rose 20 percent, while national income rose 23 percent. The conclusion is that in the average expansion of this era, the employee share of national income fell during the expansion (the source for the data above was from the research of Mitchell, 1951, based on the earliest aggregate data available from the Department of Commerce).

In each of these expansions, the employee share fell because wages and salaries remained stagnant while profits rose rapidly.

In the average of these four cycle contractions, including the Great Depression, employee income fell 14 percent while national income fell 18 percent. As always, the aggregate statistics show a decline of inequality during the contraction. This is primarily because profits fall so rapidly in each contraction. Of course, the burden of human misery is clearly on the average employee, since a 14 percent decline in compensation for employees usually means a painful constriction in their ability to purchase food, clothing, and shelter. A billionaire who loses half of his wealth, however, can still buy whatever consumer goods and services he likes.

In the 1929 to 1933 contraction, full-time unemployment rose to 33 percent of all the labor force. Part-time unemployment included 50 percent of the labor force. The remaining employees suffered wage cuts of 14 percent in real dollars. At the same time, however, total corporate profits were negative for many months at a time. Thus, the facts of the Great Depression help clarify the findings of Piketty (2014) that aggregate inequality rose to its highest point in 1928 and began its decline during the Great Depression.

Employee share and property share, 1949 to 2005

The "employee share" is defined to mean all employee income divided by the national income. "Employee income" is defined to mean wages, salaries, and benefits. "Property income" is defined to mean all rental income, interest income, and all profits, including corporate and non-corporate. "Property share" is defined to mean all profit, rent, and interest, divided by national income. By definition, all employee income plus all property income equals national income. Therefore, the employee share plus the property share equals one.

When the share of property income rises, there is more inequality. When the share of property income falls, there is less inequality. This is because the wealthiest 1 percent receive most of their income as property income. The other 99 percent are mostly employees, so in every one of the 99 percentile groups, most of the income is wages and salaries. It follows that when more income goes to the property share, more of the national income goes to the wealthiest 1 percent, so there is more inequality of income.

The previous chapter showed that inequality declined from the Golden Age until 1980 during the Age of Globalization. Table 8.1 shows how the property share is another way to measure the degree of inequality. The property share declined from 39.4 percent in the cycle beginning in 1949 down to 32.9 percent in the cycle beginning in 1980. Thus, it supports the finding that inequality did decline from 1949 to 1980.

TABLE 8.1 Employee and property share, cycle bases, 1949–2009

Cycle	Employee share cycle base	Property share cycle base
1949–1954	60.6	39.4
1954–1958	61.7	38.2
1958–1961	62.3	37.7
1961–1970	62.9	37.0
1970–1975	65.7	34.3
1975–1980	66.2	33.8
1980–1982	67.1	32.9
1982–1991	65.6	34.3
1991–2001	64.6	35.4
2001–2009	63.8	36.2

Source: Quarterly data from U.S. Department of Commerce, Bureau of Economic Analysis, NIPA, Table 1.12.

Note: Employee income, property income, and national income are in real dollars, seasonally adjusted.

Definition: Employee share means employee income divided by national income. Property share means property income divided by national income. Cycle base is the average over one cycle

Of course, the employee share rose at the same pace as the property share fell. This is still another way of demonstrating that inequality fell in that time period. The employee share rose in that time from 60.6 percent to 67.1 percent of national income. The increasing equality of income caused more consumer demand. This increased demand supported increased American production.

The previous chapter also reported that inequality rose from 1982 until the end of our data in 2009. That is shown by the fact that the property share rose from 32.9 percent in the cycle beginning in 1980 up to 36.2 percent in the cycle beginning in 2001 and ending in 2009.

Of course, in the same time span, employee share of national income fell from 67.1 percent to 63.8 percent. Thus, the data on property share and employee share further confirms the finding that inequality has been rising in America since 1980.

As noted earlier, the following are among the main reasons why inequality began to rise again in 1980: there was more global competition, which reduced the American share of global trade; labor unions declined as a percentage of the labor force; and the economic and political strength of corporations increased immensely.

Employee share during the four cycles of the Golden Age

Not only has long-run behavior of inequality changed; the behavior of inequality over the business cycle has also changed. This can be demonstrated by the movements of the employee share, whose effect on consumption will be discussed below.

Inequality in the Golden Age has many features in common with inequality during the Age of Globalization. The basics features of the cyclical process remain the same because the fundamental institutions of capitalism remain the same.

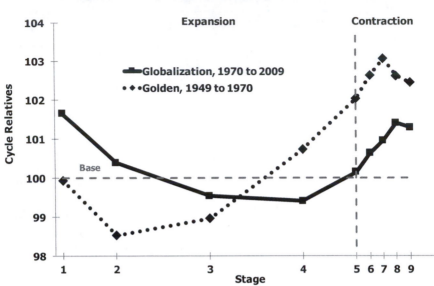

EMPLOYEE SHARE
Averages: Golden Age Four Cycles and Age of Globalization Six Cycles

FIGURE 8.3 Employee share, cycles, Golden Age, 1949–1970, and Age of
Globalization, 1970–2009

Yet there have been gradual changes in the basic features of capitalism, which have
caused some important changes in the behavior of inequality over the business
cycle in those two eras. The picture of the cyclical behavior of the employee share
in these two different eras is shown in Figure 8.3.

A fall in the employee share means an increase in inequality. A rise in the
employee share means less inequality. In Figure 8.3, a dotted line shows the behavior of the employee share in the Golden Age. The graph shows that the employee
share only fell during one interval, from Stage 1 to Stage 2. The employee share
then rose from Stage 2 for the rest of the expansion and into the beginning of the
contraction.

According to Figure 8.3, the employee share rose during most of the expansion,
so this caused the employee share to continue rising from cycle to cycle. The rise of
the employee share in each cyclical expansion meant that inequality was declining
from cycle to cycle. The rising employee share meant that profits were rising more
slowly than wages and salaries in that era. That is unusual in American history, so
it is important to understand why it happened in the Golden Age.

During the Golden Age, trade unions in America were at their peak strength
in terms of the ratio of union workers to all workers. This was a major element
causing wages and salaries to rise faster than profits in the expansions. At the same
time, corporations had not yet begun the extreme increase in their size and power
that came in the Age of Globalization. American corporations were still limited

largely to their profits in America. They were just beginning to expand to every part of the globe, as they continued to do more rapidly in the 1970s. Because of the strengths of unions, as well as the limited strength of corporations, there was still a great deal of pro-union behavior among politicians and political parties.

Another reason that America had high prosperity and continued wage increases was that the Second World War had left most of Europe and Asia devastated, while the American economy was intact and able to increase peacetime production soon after the war. The economic strength in America was reflected in the Marshall Plan, which gave massive economic aid to help rebuild Europe.

Employee share cycles in the Age of Globalization

The solid line in Figure 8.3 depicts the behavior of the employee share during the Age of Globalization. There is one major difference in its behavior compared with the Golden Age. During the Golden Age, the employee share rose during most of the expansion, but in the Age of Globalization it fell for most of the expansion.

The decline of the employee share during most of the expansion is consistent with the findings of several researchers that inequality has been increasing in the long run from 1980 to the present. From the start of the Age of Globalization, the employee share only fell a tiny bit in the three cycles from 1970 to 1982, but it fell rapidly in the three cycle expansions from 1982 to 2009. This is a major change helping to explain the difference between the Golden Age and the Age of Globalization.

Employee share and profits

Profits reach their peak usually in Stage 4 of the expansion and then decline. The decline of aggregate profits causes investment to decline at the reference cycle peak in Stage 5. The decline of investment in plants and equipment ends the expansion. At the same time, the lack of demand causes capitalist enterprises to reduce their existing production.

This lower production causes workers to be fired in that sector of the economy. Since there is no more expansion and some new unemployment, a recession or depression begins. It is clear that the decisions causing a recession or depression are made as soon as aggregate profit begins to decline, as detailed in Chapter 6.

The key question is: What is happening to all the main sectors of the economy up to the peak of profits? By looking at the main variable, such as investment and consumption at the profit peak, we can immediately see why profits begin to decline after that peak. So we must measure the expansion of each component of aggregate demand and supply up to the profit peak at Stage 4 to find out why profits decline. Therefore, from here on, measurements of the rise and fall of these components will only be made up to Stage 4, at the specific peak of profits, not up to the reference cycle peak at Stage 5.

In the four cycles during the Golden Age, the employee share of national income actually rose on average 0.7 percent from the initial trough at Stage 1 to the profit peak at Stage 4. During the average of the six cycles during the Age of Globalization, the employee share fell by 1.68 percent from Stage 1 to Stage 4, the profit peak. Thus, there was a sharp change in the behavior of the employee share during the Age of Globalization; instead of rising during most of the expansion, it fell during most of the expansion.

Actually, in the transition era from 1970 to 1980, the employee share was about constant from the initial trough to the profit peak. Inequality in America began to rise in 1980 and has continued to rise until the present, counting from cycle to cycle. For this reason, plus all the other circumstances of the Age of Globalization, there was a marked decline in the employee share in each expansion. In the average of the three expansions from 1982 to 2009, the employee share fell by 3.31 percent from the initial trough to the profit peak.

Consumer share and employee share

The employee share was defined in Chapter 7 to be the ratio between all employee income and the national income (multiplied by 100 to be seen as a percentage).

In the average expansion, the employee share falls from the beginning trough of the cycle all the way to the profit peak in Stage 4. Similarly, in the contraction, the employee share of income rises; the reason is that national income falls even faster than employee income.

In the average expansion, the employee share and the consumer share move downward together. In the average contraction, the employee share and the consumer share move upward together. The movements of the employee share determine the movement of the consumer share.

So far, this chapter has showed that consumer spending rises in every expansion, then falls in every contraction. The main cause of the consumer spending rise and decline is that national income rises and then declines.

It was also revealed that the consumer share of national income fell in each expansion to the profit peak and then rose in each contraction to the profit trough. This was true during the interwar period, including the Great Depression, and also in the Age of Globalization. It was not true in the Golden Age.

Why did the consumer share move upward in each of the business expansions during the Golden Age? The consumer share of national income is strongly influenced by the movements of the employee share of national income. During the Golden Age, the employee share moved upward in each business expansion.

This rise of the employee share in each business expansion was consistent with the fact that inequality was declining in the long run from cycle to cycle in the Golden Age. The employee share of national income reflects the degree of equality or inequality of income in the national economy.

The consumer share reflects the amount of demand for consumer goods and services. By comparing the employee share to the consumer share, one can see the relationship of inequality to demand in the aggregate economy.

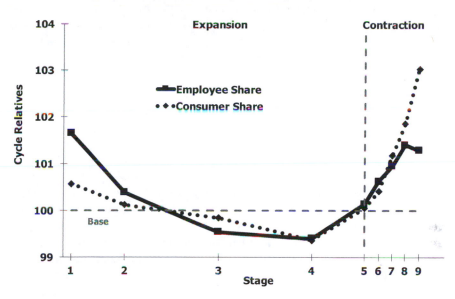

FIGURE 8.4   Employee share and consumer share, Age of Globalization, 1970–2009

Figure 8.4 shows the employee share and consumer share for the average of the six cycles of the Age of Globalization. The solid line shows the consumer share. The consumer share falls from Stage 1 to Stage 4 of the expansion. Then, the consumer share starts to rise a little up to the cycle peak. The consumer share continues to rise throughout the contraction until the next to last stage, the profit trough at Stage 8.

In other words, the consumer share mostly moves down when the economy is moving up, and mostly moves up when the economy is moving down. It is, however, a leading indicator. Therefore, it turns one stage before the reference cycle peak and again turns one stage before the trough, so it turns at the profit peak and the profit trough.

During the era of increasing long-run inequality since 1980, the consumer share declines in each cyclical expansion. Moreover, it follows closely on the path set by the falling employee share in each expansion. Therefore, it is reasonable to say that growing inequality, represented by the fall of the employee share during cyclical expansions, is a major cause of the lack of aggregate demand that leads to recessions and depressions.

Why consumer and employee shares move together

Why does a falling employee share of national income in an expansion lead to a falling consumer share of national income? Employees include lower-, middle-, and higher-income wage and salary earners. Lower-income employees are, on average, in debt, so the consumer share of their income is usually above 100 percent of their income. Most employees fall into the middle-income group in which the income barely meets the needs of consumption, so the consumer share of their income is close to 100 percent. Higher-paid employees usually save some of their income, but they spend all the rest.

In the top 1 percent of income receivers, and only in that top 1 percent, the majority of all income is from capital ownership, which produces profit. Since capital owners are far wealthier than employees on average, their average consumer share is much lower than the average consumer share for all of the income receivers.

A shift in income from employees to capital owners is reflected in a fall of the employee share of the national income. That fall in the employee share occurs in each business expansion. The decline in the employee share leads to less aggregate spending. Therefore, the consumer share of national income must also fall in each business expansion.

When the consumer share falls, less income is spent in the lower- and middle-income groups. Thus, a falling employee share in an expansion causes a lower rate of growth of consumer demand.

What happens to the income of capital owners that is not spent on consumption? It is assumed by some conservative economists that all the income not spent on consumption will be used to buy capital goods, such as buildings and equipment. This would mean that aggregate demand remains the same as before the shift of income from employees to capital owners. Actually, capital owners usually save a considerable part of their income. Some of the saved income goes to economic investments in buildings and equipment. The remaining part of the income of the wealthy and of the large corporations may be spent for speculative investment, which produces profits for its owners, but does not increase aggregate demand.

It follows that if there is a shift in the percentage of national income from poor and middle-income employees to the wealthy and the largest corporations, the average amount of spending will be a smaller percentage of all national income. Thus, the typical process of business expansions tends to reduce the consumer share of national income; that is, the percentage of national income that is spent on consumer goods and services.

Relations between inequality and consumption

The movements of the consumer share of national income, the employee share of national income, and the Inequality Ratio are briefly summarized in Table 8.2.

In Table 8.2, the three time series are consumer share, employee share, and Inequality Ratio. To avoid confusion, remember that each of these is a ratio. For example, consumer share is the ratio of consumer spending to national income. The table shows the amount of change in the ratio going up or down in the expansion. Then it shows the change in the ratio going up and down in the contraction.

TABLE 8.2 Consumer share and inequality, amplitudes for specific profit peak at Stage 4 and specific profit trough at Stage 8, Age of Globalization, six cycles, 1970–2009

Economic series	Expansion amplitude	Contraction amplitude
Consumer share	−1.31	2.45
Employee share	−2.29	1.98
Inequality Ratio	15.08	−14.79

Source: United States Department of Commerce, Bureau of Economic Analysis, National Income and Product Accounts.

Note: Expansion amplitude is Stage 4 minus Stage 1. Contraction amplitude is Stage 8 minus Stage 4. In stating the amplitudes, if the variable has declined, then a minus sign is used. If the variable has risen, then no sign is used.

Definitions: Inequality Ratio means business profit divided by employee income. Employee share means employee income divided by national income. Consumer share means consumption divided by national income.

In the Age of Globalization, the table shows that the consumer share of national income moves downward in the average expansion and upward in the average contraction. That is partly because wages and salaries increase far less than the national income or property income (profits, rent, and interest). The problem is that recipients of property income spend only a small percentage for consumption.

A large part of wages and salaries are spent on consumption. Table 8.2 verifies, however, that wages and salaries do not rise as fast as national income and output during an economic expansion. This results in a falling employee share and a rising Inequality Ratio in expansions up to the profit peak. It is this rise of inequality that is a major cause of the lack of consumer demand and aggregate demand for all goods and services.

In the contraction, the employee share and the Inequality Ratio both decline. This fall in inequality is one reason that consumer spending does not fall as fast as national income or output. Eventually, this fact is one of the factors setting the stage for a slower decline and then a recovery in aggregate profit. This describes one important mechanism of recovery in the average recession, but later chapters will show that deep depressions do not recover in this easy way.

Conclusions

Chapter 7 revealed that in those eras when long-run inequality has risen, such as the Age of Globalization from 1980 to 2015, inequality rose during each cyclical expansion. The degree of inequality has risen during each expansion, but the degree of inequality has fallen in each cyclical contraction. On average, however, economic contractions in the Age of Globalization have been shorter than the expansions. Therefore, there has been a net increase of inequality from one cycle to the next.

As inequality increased in each of the cyclical expansions, it has tended to limit the rise of demand for consumer goods and services. During the expansion, the percentage of income going to wages and salaries fell, while the percentage of income going to profit rose. This caused a decline in the growth of demand because wage and salary earners spend almost all their income on consumer goods and services, but recipients of profits spend a much smaller percentage of their income on consumer goods and services.

During the expansions in the Age of Globalization when aggregate demand slowed, production of consumer goods was reduced. This lower level of production required fewer workers. As employees were fired, they had no more wages and salaries. They were then forced to survive on a small amount of unemployment compensation. Their greatly reduced income further lowered consumer demand. This resulted in still more firings and still lower demand—a vicious downward spiral.

Additional issues to be considered

So far, only the story of inequality limiting consumer spending—which lowers aggregate demand, which lowers profits, which causes recessions—has been told. This is oversimplified and can lead to policy mistakes. In the first place, there are other types of aggregate demand beyond private investment and consumption. Aggregate demand also includes government spending (Chapter 10) and export revenue (Chapter 11).

In addition to aggregate demand, a complete model of the movements of the aggregate economy must include aggregate costs. There is labor cost (Chapter 7), interest costs (Chapter 9), taxes (Chapter 10), and import spending (Chapter 11).

Only when these additional issues are included can one have a complete view of the process that causes recessions. This complete view will show why our present economic institutions lead to recurrent recessions, while inequality still has the star role in the process.

9

CREDIT, BUBBLE, AND BUST

College students need to take on enormous debt in order to get an education. It then takes them many years, sometimes the rest of their life, in order to pay back all of the interest as well as the original debt. The average employee in America goes deeper into debt each year simply to pay for necessities. Many homeowners as well as many small business people find that in a recession or a depression, they cannot make the payments on the debts that they owe.

Why do people and corporations sometimes go so deep into debt that there is no rational expectation that the new credit will gain them anything? Why do bubbles sometimes burst and become credit crises? Why are there times when even a perfect credit rating will not get a borrower any money from a bank, a situation called a "credit crunch"?

This chapter sticks to the use of credit money in the average expansion and contraction, leaving investigation of the biggest financial crises and depressions until Chapters 13 and 14.

In Europe during the seventeenth and eighteenth centuries, the average person still bartered one product or service for another, so they seldom saw money and certainly did not use money in the form of credit. Nevertheless, there were bankers and other financiers who promoted large-scale investments in far-off countries that were held under colonial rule. Credit would expand rapidly where people expected to make overnight fortunes from, for example, a gold mine in Peru. Even if the mine made some money, it soon became apparent that profits were not going to keep rising at some phenomenal rate for much longer. At that point, the original investors who had convinced thousands of others to invest would suddenly get out with their profits. There would then be a credit crisis as the thousands of new investors suddenly found they had worthless stock they had paid for with large amounts of borrowed money.

Capitalism began to dominate the economy at the end of the eighteenth century in England and soon after spread to the rest of Europe. The credit system became closely tied to industrial capitalism. Since that time, credit has shown approximately the same pattern of behavior in each typical cycle of industrial expansion and contraction.

This chapter will show how credit rises in an expansion and declines in a contraction. It will also show that the rise of credit during the expansion allows the expansion to continue after there is insufficient demand coming from current income. On the other hand, if there is a huge expansion of credit before the peak of the business cycle, the following recession will be worse than it would be otherwise because consumers and corporations suddenly do not have the income to pay back their debts. The banks then suffer from rapidly declining profit insofar as their profits are based on expansion of credit. Now let us turn to the details of this process.

Consumer credit

The previous chapter revealed that in the Age of Globalization, the Inequality Ratio rose in each cyclical expansion. The increased inequality limited the growth of consumer spending. That was one of the causes of decreases in business profit in the last stage of expansion, which was a major cause of recession.

The source of consumer spending, however, is not just wages and salaries, but is also consumer credit. Consumers become more optimistic as they see the economy recovering and they get new jobs. Therefore, in an expansion, one expects consumers to borrow more money. For this reason, consumer credit rises in every cyclical expansion. It plays a key role in the increase of consumer demand and the expansion of the economy.

By contrast, in a contraction, consumers are generally pessimistic. Therefore, they save as much money as possible, consume as little as possible, and borrow as little as possible. At the same time, banks are afraid that people will not repay their loans because they have lower incomes, so banks reduce the amount of money they are willing to lend. The decline of consumer credit in every contraction puts a burden on consumers to buy their goods and services with less total income. The decline in consumer demand caused by the credit decline is another major reason for the deepening of a recession.

These assertions can be proven by the data. In both the Golden Age—the four cycles from 1949 to 1970—and the Age of Globalization—the six cycles from 1970 to 2009—total outstanding consumer credit expanded at a fairly steady pace throughout the entire economic expansion. In the average expansion of the Golden Age, outstanding consumer credit rose by 33 percent, or 1.9 percent per quarter. In the average expansion of the Age of Globalization, outstanding consumer credit rose by 27 percent, or 1.2 percent per quarter. In both eras, therefore, there is a strong rise of outstanding consumer credit throughout all of the expansions.

When outstanding consumer credit is examined in the average contraction of the two ages, however, there is a vast difference in behavior. During the average contraction of the Golden Age, the total outstanding consumer credit increased slightly; it actually rose by 1.1 percent during the whole contraction. This is one reason it is called the Golden Age, since it was an age in which people could and did continue to get the same amount of credit throughout the contraction period.

Did this pattern change during the six cycles of the Age of Globalization? In fact, there was an enormous and striking difference between the two eras during the contraction. It was noted above that outstanding consumer credit in the average contraction of the Golden Age increased a little. By contrast, during the average contraction of the Age of Globalization, the total outstanding consumer credit fell by 2 percent. When discussing trillions of dollars of consumer credit, 2 percent is a lot of money lost to consumers.

The pattern of the total outstanding consumer debt, including a large increase in both eras during expansions, helps explain the burden on consumers. This burden equals the outstanding debt multiplied by the interest rate, an amount that had to be paid before money was available for consumer spending. In addition, an examination of the flow of consumer credit over the cycle provides a more dramatic picture of the key role played by consumer credit. The flow of consumer credit is defined to mean the net flow of all new consumer credit per quarter minus the credit that is repaid (this is exactly the amount of change in the level of all outstanding credit from one quarter to the next). Figure 9.1 illustrates the behavior of the flow of consumer credit in the two ages.

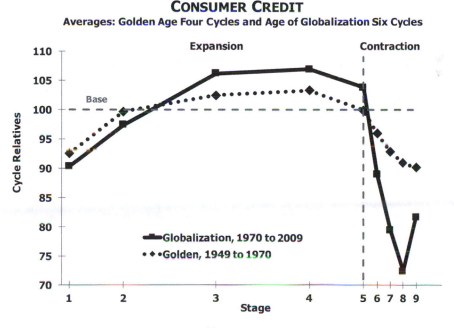

FIGURE 9.1 Consumer credit flow, Golden Age, 1949–1970, and Age of Globalization, 1970–2009

In both the Golden Age and the Age of Globalization, the flow of new consumer credit rises from the trough at Stage 1 to the profit peak at Stage 4. After the profit peak, the flow of new consumer credit declines to the cycle peak at Stage 5. Then, in the period of contraction, the flow of new consumer credit declines rapidly in both eras.

The flow of consumer credit in both ages falls by 18 percent per quarter during the contraction. The average recession in the Age of Globalization is longer, so the total decline of consumer credit is greater. Consumer credit declines by 107 percent in the Golden Age, but by 120 percent in the Age of Globalization. Both of these large decreases were a major factor reducing consumer demand and aggregate demand in the whole economy, thus helping to reduce business profits.

In both ages, credit helped create a continued expansion because it raised aggregate demand. In the contraction, however, especially in the Age of Globalization, the fact that consumer credit had grown during the expansion meant an increase of outstanding debt and interest payments. Such payments decreased aggregate demand. Moreover, to the extent that consumers could not repay the principal or the interest, banks suffered a reduction in their profit. Therefore, credit played a role in helping the expansion, but it also exaggerated the contraction.

During the expansions of the Age of Globalization, the financial system found new ways, including credit cards, to get consumers to expand their debt. This new high level of consumer credit raised demand for goods and services. In the average contraction, however, the high level of outstanding consumer debt made the recession that much worse. Consumers could not repay their debts, they lost their houses and cars for inability to make those payments, and they had to lower their standard of living.

The increase in consumer credit always means an increase in the debt owed to banks. Consumers must repay this debt by paying back the original amount plus interest. Those payments constitute a shift in income from consumers to the financial system and its owners.

Besides the cyclical instability, both the level of income and wealth inequality and the expansion of debt have risen cycle by cycle, so this is also a long-run problem.

Corporate credit

Investment was investigated in Chapter 6, where it was found that investment is mainly responsive to profit. When profit goes way up, as in many expansions, investment also goes way up. In a contraction, when profit is declining rapidly, investment declines rapidly.

In addition to the influence of profit expectations for the future, investment is also affected by the possibility of borrowing large sums of money at low interest rates to actually pay for the investments. This pool of credit for investment makes it a key character in the drama of the cyclical economy.

During every business cycle, corporate credit rose at a fairly rapid pace over most of the expansion. Corporations sometimes go deeply in debt because they are convinced of the bright future for continued profit in their business. They continue to increase their debt so long as they are confident of future profit.

This corporate credit allows enterprises to invest far beyond their own retained profits. When corporations borrow large amounts of money and spend it on plant and equipment, this becomes a major source of all new plant and equipment. Corporate spending is no longer tied only to profits, but also depends on the interest rate in the market for such capital equipment.

What has been the behavior over the cycle of outstanding corporate debt? In both the Golden Age and the Age of Globalization, the increase of total outstanding corporate debt occurred from the initial trough at Stage 1 to the cycle peak at Stage 5. There was continuous rise in the amount of outstanding corporate credit at a fairly steady pace in both ages.

In the Golden Age, the total increase in outstanding corporate debt during the expansion was 27 percent, or 1.5 percent per quarter. In the Age of Globalization, when outstanding corporate credit similarly went up for each whole expansion, the amount of corporate credit rose by 23 percent, or 1 percent per quarter, from the initial trough to the cycle peak. The total amount of outstanding corporate credit therefore rose at a considerable pace and was a central player in each business expansion.

The behavior of outstanding corporate credit in contractions is fascinating. In the Golden Age, instead of falling in the contraction, it rose by 5.3 percent. It follows that a picture of long-run behavior of outstanding corporate credit, in the years 1949 to 1970, would simply show continuous expansion of the credit with no downturns. This again reflects the golden aspect of this period. This means that banks were willing to lend and corporations were willing to borrow in order to expand the economy even during a considerable part of contractions at stages in the Golden Age.

The behavior of outstanding corporate credit in the contractions of the Age of Globalization was very different. During the average economic contraction of that age, the amount of outstanding corporate debt rose a few percent at the beginning of each contraction, then fell the same amount to the end of the contraction. Outstanding corporate debt in the Age of Globalization thus remained constant in each economic contraction, but was unable to rise. This lack of growth in the Age of Globalization indicated its weakness.

Figure 9.2 illustrates the behavior of the flow of corporate debt at each point in the average cycle of the Golden Age and in the average cycle of the Age of Globalization.

In this graph, the flow of corporate credit is defined to mean at each point the amount of new corporate credit minus repayment of corporate credit. This net increase of debt is exactly equal to the movement from the old amount of outstanding corporate debt to the new amount of outstanding corporate debt.

Figure 9.2 illustrates the fact that in both the Golden Age and the Age of Globalization, the peak of corporate credit is reached at Stage 4 of the expansion, which is the also the peak of profits. In both ages, the flow of corporate credit

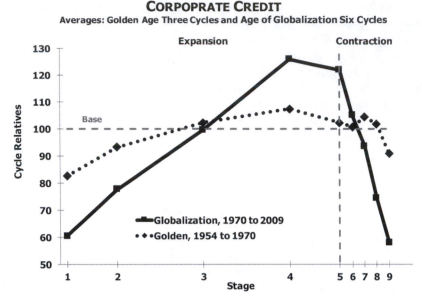

FIGURE 9.2   Corporate credit flow, Golden Age, 1954–1970, and Age of
Globalization, 1970–2009

begins to fall from Stage 4 to Stage 5, the cycle peak. The flow of corporate credit
then falls significantly in the rest of the contraction.

The rise and decline of corporate credit, that is, the volatility of the flow of new
corporate credit, is much greater in the Age of Globalization than it was in the
Golden Age. In the period of contraction, from Stage 4 to Stage 9, in the Golden
Age the net increase of corporate credit per quarter fell by 68 percent. In the average contraction of the Age of Globalization, the net increase of corporate credit per
quarter fell by 148 percent. These are large declines, with the decline in the Age of
Globalization being extremely large.

The result was that the huge decline in credit in each contraction made it
impossible for many corporations to pay their workers, to buy supplies, or to repay
their loans. It was therefore a very big factor in the spread of and deepening of the
economic and financial crisis in each cycle. Chapter 13 will measure the full extent
of the extremely large decline of corporate credit on the financial crisis of 2007 to
2008 and the Great Recession of 2007 to 2009.

The massive debt of corporations in these contractions, plus the lack of much
new corporate credit, made the functioning of many corporations impossible and
led to their bankruptcy. Even those that continued had to fire a great many workers. Clearly, the huge decline in corporate credit was one of the major causes in
increasing unemployment and the severity of each recession.

The huge increase in corporate credit in every expansion is exaggerated even
more in the minds of business people; the worry goes beyond the fall in the objective

expectation of profit. An increase in credit in the expansion beyond the growth of profits may be called a bubble. If the bubble is small, it then only leads to an average recession. When it is a large bubble, it leads to a large financial crisis and a large recession or depression.

The larger the credit bubble, the bigger its negative impact when there is a recession or depression. In order to stay afloat, a corporation must pay back the principal and interest to the financial system. If it cannot do so, it may go bankrupt. If it goes bankrupt, then it cannot repay the money it owes to the banks. Corporate bankruptcy, however, also causes enormous losses to investors and any other entities that own stocks or bonds. In addition, of course, it means many more workers unemployed, with a tiny income for purchase of consumer goods and services.

If the losses from the bankruptcy of one corporation are big enough, it can lead to the loss of confidence throughout the economy. For example, the bankruptcy of one extremely large corporation, such as General Motors, can have negative effects on the whole economy. Sometimes, corporate bankruptcy causes banks themselves to go bankrupt, thus starting a strong vicious downward circle.

The prime lending rate

During each business cycle expansion, there is not only an increase in the volume of consumer and corporate credit; there is also an increase in the interest rate that must be paid on those debts. There are many different rates of interest, but probably the most consistent indicator of rising and falling business expectations is the prime lending rate. The prime lending rate is the rate given by financial institutions to its best customers.

The cyclical movement of the prime lending rate, hereafter just called the interest rate in this section, is shown in Figure 9.3.

Figure 9.3 shows that in both the Age of Globalization and the Golden Age, the interest rate generally expanded during the business expansion and contracted during the business contraction.

Why does the interest rate rise and fall with the business cycle? During the expansion, wages and salaries slowly rise and employment slowly rises, so there is reason for optimism to increase among the entire class of employees. As their optimism increases, they are willing to borrow more from the banks. Employees generally assume that their wages and salaries will continue to increase, so they are willing to take on a larger amount of debt than seems objectively wise at the moment. Furthermore, banks tend to make the same assumption of an expanding economy with expanding wages and salaries, so banks are willing to give credit to the average employee.

During a recession, more and more employees are unemployed and the wages of those still working tends to decline. Therefore, in a contraction, employees become less confident of the future, so they reduce their debt if they possibly can do so.

Practically the same story holds true for corporations. Most corporations become far more confident in the business expansion as their profits rise. In fact, corporations

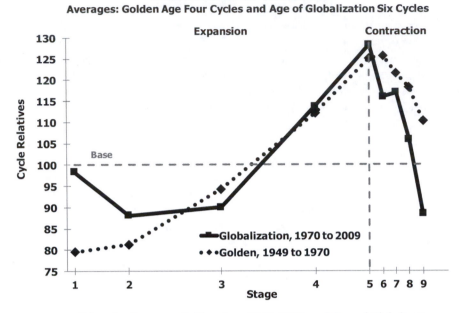

FIGURE 9.3 Prime lending rate, Golden Age, 1949–1970, and Age of Globalization, 1970–2009

almost always tend to be overly optimistic about the future at this point in time. They are therefore willing to borrow far more than the objective circumstances seem to indicate. As a result, both consumers and corporations demand more and more credit, so the interest rate can be raised by bankers, and so of course it is.

In a recession, profits rapidly decline, so extreme optimism turns into extreme pessimism. Therefore, in a recession, most corporations lean over backwards in order to not borrow any more money than is absolutely necessary. The reduced borrowing of both corporations and consumers leads to a fall in the interest rate.

In the present Age of Globalization, the interest rate is usually a lagging indicator. Figure 9.3 reveals that at the beginning of the expansion, there is still a great deal of pessimism among both consumers and corporations. They therefore are still trying to reduce their debts in the first stage of the recovery; as a result, the interest rate tends to fall further.

The interest rate sometimes does not immediately fall in a recession because both consumers and corporations are caught without enough cash. They have already become pessimistic, but they continue to borrow more for short-term cash flow needs.

In the Golden Age, the interest rate falls somewhat slowly in the recession. In the last three stages of the average recession of the Age of Globalization, however, the interest rate looks like a stone falling into the Grand Canyon. The reason is that profit expectations fall strongly, so investment and borrowing for investment plummet downward.

The stock market

Some money from the issue of corporate stock is invested in new buildings or equipment. Some new issues of corporate stock, however, are not used for productive investment. Some of the money may be used to retire debt or pay off the original investors, neither of which helps create new productive capacity in the form of buildings and equipment. Most of the transactions in the stock market do not directly affect aggregate demand because they are simply transfers of stock from one owner to another.

Broadly speaking, the stock market rises when the economy expands, and falls when the economy contracts. This can be seen in Figure 9.4.

Of course, during the business expansion, optimism over the economy leads investors to buy more corporate stock, thus raising the value of most stocks in the stock market. In any recession or depression, on the other hand, the pessimism of investors usually becomes extreme, so the value of stocks in the stock market must decline.

The most interesting fact, however, about the stock market over the business cycle is that it is a leading indicator. In both the Golden Age and the Age of Globalization, the stock market rises to Stage 4, and then falls to Stage 8. Therefore, if investors see a major decline in the economy six to nine months in the future, and they are convinced that decline will continue, they should sell their own stocks right then. The same handy advice can be given to investors around the trough of the cycle. In other words, the only reasonable advice from economists to investors is that investing in the stock market is dangerous.

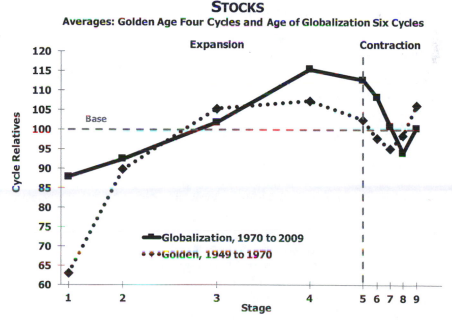

STOCKS
Averages: Golden Age Four Cycles and Age of Globalization Six Cycles

FIGURE 9.4 Stocks, Golden Age, 1949–1970, and Age of Globalization, 1970–2009

Because the stock market usually acts in an exaggerated manner both in the expansion and in the contraction of the cycle, the functioning of the stock market tends to create a greater boom, but also a greater bust. In addition to its direct effect on the wealth of stockholders and the valuation of each corporation, the stock market also has some effect on consumption. When stocks are increasing in value, people who own stocks believe that they are getting richer, so they spend more on consumption. When the stock market collapses, investors believe that they are much poorer, so they spend less on consumption. This phenomenon has been called the "wealth effect" because consumption is, in this case, affected directly by wealth, rather than the flow of current income.

It is worth noting that criminal activity has sometimes been an important factor in the stock market. Michael Lewis has two books dramatically illustrating the criminality found in the stock market. One book, *The Big Short* (2013), details how Wall Street made billions of dollars by encouraging people to buy homes they obviously could not afford. They bundled these subprime mortgages into attractive packages and then sold them. While they sold these dangerous financial instruments to investors, they knew that people would fail to make their payments on their mortgages, so the banks got rid of as many packages of mortgages as they could.

The other book by Michael Lewis, *Flash Boys* (2015), explains how some stock market participants use new technology to speed up their orders. This allows them to make an order before other investors can, which allows them to make a profit while lowering the profit of the investor.

Criminal activity is not enough to change the basic pattern of inequality or the boom and bust cycle to any large extent. It does, however, tend to exaggerate the amplitude and durations of recessions and depressions.

Other ways the stock market increases inequality

One of the big moneymakers for financial bankers on Wall Street and top corporate executives is mergers and acquisitions. It is no coincidence that the number and size of these transactions tends to increase near the end of every economic expansion. As the economy slows, the expectation of higher profits from investing in new equipment and plants dims. Therefore, in the search for higher profits for the wealthiest 1 percent, large companies begin to buy smaller rivals and each other.

The reason given for these mergers and acquisitions is that the new larger company will be more profitable and better positioned to compete in the marketplace. They explain how cost-cutting, such as closing parts of both businesses and firing massive numbers of workers, will both save money and make the new company more efficient than the two former companies.

Instead, buying other companies, either using stock or borrowed money to complete the deal, actually usually hurts the companies both in the short run and often in the long run. Often companies are forced, when the hoped for positive effects of the combination fails to materialize, to sell the smaller ones they bought for a lot less money than they paid. Other times, the combination is so toxic to the company, or the new debt load so onerous, that the new company is crippled or actually forced into bankruptcy.

Then why does this type of corporate behavior so often occur, especially at the end of every expansion during the Age of Globalization? First, the financial bankers make fortunes on fees and expenses, no matter if the deal goes through or not. Second, upper management, who are part of the wealthiest 1 percent, get paid large bonuses and often higher salaries once the deal is done.

So why are these mergers and acquisitions so bad for the economy, and often the new larger company, in the long run? Large numbers of workers, who are part of the 99 percent of the population who make their income mostly from wages and salaries, lose their jobs or are forced to take new positions that may not pay as high a salary. These job losses are often permanent, as older workers are often the first to be laid off, again in the interest of making the new company more efficient and competitive.

As noted in several places in this book, job losses or lower wages and salaries lead to less aggregate demand in the economy, as the new unemployed workers or lower-paid employees can no longer afford as many products or services. Although the effect of just a few companies doing this would not have much effect on the economy, the enormous number and size of the companies going through mergers and acquisitions has a negative effect on aggregate consumption.

These new companies are also sometimes made a lot less competitive in the long run. Often the cost of combining the companies is larger than the economic benefits. Additionally, the loss of experienced workers decreases the remaining workers' morale, as they watch so many other workers once loyal to the company fired. Although this damage to the company is hard to measure, it is surely not good for their long-term performance.

The average middle-class American is hurt in two ways. First, in those mergers that result in successful companies with more market power, consumer prices will rise. Second, as noted above, many employees are fired after almost every merger. The combined effect of higher consumer prices and lower employment creates still more income inequality in America.

Comparing the rise and fall of credit

Table 9.1 contrasts the expansion amplitudes and contraction amplitudes of each of the four variables affecting credit over the business cycle during the Age of Globalization. These variables are: consumer credit, corporate credit, prime rate of interest, and the stock market.

Consumer credit in the Age of Globalization rises during expansions and falls during contractions, but the rise and fall most of the time is at a fairly moderate pace. This reflects the slowness of change in the income level of consumers, since most wage and salary income moves slowly up or down. Corporate credit, on the other hand, rises rapidly in the expansions and falls rapidly in the contractions. This is due to profit expectations rising rapidly in expansions and falling rapidly

TABLE 9.1 Credit, amplitudes for specific profit peak at Stage 4 and specific profit trough at Stage 8, Age of Globalization, six cycles, 1970–2009

Economic series	Expansion amplitude	Contraction amplitude
Consumer credit	17.38	−34.84
Corporate credit	62.73	−56.89
Prime rate of interest	16.71	−10.01
Stocks	27.08	−19.71

Definition: Consumer credit means total consumer credit owned and securitized. Nominal dollars deflated by GDP deflator.

Source: Federal Reserve Board G19, DTCTL.M. National Income and Product Accounts, Table 1.1.9, line 1.

Definition: Corporate credit means Nonfarm Nonfinancial Corporate Business; Credit Market Instruments; Liability. Nominal Dollars deflated by GDP Deflator.

Source: Federal Reserve Board Z1, FA104104005, NIPA, Table 1.1.9, line 1.

Definition: Prime rate of interest means average majority prime rate charged by banks on short-term loans to business, quoted on an investment basis, in percent per year.

Source: Federal Reserve Board H15, RIFSPBLP_N.M.

Definition: Stocks means Standard & Poor's (S&P) 500 index. Daily data aggregated to monthly data aggregated to quarterly data.

Source: Yahoo finance symbol GSPC, at http://finance.yahoo.com, or Google finance symbol INX, at http://finance.google.com.

Note: Expansion amplitude is Stage 4 minus Stage 1. Contraction amplitude is Stage 8 minus Stage 4. In stating the amplitudes, if the variable has declined, then a minus sign is used. If the variable has risen, then no sign is used.

in contractions. Thus, corporate credit plays a large role in the expansion of the economy during business expansions. Yet corporate credit also plays a large negative role in contractions because of the large percentage decline it suffers.

During the average cycle of the Age of Globalization, the prime lending rate rose and fell at a moderate pace. In addition to the economic forces that cause interest rates to rise over the expansion and fall during the downturn, monetary policy as carried out by the Federal Reserve (Fed) adds to this—as the economy nears its peak, the Fed will often adopt a tight money policy, designed to raise interest rates, to stop what they fear is the "overheating" of the economy—in a downturn, the Fed slashes interest rates as a way of reducing—and attempting to reverse—the downturn.

In this era, therefore, the interest rate did have an effect in causing recessions and in helping the recovery from recessions. On average, however, the interest rate did not have a strong effect on the economy.

The price of stocks always moves in an exaggerated manner in both expansions and pessimism, compared with the objective movements of corporate profits. Therefore, stock prices move up and down fairly rapidly in the expansions and contractions. They rise and fall somewhat more than interest rates, a factor that affects the way money gets invested in the stock market or in bonds.

Effect of credit on inequality

If everyone had high incomes that were roughly equal, then no one would require or desire a large amount of credit. If everyone had low incomes, then there would be plenty of reason for borrowing merely to remain at a reasonable level of subsistence, but there might also be more borrowing for the reason of "staying ahead of one's neighbors." In the reality of extreme inequality in America, people go into debt both because they are forced to do so by economic circumstances and because they wish to outdo their neighbors in the consumption of goods and services.

Once one is heavily in debt, it is difficult to get out of that situation. Repayment of the debt as well as interest payments is a considerable burden on the borrower. The current debt makes it that much harder to gain a subsistence level for oneself and one's family without going further into debt.

The existence of large-scale debt for a considerable chunk of the population under conditions of inequality means that the economic situation becomes more and more fragile. If there is a recession, then consumers cannot pay back their loans. Corporations also cannot pay back their loans. Householders cannot afford to pay their monthly mortgage payments. The effect of these defaults greatly exaggerates the economic contractions.

More specifically, if people start to lose their jobs, then they are unable to pay back their debts. If they are not able to pay back their debts, then those industrial or financial corporations that own their debts may themselves be weakened and faced with possible bankruptcy.

The same arguments are equally true of corporations. If a medium-size corporation becomes deep in debt, then it becomes more difficult to meet their obligations each year and it becomes even more difficult to get new credit. Thus, the debt that was taken on in their time of extreme optimism becomes a huge burden that pains the corporation, thus further weakening the economy in a recession or depression.

The low wages and salaries of employees under conditions of extreme inequality leads to the impossibility of their paying back their loans in a recession. This inability to pay back their loans leads not only to their own disaster, but also to the weakness of corporations who lose money when the loans are not paid back.

Large corporations sometimes have enough reserves to get them through a brief recession. Small corporations often have no reserves, so even a small recession can lead to bankruptcy. Thus, income inequality for both consumers and corporations tends to mean large amounts of debt, which worsens recessions.

One of the points of this chapter is that employees with low incomes generally have high percentages of debt to income. In any recession, consumer debt becomes a larger percentage of their income. Therefore, in a recession, it is harder for consumers to pay off existing loans or to obtain new credit.

Mystery of credit

Both consumer credit and corporate credit increase in the last half of an expansion. This increase raises aggregate demand. But the increase of credit means an increase of debt and interest rates. The higher debt and higher interest that must be paid are a burden on consumers and on corporations that would seem to lower aggregate demand. So what is the effect on aggregate demand and profit?

Resolving the mystery

As long as there is some growth in national income, the additional consumer credit and corporate credit raises aggregate demand, regardless of interest rates and repayment. As soon as a recession begins, however, it becomes impossible for many consumers and corporations to continue to make repayments, causing bankruptcies and other harm to the economy. The correct answer, therefore, seems to be that the existence of credit during the expansion tends to increase and prolong the expansion, but it also makes the system more fragile, since the debts become more and more difficult or impossible to pay back on time. Therefore, in the contraction, the large debts greatly exaggerate the crisis and make an economic recovery far more difficult.

Conclusions

In the average business cycle, consumer credit, corporate credit, and the value of stocks are all leading indicators. This means that they usually expand until Stage 4 of the expansion (at the peak of profits).

Consumers must spend a higher proportion of their income on debt repayment and further credit becomes more difficult to obtain, thus lowering the demand for consumer goods and services. The huge amount of consumer credit also prevents people from paying off all of their debt to corporations, so some of those corporations are made weaker and may go bankrupt.

During the expansion, when their debts increase, consumers must pay an increasing proportion of their income to the banks and other financial corporations. This is another way in which inequality increases during the expansion.

Corporations, since their profit has been growing, likewise expand their credit to an unsustainable level until Stage 4 is reached. As soon as profits begin to decline, however, they attempt to lower the amount of their credit. Because of the need for cash flow to meet current obligations, their debts can only decline slightly. Due to the financial emergency, some are forced to actually increase their debts at this time.

The huge amount of corporate debt prevents non-financial corporations from being able to pay off all of their loans from financial corporations, which then drives some of the financial corporations into bankruptcy.

The prime lending rate is usually a lagging indicator. This means that even after profit has reached its peak, the interest rate continues up for some time. It may even continue to rise, or at least not fall, after the general cycle peak is reached. The reason is that people and corporations need emergency loans, but the impact is to raise the interest rate burden just when the economy is going into a recession or depression.

The high level of the prime lending rate as the economy begins to contract makes it even harder to obtain financing to cover emergency business expenses.

The stock market is a leading indicator, so it declines at about the same time as profits decline. The enormous amount of stock that has been issued is much higher than the value of the assets it is supposed to represent. This leads to the loss of investor confidence, which causes a further decline in the value of stocks. The decline in the stock market before the general cycle peak is reached tends to further lower business confidence.

Each of these four processes contributes to the problems causing a recession or depression.

10

GOVERNMENT

Economic inequality and political inequality

To understand government behavior in relation to economic crises, as well as its relationship to inequality, one must first understand the political and economic structure within which the government operates.

The impact of democracy and plutocracy

By definition, democracy means the rule of the people. Two basic features of democracy are open, universal elections leading to the rule of the majority, but also the right of the minority to effective criticism of the government or the society. Plutocracy, on the contrary, means the rule by a small group of the wealthiest individuals.

In American politics today, money seems to dominate on all major issues of policy. The control of the Republican Party by the plutocracy is obvious from how they follow the wishes of the plutocracy on every issue. For example, they oppose the two years of free community college education that was proposed by President Obama. They also oppose free lunches in schools for children who may not be able to buy lunch. Their argument is that such help for the middle class and the poor will cause the taxes of the wealthy to rise.

In addition to political parties, the wealthiest 1 percent of the wealth pyramid also controls the corporations that own the media. The media are given some measure of freedom, but it's a small amount of freedom, and does not include fundamental criticism of the political and economic system. It will be shown below how the control of the political system by the plutocracy is also exercised in many other ways.

Some progressive economists would say there is a danger of America becoming a political dictatorship of the plutocracy. There is certainly still some freedom for political opposition. Under the Trump Administration, however, there has been an attack on the liberal media, arguing that most of its news about President Trump is fake. President Trump has also tried to get the Chair of the Intelligence Committee of the House of Representatives to sabotage the committee's investigation of the ties between the Trump organization and Russian intelligence.

Conservative economists such as Milton Friedman (1962) contend that the millions of small businesses represent a healthy middle class that supports democracy and prevents plutocratic dictatorship. In every recession or depression, however, a large number of small businesses go bankrupt. Some disappear and some are eaten up by larger businesses. Therefore, in many sectors, there is an increasing degree of concentration of production in the hands of a few giant corporations. Particularly noticeable is the trend in banking toward the disappearance of small banks and the growth of very large ones. Usually, there is a large increase of small businesses in every expansion. Small business recovered very slowly in the Obama expansion.

Progressive economists, on the contrary, point out that the wealthiest 1 percent own 42 percent, at present, of all the wealth in America (as discussed in Chapter 7). The wealth of the plutocracy includes majority control of many of the giant global corporations. The wealthiest 1 percent can thus use their personal wealth, as well as the wealth of the global corporations, to affect politics.

In other words, the trend toward dictatorship over the economy by a small minority allows them to also dictate in the political sphere. In recent years, as inequality and concentration of wealth have increased, so has the control of politics by the wealthy. The wealthiest 1 percent have even used their wealth and influence to attempt to control the Supreme Court of the United States.

The Supreme Court decided in the case called "Citizens United" that it is constitutional for the wealthy and corporations to spend as much money as they like to control elections. In its opinion justifying this decision, the Supreme Court said that when corporations spend money for political purposes, they are only exercising their right to free speech. By using this extreme definition of freedom of speech, the court gave enormous help to the wealthy in their attempt to control political power.

America still has a flourishing opposition to the wealthiest 1 percent and its plutocratic control of politics. Yet the continued escalation in recent years of the use of money to determine the political process has brought America closer and closer to a plutocracy. If the trend continues much longer, it will become more and more difficult to reverse the control by the wealthiest 1 percent and restore a more democratic political procedure.

The process of control by the wealthy has reached a new peak with the election of Donald Trump to the presidency. His cabinet is almost all very wealthy, including five billionaires. They are discussing a new tax law that would give immense tax cuts to those billionaires. On the other hand, the beginning of the Trump Administration has also witnessed a historically unprecedented level of resistance to the new administration.

Economic democracy

Democracy may be applied not only to the political sphere, but also to the economic sphere. Most of the economy is controlled by a small number of men and women, the wealthiest 1 percent. Economic democracy, on the contrary, is by definition an economy controlled by democratic means.

In order to reverse the control of the economy by a tiny minority, two sorts of structures have been used by the citizens to ensure democratic control. One structure, or process, is embodied in cooperative ownership and control. There are many cooperatives in America, though they do not control a large part of the economy.

In some towns, the taxi drivers work together in a cooperative. This means that they democratically elect leaders in a corporation, in which each taxi driver has one vote to determine the board of directors and other general policies, including the distribution of corporate income.

Most cooperatives are based on groups of people that work together, though there can also be consumer cooperatives. How cooperatives can contribute to greater equality and to greater stability of the economy will be discussed in Chapter 15.

Another form of economic democracy is a corporation in the public sphere, whose officers are appointed by a democratically elected government. For example, a town council may decide how to run a school for children. The town council is democratically elected. It may then appoint someone to run a school according to the rules and money given to the school by the town council.

Some public corporations are also run by the state; for example, North Dakota runs the Bank of North Dakota. Some other public corporations may be run by the federal government. For example, the Tennessee Valley Authority (TVA) is a corporation that spends money to create power as well as irrigation. The officers of the TVA are appointed by the American government. All the profits of the TVA from the sale of water and power go back to the American government.

Those who own the economy, mostly the wealthiest 1 percent, make most of the decisions on the economy and reap most of the profits from the economy. Thus, profits may go to private owners, or to cooperative organizations, or to the general public.

The degree of inequality in the economy is merely one measure of the power of plutocracy. The degree of democracy in the governance of each American business determines the degree of inequality in the economy. The degree of inequality in the economy then affects the degree of inequality in the control of the government.

The economic process and the political process affect each other. Thus, the degree of inequality in the economy strongly affects how much the American government follows the democratic will, while the power of the plutocrats in the government will determine how much the American government helps or hinders economic inequality. Policies in favor of both political and economic democracy are discussed in Chapter 15.

How the wealthy practice class warfare

The average person thinks of themselves as an individual with individual interests. They do not think of themselves as a member of some class. The average person reacts to the class warfare practiced by the elite only if it actually affects them or their friends.

It is the elite, however, who take the initiative in launching class warfare. For one thing, they tend to know each other in society and to intermarry to a large extent. Since they have an enormous amount of money, they are clear about their interests in preserving it and expanding their influence as rapidly as possible. Therefore, in many cases, they do practice class warfare by individuals, by small groups, or by a whole class.

Some issues affect every member of the wealthiest 1 percent, no matter how concerned or caring they are about other issues. One issue that unites them is to pay as small an amount of taxes as possible. Many of the wealthy consider it an insult that the government takes any of the enormous amounts of profits, rent, and interest that they receive. It is worth emphasizing that only the wealthiest 1 percent receive a majority of their income in the form of profits, rent, or interest, rather than wages or salary. Therefore, as a class, they have an interest in reducing taxes on property income, but increasing taxes on labor income.

In January 2015, when a compromise was reached between the Republicans and Democrats on a budget for the coming year, the Republicans then added a few "small" points at the last moment, all of which helped the wealthiest 1 percent.

The part of the tax code dealing with the inheritance of stock is one of the most millionaire-friendly parts of the code. This law allows the wealthy to pass on wealth from generation to generation. Under the code, there is no need to pay taxes on gains if the stock is never sold.

The inheritance tax is an issue that is clearly a class interest. The wealthiest 1 percent are willing to spend large amounts of money on lobbyists and other means of fighting to keep this tax as low as possible. The Republican Party, under the influence of the wealthiest 1 percent, has spent a lot of time attacking all inheritance taxes by calling them death taxes. Their argument is that if a wealthy person is allowed to give a billion dollars to their children without tax on the money, then the wealthy person will have a stronger incentive to work harder to earn another billion or two.

As a result of intense lobbying by the wealthy, the American inheritance tax is relatively small compared to the same tax in other countries. The American inheritance tax falls lightly on the wealthiest 1 percent. Yet the inheritance tax is clearly one of the best possible ways to reduce the current extreme inequality.

Power and alienation

There are two kinds of alienation with regard to political power in America today. The wealthiest 1 percent know that they have enormous influence over the political process. Some of them even believe they are above the political process.

On the other side of the fence, millions of people in America believe that they have no political power. As a result, even when they are angry, they do nothing about it. They do not vote because they feel their vote will not count, or they simply feel defeated and helpless.

How political power affects inequality

Some of the increases in inequality from 1980 to the present were caused by changes in government policy. Stiglitz (2015b) details many of the changes made by the conservatives in government in their class warfare on behalf of the wealthiest 1 percent. Most famous were the tax cuts made for the wealthy at various times. There were also a considerable number of changes in the labor laws that made unionization more difficult. Other changes make it harder to collect overtime pay at a higher salary.

There have also been changes in the laws so that corporations may employ so-called "independent contractors." Workers are then forced to accept the honorable sounding title of independent contractor. By this change in name, although there was no change in the work that the person does or in the supervision that they receive, the person is no longer considered an employee.

As an independent contractor, they are not covered by the laws on labor relations, healthcare laws, or safety laws. Therefore, the fact that corporations are now allowed to hire people with this title means that the corporations save an enormous amount of money, while the person loses a large amount of money and security.

Stiglitz identifies a large number of other changes in government policy that help the profits of the wealthiest 1 percent but harm most employees. In addition to what the Republican Party has done, the Democratic President Bill Clinton eliminated a large part of the existing welfare system by getting rid of the program called Aid to Dependent Children.

Elizabeth Warren and class warfare

In her book *A Fighting Chance*, Elizabeth Warren (2014) provides three personalized, dramatic examples of class warfare by banks and other giant corporations against the rest of the people. Since they own these corporations, the interests followed are those of the wealthiest 1 percent. The three examples are the struggles over the bankruptcy laws, the Troubled Asset Removal Program (TARP), and the Consumer Protection Agency.

Before she was a Senator, Warren taught law. She chose to teach a course on bankruptcy law. When she studied the bankruptcy laws, she found that the laws were extremely biased toward the interests of business and against the interest of people trying to get rid of debt by going through bankruptcy. She decided that the bankruptcy laws should become more pro-people.

After many years of struggle, the laws reached the American Congress. When the legislative battle reached Congress, however, the proposed laws were made less friendly to the interests of the 99 percent of the population. Instead of allowing easier bankruptcies, the bankruptcy laws were strengthened to make them even more in the interests of the banks and the wealthiest 1 percent. In that form, in spite of Warren's best efforts, they were passed into law and have harmed thousands of people since then.

In her second major fight, Warren had been made head of the committee appointed by Congress to oversee the creation of the Troubled Asset Removal Program (TARP). She eventually discovered that the Federal Reserve and Treasury were taking many steps to help the biggest banks under this program without ever telling her about it.

The collusion of the government and the big banks helped create hundreds of billions of dollars in loans to the banks at extremely low interest rates while never seriously considering other alternatives. This action harmed the taxpayers.

Instead, the government could have taken over the failed banks (such as Bank of America and Citibank). The banks could then have been used to help the economy recover. This would have provided new profits for the taxpayers, instead of them having to pay to bail out the banks. The bailout of the banks also did not solve the problem. The largest banks are now much bigger and in even more danger of bankruptcy in the next financial crises.

The third major fight of Warren's career before becoming a Senator was her leadership of a coalition that helped create the Consumer Protection Agency. The Consumer Protection Agency was designed to stop some of the most immoral actions against consumers by the banks and other financial corporations.

For example, if a person gets a little behind the deadline in making a payment on a loan to a financial corporation, then the new law prohibits these financial corporations, including the banks, from raising the interest rates on those loans. Before that law, the financial corporations raised the interest rates on overdue loans so much that the person then fell further and further into debt while trying to pay the extremely high interest on their loans.

All of the changes in financial regulations in the new law, designed to help the consumer, were fought tooth and nail by the banks. The banks succeeded in softening many of the regulations and removing their power. Even when some strong regulation was adopted by Congress in spite of the banks, the bank lobbyists then proceeded to soften them during the process of writing the detailed regulations by the consumer agency. Once those much-weakened regulations went into effect, the bank lobbyists then worked to have the enforcers do as little as possible. The Act was also attacked in court. Nevertheless, the Consumer Protection Act has saved millions of dollars for consumers.

The lobbyists for big business and the bankers continue with great success to remove any teeth from regulations of the banking industry or of other corporations. When the legislation becomes law and is sent to an agency to draft, the fight continues so as to interpret all legislation in the interests of the largest banks and corporations. Any law that succeeds in retaining any teeth at all is then further attacked in the courts.

Perhaps the most impressive example of this was the Sherman Antitrust Act in 1890, which was intended to cure the tendency in America toward monopoly control of industries. So much of its power was taken out during the congressional struggles that the remaining bill did little, if anything, to prevent monopolies. It was only many years later that further legislation finally gave some teeth to the Sherman Antitrust Act of 1890. During the conservative era of the 1970s, however, the courts altered the antitrust legislation in such a way that few cases have been successful in recent years.

Economic myths

This chapter exposes the truth about economic myths about government and offers a more realistic view of the facts. One economic myth is that there are no opposing group interests in America, so it should be possible for the two political parties to find harmonious agreement on all issues.

The examples given above by Elizabeth Warren clearly show that there is class warfare in America initiated in all areas by the wealthy and their corporations. Those who deny there is any class warfare, or accuse Democrats of class warfare, are the first to use class warfare whenever it suits them.

Another good example of the effects of class warfare is set up by a question that was asked by Thomas Piketty (2014). Piketty asked why inequality rose from 1980 to 2010. The answer is that class warfare through the use of government policy, both in America and in many other countries, increased inequality. A major example was that a large number of public assets in Europe and in America were privatized. Privatization means, in practice, selling public facilities and land to private capitalists at extremely low prices.

A second economic myth is that the federal government is free to make decisions about economic policy at any time. This would imply that every administration would have a different pattern of economic policy over the cycle.

Actually, every government decision is made according to the balance of class interests under given economic conditions of prosperity or recession. Revealed below are the exact patterns of the government behavior under different economic conditions. The object of the wealthy capitalist class in each situation is to get the government to do that which both keeps the economy at some high level of production, but also increases inequality of income and wealth.

The problem for them is that these two desires do not coincide with each other in the real world. The results of their interests, as well as the resistance of the rest of the population, are revealed in the behavior discussed in the following sections. The story begins with government spending, followed by government taxation, and ends with the government deficit.

Federal spending in boom and bust

The typical behavior of American government spending during the average business cycle expansion is a fairly slow increase in spending. That spending corresponds to the rising needs of society, in a capitalist economy, for such goods and services as healthcare, education, and infrastructure. Expenditures that the government needs to do for society automatically rise with the growth of population and production.

For clarity, the reader must distinguish between automatic government spending and discretionary government spending. When the government passes a new law to increase or decrease government spending, that is called "discretionary" spending. An example of "discretionary" spending would be a government decision to raise spending for military purposes by $100 billion.

If there is a law, however, which states that the government must increase spending in some circumstance, then that will be automatic spending. For example, the government may pass a law which says that in a recession, all workers who are fired from jobs automatically get unemployment compensation. This unemployment compensation is an example of automatic government spending that occurs in a recession. Many of the increases in government spending that occur in every recession are automatic, having been in the law for decades.

The growth of federal government spending can be seen in Figure 10.1.

Figure 10.1 shows that government spending rises slowly throughout the expansion. It also shows that government spending rises rapidly during the average economic contraction.

All other things being equal, we can conclude that government spending tends to follow the economy upward during business expansions, but it does not expand more rapidly than the private economy. In the contraction, however, the story is very

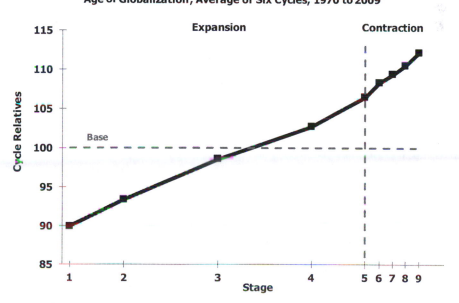

FIGURE 10.1   Federal spending, Age of Globalization, 1970–2009

different. The private economy is declining, but government spending rises more rapidly than during the economic expansion. This means that the average government behavior in the contraction tends to stimulate the economy and push it upward.

Why does government spending rise rapidly during the contraction? The basic answer is that the American government automatically spends more in every contraction because the laws require it. First, it is obvious that as unemployment rises, the law requires that the compensation of the unemployed must rise. Second, there are a number of different business subsidies built into the laws. These subsidies are such that in certain situations, in the interests of certain economic groups, the government must provide funds to a part of the private business economy.

Third, some types of government welfare spending need to increase because poverty increases in a recession. Finally, Congress appropriates more money for private industry in a recession. This money is given to business when most of Congress believes that government stimulus will help to end the recession.

How government spending affects inequality

Every item in the American budget brings income to some group. For example, there are subsidies to farms. It turns out that large farms are given a large amount of money, and that small farms get almost nothing. For many years, large subsidies went to tobacco growers.

Why did government money go to tobacco growers when this crop is harmful to the health of Americans that become addicted to smoking it? The answer is that tobacco growers were an important voting bloc in some states. They used money to support candidates pledged to help them get subsidies.

Even though it was only a few states, those who received the money and were elected to Congress formed a vociferous chairing committee for subsidies going to tobacco farms. Representatives of other states did not care about how much money went to tobacco farms, provided that the representatives of tobacco states would support special interest legislation for their states.

One of the largest lobbyist groups in Washington has always been the road- and highway-building lobby. Building roads for the public sounds like a good idea, but it also generates huge profits for the companies that build the roads. Similarly, one of the greatest scandals in American history took place in the 1870s when the companies that built the first intercontinental railroad received from the government fantastic sums of money and the rights to own land around the railroad. It was not enough that the railroad companies were paid an extraordinarily high price for the rails they laid. They also created a complex set of corporations, so that the government sometimes paid them twice for the same thing.

The case is similar with public schools and public hospitals. These are valuable and important items for the whole population, but they also involve high profits for those who build them.

Another example is the healthcare system under the Affordable Care Act, signed by President Obama. It is a good thing that the government has expanded the healthcare system of insurance to millions of more people. Yet it is a bad thing that so much of that money goes to healthcare insurance companies who do their best to make maximum profits while producing minimum healthcare services.

Worst of all is the military-industrial complex. The military industries produce no useful goods and services. Instead, they produce goods and services that kill people. By providing weapons that are used in war, the military industry receives an extremely high profit rate, sometimes as high as three times the average rate for all other industries (e.g. see Sherman, 1967).

Investigative reporting has found hundreds of wasteful examples of military purchasing, such as toilets sold to the military for thousands of dollars. In most cases, there is little or no competition among military enterprises. Haliburton, an engineering and construction company, received $39.5 billion in government contracts from 2003 to 2012 for services rendered in the Iraq War. Their quarterly reports during those 10 years would state their enormous profits were "from favorable government contracts." Most of those were for services only Haliburton was allowed to bid on.

Furthermore, the military producers and service providers have the largest single lobby in Washington, DC. These lobbyists help pass enormous military budgets, filled with high-priced items. In the end, the taxpayer is stuck with the bill; thus, inequality is increased both by obscene profits to the military-industrial complex and by a heavier burden of taxes. There is a large amount of literature going back to the nineteenth century to show that almost every country loses every war in terms of expenditures and debt.

It is often argued that the military industry provides jobs to many people. That is certainly true. But is there any reason that in a sane economy, in a sane world, the same people could not be employed by industries producing useful, peaceful goods and services?

Military production, military intelligence agencies, military security services, and employment in the armed forces all directly increase the short-run amount of production in America. In the long run, however, putting a large part of American spending into war production takes away from the funds needed for health, education, infrastructure, and non-military industrial expansion.

Although military production receives an amazing amount of money from the American budget, it should be emphasized that it does not produce a single item for the peaceful economy. As a result, if military production is a large part of all American production, then that part contributes nothing whatsoever to the expansion of peaceful production capacity. The exception is that some military innovations are then used in peaceful industries.

Instead of so much of our national treasury being used for research and development of weapons to kill people, those funds could be spent on positive and innovative ways of meeting human needs. This could include creating more environmentally sound consumer products, in which the production is exclusively from renewable sources.

President Eisenhower, in his last speech as President, warned that the military-industrial complex, composed of military producers, security providers, plus generals and admirals, always tends to pressure for preparation for war. Because they control a very large part of the American budget, and they use part of their enormous profits to push for more military production, the military producers and military leaders are a huge threat to the existence of a democratic government. Their power is often unseen but extensive. They have often helped to push the country over the brink into unnecessary wars, such as the Vietnam War and the Iraq Wars.

In recent years, the Republican Party, which represents most of these business interests, has frequently argued against extension of unemployment compensation to workers suffering from long-time unemployment, while supporting those goods and services produced by the military, which generate a large profit for those who donate to the Republican Party.

Federal taxation

American government spending has in the long run risen to meet the perceived needs of the nation. Government taxation has generally risen to cover the amount of spending, although there have been periods with large deficits.

During the 1920s, when federal taxation became the law after an amendment to the Constitution, a series of Republican Presidents generally tried to reduce both spending and taxation. In 1929, government spending was only 1 percent of the Gross Domestic Product. Taxes were almost as large, so there was only a small deficit. The fact that there were three recessions in the 1920s, with almost no government intervention, shows how wrong is the idea that government policy is the main cause of recessions.

During the 1930s, the American budget rose because the Roosevelt Administration considered it necessary to spend money to relieve starvation and to give jobs to a few million people. With all the spending of the New Deal, there was still a small deficit amounting to about 3 percent at its peak.

Franklin Roosevelt ran on a platform in 1932 that he would balance the budget. After he took office, he found that he needed to experiment with various kinds of government spending in order to give people jobs and to expand the economy. From 1933 to 1937, he did in fact expand the economy through government deficit spending.

In 1937, however, he was convinced by conservative economists that he needed to reduce government spending drastically or there would be runaway inflation. The American budget was reduced, which reduced aggregate demand in America. The result was a new, sharp recession in 1938, causing 18 percent unemployment.

America was rescued from the Great Depression by the Second World War. The government spent most of its money on the war effort, so that the total government spending amounted to 40 percent of GDP. Taxes were raised, but a huge gap was left to be filled by deficit spending. The predictable result was that there was excessive aggregate spending. This aggregate spending was greater than the aggregate supply, which caused inflation.

The inflation was managed during the war by a system of price controls for all goods and services. The price controls created a situation where prices were relatively low compared with the high wages of fully employed workers. If nothing else had been done under price control, then the first person to shop in a butcher's store could have bought all the steak and left none for others. To ensure everyone got their fair share, a system of rationing was also created.

Government revenue (mostly taxation)

Since the Second World War, many small wars have continued to cause large government spending. In peacetime eras, government spending grew slowly during expansions. Federal taxes rose faster than spending in every peacetime expansion. The behavior of federal revenue, primarily from taxes, during the six cycles of the Age of Globalization, from 1970 to 2009, can be seen in Figure 10.2.

Figures 10.1 and 10.2 show the dramatic differences during the Age of Globalization between the cyclical behavior of federal spending compared to the cyclical behavior of federal revenue, which is primarily from taxes. Both spending and taxes rise during the expansions. Government spending usually rises fairly slowly over the expansion, but taxes rise much faster.

It was shown above that government spending during the expansions simply rises at the long-run rate of growth in the needs of the population, such as for roads and hospitals. Federal taxes, however, mostly derive from income. National income rises with the expansion of the economy; therefore, taxes rise with the expansion of the economy. To the extent that federal taxes are still somewhat

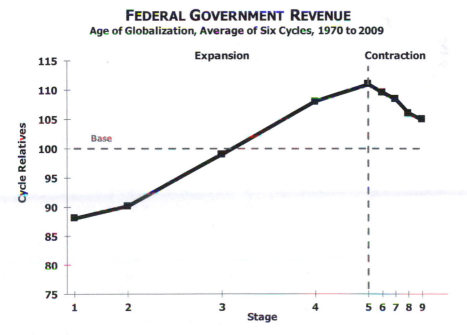

FIGURE 10.2   Federal revenue, Age of Globalization, 1970–2009

progressive, with higher tax rates on the wealthy than the poor, federal taxes tend to rise somewhat faster than the whole economy.

What is the result of the fact that federal taxes tend to rise faster than government spending in the expansion? As government taxes and revenue rise faster than government spending, less money is flowing from the government into the economy. This reduces aggregate demand. The lower demand leads to lower economic growth, and may help cause a recession.

During the expansion, the current tax laws automatically insure that taxes will rise faster than spending. Therefore, this is the reason why the deficit usually falls in each peacetime expansion. It is that automatic rise in taxation which lowers the deficit in each economic expansion. This lowered deficit does not happen mainly because of any conscious new policy of the President and Congress. Rather, it happens because government taxes automatically rise faster than government spending in each expansion.

The difference between federal spending and federal taxes is far more dramatic in the recession or depression. It was noted above that government spending automatically increases during economic contractions. These increases are due to such things as unemployment compensation and subsidies for certain businesses. When the economy declines, however, federal income taxes also decline. They always do so with somewhat of a time lag, depending on the exact system of tax collection.

Types of taxes and their impact

Taxes may be divided into regressive and progressive types. The progressive type of tax is one that rises as a percentage of income as income rises. The federal income tax is progressive. Under President Franklin Roosevelt, the income tax became more progressive. The tax on the highest tax bracket was 90 percent. Those with low incomes paid no income tax. Since the death of Roosevelt, Republicans have worked hard to lower the rates on high-income individuals, so the federal income tax is no longer as progressive as it was under Roosevelt.

There are many loopholes that allow the wealthiest 1 percent to pay less tax than many of their employees. For example, the billionaire Warren Buffet pays a lower tax rate than his secretary.

Since most of their income is from profits, rent, and interest, they pay a lower tax rate than from wages and salaries. When selling stock, bonds, or land, a special low tax of only 15 percent was given in order to encourage the wealthiest 1 percent to invest in stocks, bonds, and land. Thus, for no reason other than their economic power, the wealthiest 1 percent can legitimately sell and make profit at a much lower tax rate than the average employee has to pay for doing labor all year long.

It is still the case that the federal income tax is somewhat progressive, at least for everybody below the wealthiest 1 percent. It is certainly progressive for those individuals whose only income is from wages and salaries, because there are almost no loopholes for those earning only labor income.

In addition to federal and state income taxes, the federal government also taxes all employees to obtain Social Security tax payments. This tax rate does not rise as the level of income rises, but remains the same percentage at every level of income. Furthermore, it has an income ceiling beyond which no more Social Security taxes need be paid; thus, it most heavily falls on lower-income groups.

In addition, most states receive a large part of their revenue from sales tax or property tax, both of which are highly regressive and fall most heavily on the lower-income groups. The sales tax is a tax on all goods and services. It is large relative to the money that a low-income person has to spend. The property tax remains fixed for a long time in most states and is usually at a rather low level compared with the average level of income of the wealthiest 1 percent.

Therefore, the tax system as a whole benefits the wealthiest 1 percent versus the middle class and the poor. The American tax system once was a progressive tool to help produce more equality of income and wealth. Today, it probably has a net effect as a producer of more inequality.

The present tax system is thus one more cause for the lack of aggregate demand in the economy.

Deficits: the result of federal spending and revenue

Federal spending and revenue can be compared at each of the four phases of the business cycle: Recovery, Prosperity, Crisis, and Recession. Figure 10.3 shows the average percentage rise or fall of both spending and revenue for these four phases during the six cycles of the Age of Globalization, 1970 to 2009.

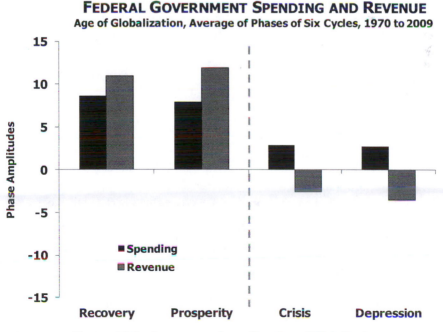

FIGURE 10.3 Phases of federal revenue and spending, Age of Globalization, 1970–2009

Figure 10.3 clearly shows the typical behavior of federal government spending and revenue for each phase of the cycle, a behavior that is repeated cycle after cycle because our political and economic institutions remain roughly the same.

In the Recovery phase of the average cycle, Stages 1 to 3, revenue (mostly taxes) rises faster than government spending. That is because government spending rises only enough to meet the rising necessities of the population, and sometimes not even that much. On the contrary, federal taxes pour in automatically as the national income rises. The result of spending rising less than taxes is that the government deficit decreases.

In the Prosperity phase, Stages 3 to 5, taxes and other revenue again rise much faster than federal spending. The reason is the same as in the Recovery phase; spending rises slowly while taxes rise faster. Again, the result in every peacetime cycle has been a falling deficit in the Prosperity phase.

Then comes the Crisis phase, Stage 5 to 7. In this phase, income taxes always fall. At the same time, the government is forced to spend more for unemployment compensation and other expenditures due to a contracting economy. Since revenue is falling while spending is rising, the federal deficit always rises in the Crisis phase. The rising deficit spending always helps to increase aggregate demand, even though it is not enough to stop the recession or depression.

Finally, in the last phase of the cycle, the Recession phase, government spending continues to rise. It rises because it has increasing obligations during the recession. At the same time, income taxes continue to fall. Therefore, since revenue is rising more slowly than spending, government deficit spending continues to rise. The rise in deficit spending is one of the factors that raises aggregate demand and helps to end the average recession. This automatic spending, however, is only a drop in the bucket during deep recessions or depressions. In a deep recession, new conscious policy actions are necessary.

Federal deficit

The deficit is discussed a lot, but remarkably few people seem to know its exact behavior, so let us begin by discussing how it acts.

The above section explained what happens to the deficit in the cyclical expansion and in the cyclical contractions. In brief, the deficit has almost always gone down in both phases of the expansion, but has almost always gone up in the two phases of contraction. Table 10.1 summarizes the expansion numbers and the contraction numbers.

The table shows the movements of revenue, spending, and of deficits up to the peak of profits. Previous chapters have demonstrated that aggregate profit reaches a peak usually in Stage 4, usually six to nine months before the reference cycle peak. The issue was why profits reach that peak and then start to decline, bringing on a recession.

Previous chapters also demonstrated that both the employee share and consumer share of national income usually reach a trough at the same time that profit reaches a peak. The Inequality Ratio reaches its peak at the same time as

TABLE 10.1 Federal spending, revenue, and deficit, amplitudes for specific profit peak at Stage 4 and specific profit trough at Stage 8, Age of Globalization, six cycles, 1970–2009

Economic series	Expansion amplitude	Contraction amplitude
Federal spending	12.4	7.3
Federal revenue	20.0	−2.3
Federal deficit	−7.6	9.5

Source: US Department of Commerce, Bureau of Economic Analysis, NIPA, Table 1.1.6, line 15, and NIPA, Table 1.1.6, line 18.

Note: Expansion amplitude is Stage 4 minus Stage 1. Contraction amplitude is Stage 8 minus Stage 4. In stating the amplitudes, if the variable has declined, then a minus sign is used. If the variable has risen, then no sign is used.

profit does. Both consumer demand and investment, however, reach their peak at the reference cycle peak.

How does government contribute to the profit peak? Does it enhance aggregate demand and profits, or does it harm aggregate demand and profits?

Table 10.1 illustrates the behavior of federal spending, taxes, and the deficit, up to the profit peak in the column on expansion. Government spending rises relatively slowly during the expansion up to the profit peak. Government revenue, mostly income taxes, rises much faster to the profit peak. Therefore, the deficit falls from the initial trough to the profit peak.

A more detailed look at the movements of the deficit over the expansion of the business cycle shows the following. The total deficit usually continues to rise in the early stages of expansion because taxes are slow to recover from the recession. In the last half of the average peacetime expansion, however, the total deficit usually declines. Certainly, in the last half of expansion, the government deficit falls as a percentage of the Gross Domestic Product.

What is the impact of a declining deficit, and the even stronger decline in the deficit as a percentage of GDP, in the last half of expansion? The deficit is the difference between spending and revenue. Deficit spending is the amount of spending that goes beyond the revenue from taxes and other sources.

Many political leaders in America cry out that the problem is rising deficits. Yet one of the problems at the profit peak is the decline in deficit spending. The falling deficit spending means less aggregate demand, which means less aggregate profits. Less aggregate profits inevitably lead to a recession.

In the Age of Globalization, the deficit has fallen in the last part of each expansion. The pattern has mostly been a falling deficit in expansions and a rising deficit in contractions. It is, however, possible to have a surplus, depending on conditions and policies. For example, the information revolution of the 1990s created a surplus in the federal budget for three years in the late 1990s under President Clinton.

A surplus in the federal budget means that more revenue is being taken in by the government than the government spends in the economy or gives to people.

Such a surplus means a reduction of aggregate demand relative to what it would be without a surplus.

In the average expansion of the Age of Globalization at the profit peak, consumption and investment demand were rising only at a snail's pace, while interest costs and taxes continued to rise. The result was that profit rose ever more slowly up to the peak. Add to this mix a declining amount of deficit spending and one can see why aggregate profit finally declined.

How the deficit or the surplus may have positive or negative effects on the economy

Suppose the economy is in a depression. If the government spends a lot more than the revenues it receives, thereby creating a large deficit, then this helps to create aggregate demand, which helps to create more jobs. Thus, the deficit in this case clearly has a favorable effect on the capitalist economy in the short run. Taking a longer-run view, however, the higher the deficit, the higher the national debt. A higher national debt requires the payment of interest, so the burden on the average taxpayer increases. Over 90 percent of the interest goes to the wealthiest 1 percent. Therefore, this increase of the national debt due to deficits increases the Inequality Ratio in the country. In the long run, this effect clearly harms the economy and the country.

Suppose, however, that there is full employment in the American economy. If there is a large amount of deficit spending, then the large spending increases can only lead to inflation. Since there can be no further increase in production, the short-run effect of deficit spending is to cause higher inflation, which is harmful to the economy. This has happened to the American economy only under conditions of a large war.

War spending

As discussed above, economic expansions based solely on the military are very different from an ordinary expansion. There is excessive demand caused by military spending. This excessive demand leads to inflation, then price controls, then rationing. It means enormous profits for military producers.

How does the war economy affect inequality? In any all-out war, the government puts everyone to work, so there is full employment. Full employment means that all employees are getting paid a regular income. Employees therefore increase their real income individually and as a class.

Since real employee income increases, do employees get all of the continued increase in production? Suppose there is full employment, but wages and salaries are not allowed to rise further. Then private capital will obviously make larger and larger profits, and in this case inequality will rise.

If there are no controls on prices, then the upward movement of profits will produce growing inequality. In practice, American wars differed greatly in the amount of regulation, so each war had a different effect on inequality.

Mystery of the government

American government is politically democratic in form. If the political process was truly democratic, then the members of Congress should reflect the interests of the bottom 99 percent of the income pyramid. Yet a great many of the policies of the American government clearly help the interests of the wealthiest 1 percent and harm the 99 percent. Why does this mysterious contradiction persist?

The answer to the mystery was given earlier in the discussion of class interests. The richest 1 percent and the largest corporations use their wealth to exert considerable control over the political process. As a result, America continues to have the forms of political democracy, but the process has been dominated more and more by the richest 1 percent. This trend has culminated in the control of the government by the billionaire President Trump and his billionaire Cabinet. Nevertheless, there is enough remaining power in the least affluent 99 percent so that they have been able to mount a very strong resistance to the policies designed to help only the richest 1 percent. How this conflict will play out in the near future remains unknown.

Conclusions

The extreme and increasing economic inequality in America undermines the democratic form. It often allows the interests of the wealthiest 1 percent to dominate the policies of the American Congress. The result is that the political power of the wealthiest 1 percent is used to increase economic inequality through government policy. This is a true example of the vicious circle downward.

The increasing use of money and wealth to control American ideology and politics has caused a drift away from effective democratic processes. There has been a considerable movement toward those with money having power in the government; that is, a movement toward plutocracy.

The interests of the plutocracy, especially the top 1 percent of wealth holders in the United States, influences major trends in the U.S. economy. Two points in particular should be noted:

1. Any and all means have been used to control government policy so that economic inequality has increased rapidly since about 1980.
2. Private financial corporations have been able to abolish or disregard many regulations. This made the economy ever-more risky.

These movements have made the economy ever-more risky. As a result, this increase in inequality caused the recession of 2007 to 2009. A major financial crisis, which was in the middle of the recession, made the recession much worse. This very bad recession or depression caused very large unemployment and rising poverty levels. The reason was that more government spending was obstructed by the richest one percent who wanted to avoid paying more taxes. This caused increasing inequality and increasing lack of economic growth. These issues on inequality and other crises will be explored further in Chapters 12 and 13.

Appendix 10.1

Systematic government policy tools and stagnation

The government mainly uses three types of policy tools to control the macroeconomy. Government fiscal tools include spending and intake of revenue, mainly taxes. Government monetary tools include Federal Reserve policies designed to raise or lower the interest rate, decide on requirements for what banks have to hold in reserve, and printing and spending more new money. A third means of influencing the economy is the use of regulations on the finance system, such as limits on a bank's total liability. These three policy areas are now examined in detail.

Fiscal policy

It was shown above that government spending during the expansion rose more slowly than government taxation. Therefore, in the average expansion, there is less and less stimulus to the economy from the net flow of spending after taxes. It follows that at the end of the expansion, the weaker government stimulus is a factor reducing aggregate demand and harming aggregate profits. The usual government behavior of spending and taxes in the expansion tends to help bring about instability and recession.

In the average economic contraction, total government tax revenues fall rapidly as income falls, but automatic stabilizers, such as rising unemployment compensation, actually increase government spending more rapidly than in the expansion. Therefore, government automatic fiscal policy in the recession helps create the conditions for further expansion.

Government spending, by definition, is divided into two parts. One part is discretionary spending, which means that amount of new purchases of goods and services decided by the government at a particular time. One example of discretionary spending would be the decision to build a new public hospital. The wages paid by the government to construction workers for building the hospital would be used by those workers to buy consumer goods and services. Such a new demand for consumption would help economic growth.

The other part is automatic spending, which occurs because of previously passed laws. One example of automatic spending would happen when a law requires a certain amount of spending paid to the unemployed whenever unemployment goes beyond a certain limit.

When there is a recession, the government may set up a large package of various projects, each of which stimulates demand by consumers or demand by investors. In order to restore economic growth, the government may use a package consisting of hundreds of different projects; these may include road-building by construction workers, addition of new teachers to expand education, and hiring new forest rangers to conserve and improve national parks.

The amount of stimulus to the economy depends on the difference between government spending and government taxes. Government taxes flow from workers and businesses into the government treasury. This flow out of the pockets of workers and business means less money being spent to buy goods and services. Therefore, taxes reduce the total demand in the economy. Government spending, on the contrary, is money that flows into the pockets of workers and business, and helps to expand the economy. In other words, the net effect of government actions depends on how much more the government spends beyond how much it takes in taxes.

In 2009, the Obama Administration used the largest government stimulus package ever to help bring about recovery from the Great Recession of 2007 to 2009. Unfortunately, the Obama stimulus package was far weaker than it should have been. In the first place, although the President's economic advisory committee advised that the spending must be at least $1.3 trillion, the actual spending, as passed by Congress and the President, was only about $750 billion.

A second problem with the Obama stimulus was that, under the pressure of Republicans and fiscally conservative Democrats, a large portion of the stimulus was not direct spending for jobs, but only reduction of taxes. Tax reduction always has a far weaker stimulus effect than direct spending. Some of the money from tax cuts going to the upper middle class is saved. A high percentage of the money going to the wealthy is also saved, rather than being spent.

When the government directly pays workers for conservation jobs in a national park, the money goes directly into their pockets and is immediately spent for their consumer goods and services. That first round of spending immediately helps the economy to get out of recession. In addition to the money spent by the workers, the shop owners and their employees who get the money paid out by the workers will re-spend most of it. Thus, the total amount of stimulus to the economy results from the initial spending by recipients of government money plus the re-spending by all of those who get it at second or third hand.

When taxes are reduced, the individual may decide to save some of it rather than spend some of it. Therefore, the increased purchasing power from tax reduction starts out in the first round already lowered by some saving. In the jargon of economists, the multiplier effect of reduced taxation is always much lower than the multiplier effect of increased spending for the whole economy.

Government spending and taxation, that is, fiscal policy, not only affects the aggregate growth of the economy; it also affects the degree of inequality in the economy. Every dollar spent by the government goes to some specific class; it either goes to the wealthiest 1 percent, who are capitalists making profits, or it goes to the other 99 percent, who are mostly employees making wages and salaries.

The spending by the Obama Administration went in large part for items such as increased unemployment compensation and payment of wages to construction workers, though it also contained considerable profit and tax cuts for the wealthy. The overall effect of the stimulus package under the Obama Administration was the reduction of economic inequality in America.

Conservative American governments, such as the Trump Administration, always direct most of the stimulus into tax cuts for the very wealthy. One proposal in May 2017, passed by the House of Representatives, gave tax cuts only to those with over a $200,000 income. The overall effect of all tax–cutting and profit–making projects by the Trump Administration will be a large increase in the Inequality Ratio for the whole economy.

Monetary policy

Under the Obama Administration, all further fiscal stimulus policies were stopped in the Senate by Republican filibusters. Therefore, the administration used monetary policy to try to expand the economy. The monetary actions began with the bailout of the big banks, in which an enormous amount of money went from the taxpayers to the banks. This bailout had a two-sided effect. As shown in some detail above, it did succeed, along with the fiscal stimulus, in preventing an enormous depression and equally enormous financial crisis. The flow of money to the big banks not only gave liquidity to the banks, so that they could give more credit if they desired to do so, but also strengthened the confidence of the capitalist class. This was seen in the recovery of the stock market following soon after the bailout and the first steps of fiscal stimulus.

In addition to the money given to the large banks, there was also an attempt to reduce the interest rate on loans made by the Federal Reserve to the banks. The hope was that the banks would make the cheap money more available to industrial capitalists. The interest rate was reduced to 1 percent or lower and was kept that way for many years.

Stagnation and policy

Unfortunately, the Obama stimulus package was too small and was directed, in part, toward considerable tax cuts, rather than giving funds that go into the hands of employees and businesses. As a result, the Obama stimulus package was insufficient to raise economic growth to a consistent and healthy level. Instead, the overall rate of economic growth under the Obama Administration was weaker than in any previous economic expansion since the Great Depression. These seemingly endless years of very low growth deserve to be called "stagnation." The stagnation resulted from a combination of a bad economy with bad policy. The very deep recession, called the Great Recession, plus the major financial crisis of 2008 and 2009, tended to produce a very weak economy for many years. A similar weakness could be seen after previous recessions or depressions, especially when they included major financial crises. In addition to the underlying economic trends, the stagnation was also caused by the lack of economic policies produced by the inability of Congress and the President to work together.

The necessary stimulus could not be passed into law because of the struggle between the liberal administration of Obama and the conservative actions of the

Republican Congress. Senator McConnell, the Republican leader in the Senate, stated explicitly that the Republican policy would be to prevent any major actions by the Obama Administration. When the House of Representatives was under Democratic control, it passed over 400 laws that were rejected by the Republican filibuster in the Senate.

The inability to work together prevented any useful fiscal stimulus. The burden of stimulating the stagnant economy was left mostly to monetary policy. One part of the monetary policy was the reduction of interest rates to a very low level, discussed above. Although this monetary policy continued throughout the Obama Administration, it had little effect in increasing the rate of economic growth. The reason why it was ineffective was that the underlying economy was so weak. Because demand was very limited, investors had very low profit expectations from new investment. The corporations actually accumulated a huge amount of money of their own, about $3 trillion. Since there was no clear expectation of profit, however, the corporations neither used their own money nor the easily available borrowing at low rates to make productive investments. They simply used their money in financial speculation, such as the purchase of their own stock, designed to make the remaining stock more profitable.

The other monetary action taken was the so-called "Financial Easing." The Financial Easing meant the policy of the Federal Reserve to give trillions of dollars over the years to the large banks through various means. These unsuccessful monetary policies, designed to encourage banks to lend and corporations to borrow, remind one of the old saying that you can lead a horse to water, but you cannot make it drink if it does not wish to do so.

The monetary policies did not prevent the stagnation from continuing for many years, but the transfer of large amounts of money to the banks did result in a further increase in economic inequality in the United States. This aspect of the monetary policy of the bailout and the Financial Easing is discussed more fully in Chapter 14.

The role of financial regulation

During the Great Depression, many regulations were passed to ensure that there would be no repetition of the financial crisis that engulfed the nation for several years. These policies included the Federal Deposit Insurance Corporation (FDIC), which ensures that depositors in failing banks will be reimbursed for their lost deposits, up to a certain level of money. Another very important regulation was the Glass–Steagall Act. This Act prohibited the integration of two types of banks. One type is the ordinary function of keeping money for depositors and making loans to customers and businesses. The second type of bank is one that focuses primarily on putting enormous amounts of capital into speculative investments. Henceforth, banks had to be the ordinary deposit and loan variety or else be an investment bank, but not both. In addition, the Federal Reserve was given wider power to regulate the banks against making loans that were vastly larger than their capital. The Securities and Exchange Commission (SEC) was also formed to regulate the stock market.

All of these measures did help to prevent a large financial crisis for many years. By the 1970s, however, conservative economists, bankers, and conservative politicians were proclaiming the need to reduce government regulations. They accused government regulations of slowing economic growth by adding a burden and preventing many activities of business. Several presidential administrations beginning with the Reagan years went along with these ideas, and there was extensive deregulation of all kinds for several decades from the 1970s until 2007. Especially prominent was the destruction of the Glass-Steagall Act, but each of the other acts of deregulation also weakened the financial structure, so as to allow the possibility of a new financial crisis.

The story of how these acts of deregulation, plus the weakening economy, led to the financial crisis of 2008 and 2009 will be told in Chapter 14. That chapter will also tell the story of the attempt to put back the most important financial regulations in the Dodd-Frank Wall Street Reform and Consumer Protection Act. The limitations of this Act will also be discussed.

11

GLOBAL CAPITALISM, INEQUALITY, AND CRISIS

There are many sources and types of inequality in the global economy. For example, there are rich nations and poor nations. This division is partly because for several centuries, the rich nations held most of the poor nations as colonies, from which they extracted every bit of profit they could. They also smashed the beginnings of industry in any colony when it might have competed with their own industry. This process of colonization and underdevelopment was powerfully described in the pioneering book *The Political Economy of Underdevelopment* by Paul A. Baran (1952). This is one clear source of inequality.

From the time of slavery in the Greek and Roman Empires, there has been sexist oppression against women. That oppression had economic, political, and psychological aspects, which changed in every new society that developed. The oppression of women has continued unabated to the present day. It has been greatly reduced, however, by the struggle of women in every political and economic system to liberate themselves and develop fully in a society where all people are treated equally. This process was fully explained in the pioneering book *The Women's Movement* by Barbara Sinclair (1983).

Another major source of inequality has been racial discrimination. Racism was the main ideological defense for the vast amount of slavery in the past, including slavery in nineteenth–century America. Although slavery supposedly ended in most of the world during the nineteenth century, racism and racial discrimination has continued to the present day.

For example, slavery officially ended after 600,000 people were killed in the American Civil War. Yet racial discrimination, especially against African Americans and Latino Americans, has continued to the present day. Some aspects of racial discrimination were prohibited by law in America, but other aspects, especially in the economy, still continue. Current economic articles on this subject, which investigate the relationship of racism to global capitalism, may be found in the journal *Review of Radical Political Economics*.

Another type of inequality of considerable importance is the inequality of income and wealth between small, medium, and large corporations. There are major differences in the behavior and success of corporations according to their size in the overall global economy, as well as their size relative to a given industry. The small ones usually go bankrupt within two years, especially during recessions or depressions. The most obvious difference in behavior is that most small corporations are limited to a single country. Only the largest corporations normally do business in every major country of the world. The degree of power held by the top 100 global corporations in both the economic sphere and the political sphere is enormous (see the discussion of the American example in Sherman, 1967).

The focus of this chapter is the discrimination by income and wealth among the entire population in the global capitalist economy. The reader should remember, however, that the sources of discrimination discussed above all contribute to the inequality by income and wealth.

In recent years, a large amount of data have been published about inequality by income, wealth, and opportunity. There are four especially helpful books: the outstanding book *The Price of Inequality* by Joseph Stiglitz (2012); an extremely useful book of essays, *The Great Divide*, by Joseph Stiglitz (2015a); a book on changing the rules, *Rewriting the Rules of America*, by Joseph Stiglitz (2015b); and the excellent book *Capital in the 21st Century* by Thomas Piketty (2014). Piketty's book has extensive data comparing inequality in different countries; he also has a large number of historical data series on major countries, as well as some global data. All of the data in the rest of this section are from Stiglitz (2015a, 2015b). Additional statistical investigations can be found in a wide variety of progressive economic journals, such as *Review of Radical Political Economics*, *Monthly Review*, *Review of Economic Issues*, and *Challenge*.

Among the many important facts about global inequality, two in particular show the rapid growth of inequality in the global economy. In 2014, a total of 80 billionaires in the global economy had as much wealth as the bottom one-half of all the people in the global population (Stiglitz, 2015a, Chapter 1). Surely the fact that 80 people owned as much wealth as over 3 billion people has an extremely powerful effect both on economic power and on politics. They can use their political power to influence the making of laws that benefit their economic wealth. Therefore, there is a vicious circle in the global economy in which economic power leads to political power, and then that political power leads to more economic power.

The second amazing fact is that in 2014, the wealthiest 1 percent of the global population owned half of all the wealth in the global economy (Stiglitz, 2015a, Chapter 1). It is striking that the wealthiest 1 percent in America own "only" 40 percent of all the wealth, but the wealthiest 1 percent in the global economy owns 50 percent of all the wealth. Thus, there are many countries in the world, mostly among the poorest, that have even more extreme inequality than America.

The 80 billionaires and the wealthiest 1 percent of the global economy are mostly from the racial majority in their country, not racial minorities. Most of the billionaires in the world are men, not women. Over half of the most powerful

100 corporations that control most of the global economy are owned by the wealthiest 1 percent of the global population. In America, the wealthiest 1 percent are mostly white males.

Global trade

Both inequality and the cycle of boom and bust have changed greatly from the time of little globalization to the present era of extreme globalization.

The economic cycle of boom and bust is a global fact, not a phenomenon limited to just one country. Similarly, inequality is not limited to one country, but is an interlocking system around the globe led by about 100 giant corporations and a significant number of billionaires.

Globalization, as defined here, is composed of a system of instantaneous global communication and rapid transportation of goods and people. It also represents a concentration of power and wealth within a system of global capitalism. The process by which crises and inequality are spread from one country to another includes global trade, global investment, and global finance, each of which is discussed below.

Money flows into each country according to the exports that it sends to other countries. Money flows out of each country according to the imports that it buys from other countries.

Global exports and imports do not behave randomly over the business cycle. Rather, exports almost always rise more slowly than imports in the last half of an expansion. America is used as an example because it has the largest trade of any developed capitalist country. As a result, it has the largest single effect on global trade. China is rising fast and may soon challenge America for the top position in trade.

American exports

How have American exports behaved in the Golden Age and in the Age of Globalization? Figure 11.1 shows their typical cyclical behavior.

Figure 11.1 depicts the rise of American exports during the average economic expansion of the last 10 cycles. Its behavior is similar to that of American GDP or national income. Yet the reason for its expansion is quite different. It is not directly affected by the American economic expansion, but instead is based on the expansion of national income in each of the other countries of the global economy. When a country, such as Germany, expands its national income, then it has more money to import American goods and services. Thus, the amount of American exports is dependent on the aggregate demand for American goods and services by the rest of the world (note that the term "American" is used here to refer to the economy of the United States, not the economies of other North and South American countries).

Why does the shape of aggregate demand in the global economy resemble the shape of aggregate demand in the American economy? The answer is that all capitalist

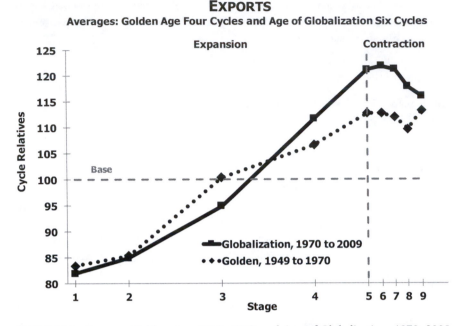

FIGURE 11.1 Exports, Golden Age, 1949–1970, and Age of Globalization, 1970–2009

countries in the global economy tend to rise and fall together. It is important in studying the global economy to remember that American exports usually do not rise as rapidly as aggregate American demand.

In any expansion of the global economy, the different economies take off at different times and rise at different rates of speed. If the American economy is rising at a moderate rate, but other economies are rising more slowly, then both their aggregate demand and their imports from America will fail to rise as rapidly as the American economy. This presents a problem because the total income of all the economies in the world determines the purchase of American exports. If a lack of global demand prevents American exports from rising as rapidly as American production, then this gap will weaken the American economy.

Toward the end of each American expansion, imports grow faster than exports, thereby contributing to an American trade deficit and the slowing of the American economy.

Similarly, in the average economic contraction of these 10 cycles, American exports fell. At first glance, the fall seems the same as that of aggregate American demand. Actually, however, because all the capitalist economies are not fully synchronized, the demand for American exports usually falls more slowly than aggregate American demand.

Another interesting fact is revealed in Figure 11.1. American exports in both the Golden Age and in the Age of Globalization rise in the expansions and fall in the contraction. That may seem uninteresting, but it is also clear that exports tend to rise and fall more sharply in the Age of Globalization than in the Golden Age. This reflects the fact that the present Age of Globalization is far more volatile in all respects than the Golden Age.

American imports

American imports and exports have entirely different reasons for their growth. The aggregate national income of America is the source of American imports. For example, if American consumers have more money, they may buy more German cars. If American corporations decide to produce more goods and services, then they may import more raw materials from Brazil.

The actual behavior of American imports over the business cycle is shown in Figure 11.2.

Figure 11.2 pictures the rise of imports in the American business expansion and the fall of imports in the American business contraction. The basic reason for that rise and fall is that import behavior closely resembles the behavior of national income in America. Some percentage of aggregate demand always goes into buying imports.

Notice that this diversion of money to buying imports from foreign countries reduces the income available for demand of domestically produced goods and services. Of course, demand for American exports has the opposite effect, in that it increases aggregate demand in America.

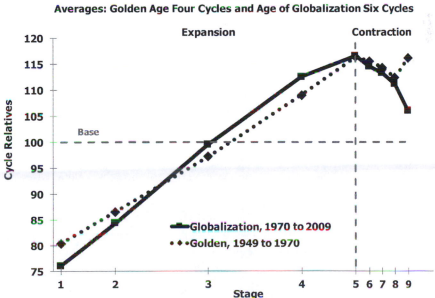

FIGURE 11.2   Imports, Golden Age, 1949–1970, and Age of Globalization, 1970–2009

It's also worth noting that the increasing import demand in expansions and its fall in contractions is a stronger movement in the present Age of Globalization than it was in the Golden Age. Again, this conforms to the fact that the Golden Age movements were all somewhat milder.

Finally, it must be emphasized that the rise and fall of demand for imports by Americans is much greater than the rise and fall of demand for American exports by foreign individuals and corporations. Why is that? The reason is that all capitalist countries tend to expand and contract their economies together, but the similarity of the movements is far from perfect. Foreign countries almost always begin a recession sooner or later than America. Since they are not synchronized, imports rise and fall faster than exports because imports are tied directly to American aggregate demand. Exports are tied, on the contrary, to global demand.

American trade deficit in the Age of Globalization

Exports and imports rise and fall at different paces, which affects the trade deficit, so Table 11.1 compares them and illustrates their effect on the trade deficit.

American trade deficits rise in each expansion where American exports are rising more slowly than American imports. Obviously, the rising trade deficit as shown in Table 11.1 will mean that more money is flowing out of America than into America. As a result, the rising trade deficit reduces aggregate demand in America. The reduction of aggregate demand will be one more factor causing profit to fall.

The opposite tendencies are also usually seen in every recession. In the Age of Globalization, average imports fell in each recession because the national income fell.

TABLE 11.1 Imports, exports, and trade deficit, amplitudes for specific profit peak at Stage 4 and specific profit trough at Stage 8, Age of Globalization, six cycles, 1970–2009

Economic series	Expansion amplitude	Contraction amplitude
Imports	36.3	−1.8
Exports	29.2	6.4
Trade deficit	7.1	−8.2

Definition: Imports is the value of all goods and service bought from other countries.

Source: Imports from US Department of Commerce, Bureau of Economic Analysis, NIPA, Table 1.1.6, line 18.

Definition: Exports is the value of all goods and services sold in any other country, in real dollars, seasonally adjusted, quarterly data.

Source: Exports from US Department of Commerce, Bureau of Economic Analysis, NIPA, Table 1.1.6, line 15.

Definition: Deficit is imports minus exports.

Note: Expansion amplitude is Stage 4 minus Stage 1. Contraction amplitude is Stage 8 minus Stage 4. In stating the amplitudes, if the variable has declined, then a minus sign is used. If the variable has risen, then no sign is used.

On the other hand, in the average recession of the Age of Globalization, American exports did not usually fall as quickly. In most recessions, since imports fall more rapidly than exports, the trade deficit decreases.

This fall in the trade deficit during most contractions is usually welcomed as a miracle achieved by the American President according to the press releases of the administration. At any rate, the fall in the deficit does help to stop aggregate demand from falling as rapidly as it would otherwise do.

Inequality and trade

The increase in trade during an expansion helps aggregate demand and prosperity. Trade, however, affects different economic groups in different ways. Different groups have different political power. Therefore, they have different success in affecting trade negotiations. Most trade deals have resulted in reducing American jobs and wages in a number of sectors.

The trade deal may also make it easier to import some products at a cheaper cost than it can be produced in America, which will result in fewer American jobs. Large corporations, however, can make higher profits by importing these cheaper goods.

A trade deal may also make it easier to import goods that contain toxic substances, unknown to American safety authorities. An example was how some cheap toys imported from China had major safety problems that were not known to the American importers. They caused illness or even death to some American children.

In May 2015, these issues were debated in the American Senate. The President asked for the authority to conduct secret negotiations followed by an immediate yes or no vote in the Senate. This is called a fast track procedure. It enables a bill with many provisions that are anti-labor or anti-environment to be more easily passed by the Senate.

The problem is compounded by how, in addition to the main negotiators from the government, there are also important working groups appointed for each detailed area. Since labor issues and environmental issues are the most controversial points in the negotiations, one would hope that the President would appoint numerous labor leaders and leading environmentalists.

Instead, according to data presented by Senator Elizabeth Warren, 85 percent of the American appointees to the working committees are either top executives of large corporations or lobbyists for those corporations (statement by Senator Elizabeth Warren on the Rachel Maddow television show, April 22, 2015).

This is a blatant example of how large corporations use their economic power to affect the political process to add billions of dollars to their profits. It means that the interests of the wealthiest 1 percent of Americans control the negotiations, not what is best for the other 99 percent of Americans. If the fast track procedure is approved, then a trade treaty prepared by and for the interests of the global corporations will easily be approved. In this way, democracy is limited and the rule of the plutocrats made much stronger. Inequality is then increased by the trade deal conducted under these rules because the profits of the wealthiest 1 percent increase, while everyone else suffers the costs.

Global investment

If one travels to the capitals of all the major countries in the world, one finds that the most common business names encountered are the top 100 corporations in the global economy. The top corporations in the global economy now have more concentrated economic power than at any time in history. That economic power translates to some control of the economy in many countries, and also some power over governmental decisions in those countries.

How do these corporations decide how much and where to invest? The answer is they use the same general rules for making an investment within any country. They put their money in enterprises in each country according to the criterion of which enterprise has the most expected profit in the future. In addition to issues of expected supply and demand in each industry, they also calculate which countries are the safest for investors.

Such as, in which countries are the governments most willing to do whatever is suggested by the global corporations? Or in which countries is there less risk that the population may change the government and remove the special favors given to the global corporations?

A lack of investment causes a recession in one country, such as America, which then leads investors to reduce investment in all other countries. One reason is that the recession reduces the income of investors, so they have less to invest in other countries. The second reason why other countries suffer reduced investment is the psychology of investors in which a panic in one place tends to spread to panic in other places. If there is recession in a large country, such as America, then the subjective concern is that recession will spread to other countries. As a result, investors are afraid to invest in any country. Their own panic then helps to make the worry come true.

Although knowledge of the situation spreads instantaneously in the present era, it still takes time for investors in each country to make up their mind whether to change the location of massive amounts of money. In practice, this has led to investors following a wave of pessimism or optimism. Nevertheless, the optimism or pessimism rises or falls with the level of profit, although with a considerable time lag.

For example, when the American recession became deeper and stronger in 2008 and 2009, investors from other countries eventually left in wave after wave. When the American economy and its stock market began to improve in 2009, the deep erosion of confidence prevented a return to the American stock market for some time.

The spread of the top global corporations to all of the main countries of the globe has meant a large increase in global inequality. There is, of course, inequality between different countries. Global recessions tend to increase the gap between countries because the smaller, less developed countries tend to suffer more from the recession. Many of these countries still follow the neocolonial pattern in which they produce primarily raw materials, so they are completely dependent on the prosperity of industry in the more advanced countries.

When a poor country suffers from global recession, it is usually the poorest people in the country that suffer the most. Many people have small farms, which suddenly lose their major markets. Others work for the major export firms, which also lose their markets. When an exports firm loses its market, it always tells the workers that they must lower their wages in order to compete.

Global finance

The current enormous global banking and finance system is the main source of all loans for new investments or for major expansions of investments. This means that global finance has a hand around the throat of all industry around the world. Those industries it chooses to support will grow, while those industries it refuses to support will wither away. In a period of average prosperity, there is a vast flow of money from every country into the global financial system.

If a recession in one country causes large problems for the banks and other financial institutions, including bankruptcies, then there is a strong tendency to panic within the financial system. To some extent, this has a true, objective base, but it is also likely to cause a vast overreaction, leading to a great increase in panic among the great financial organizations. That panic spreads immediately to the rest of the world.

When there are financial panics, all the banks and other financial institutions immediately refuse to make further loans, even to the healthiest of businesses. They naturally also refuse to make new consumer loans.

One reason why they refuse to make new loans is that they finally figure out that they have created far too risky and fragile a system, which causes the recession to be much worse than it otherwise would have been. The fact that some of the largest banks and insurance companies are threatened with bankruptcy causes their thinking to be fairly clear, once it is much too late.

Greece and the bankers

During the great recession of 2007 to 2009, including the financial crisis of 2008 and 2009, one of the hardest hit countries was Greece. One of the problems was that a conservative Greek government had borrowed billions of dollars for questionable purposes. The details of the transactions, plus the details of the Greek international debt, were kept as secret as possible from the Greek public and from all politicians except a few insiders.

When a new election placed the old socialist party, Pasok, in power, it found that the country owed an incredible amount of money, mostly to foreign bankers. It faced a situation where the country was in a significant depression and certainly could not pay back their loans on time. It badly needed help to pay or postpone immediate loans and to bring the country out of depression.

The socialist government, however, was a moderate socialist government, with few socialist ideas or actions. On the contrary, the socialist party largely relied on conservative economic experts. These so-called experts relied on the theories of the conservative economists, who had been arguing that aggregate demand does not matter ever since the days of J.B. Say in the 1800s.

The socialist party was told by the experts, especially the experts of the European Central Bank, that the most important thing to do was to pay back all the loans to foreign bankers immediately. In order to pay back these loans and to improve the Greek economy, what was needed was a firm austerity program that would greatly reduce Greek governmental spending for all kinds of goods and services.

For example, thousands of Greek teachers needed to be fired. All pensions held by Greeks from the government needed to be cut back or eliminated. In general, most services of the Greek government to the people needed to be eliminated or at least cut way back.

This program meant that a large percentage of government jobs needed to be eliminated. This would save a great deal of money, so Greece would be able to pay back the loans made by foreign bankers. If Greece was willing to do this, it would be given additional new loans to help pay back the old ones.

This was a program of austerity for the middle class and the poor, who lost their jobs and also lost their government services. It turned out that it was not a program of austerity for the rich, whose high incomes and fortunes managed to escape the eyes of the tax collectors.

What was the effect of this austerity program? The effect was quite predictable and followed the predictions of leftist economists. It reduced jobs and income, so it reduced aggregate Greek spending by a large amount. As a result, aggregate Greek demand for goods and services fell drastically. Because demand fell drastically, jobs were further reduced, income was further reduced, and spending for all goods and services was forced to decline. This meant that the depression became deeper.

Furthermore, because demand fell drastically, government revenues were further reduced. The reduced government revenue meant that the government deficit increased, so there was even less money available to pay back the foreign bankers. Thus, the result of the austerity policy was to make all aspects of the Great Depression and the financial problems in Greece much worse.

Amazingly, the socialist government, with conservative support, not only followed this disastrous policy once, but three times. After each new round of bailouts by foreign bankers, repayment of all loans, and austerity for the government and the people of Greece, the effects were the same. In each case, aggregate demand fell, aggregate employment fell, aggregate spending for goods and services fell, and so the depression deepened. In addition, the revenue of the Greek government fell, so its annual deficits grew higher, and it was able to pay back even less of the loans without new foreign bailouts.

After six years of austerity policy, including three devastating deals with foreign bankers, the Greek economy was in a deep depression. Many people voted with their feet by moving to other countries to find jobs. In a new election in January 2015, the Greek people chose a government that had almost half the seats in the parliament. This government was a coalition of a number of Greek parties, all of which were to the left of the socialists.

Though it did not include the communists, this left-socialist coalition was the first such elected in Europe in many years. Its policy stand during the election was clear. It stated that it would no longer bow down to the foreign bankers, it would no longer have an austerity policy, but would do all it could to increase Greek jobs, income, and aggregate spending. When it took power in January 2015, it repeated this pledge to the Greek citizens. It even won a referendum which stated that Greece would not bow to austerity, but would maintain strong government programs for the benefit of the citizens.

Yet the pressure on this government was enormous. Every well-known conservative economist in Europe repeated the view of the European Central Bank. This view stated that Greece would be lost forever if it did not immediately pay back its debts and further cut all government programs. On the contrary, the Greek government at first stated that it would take no more austerity actions, but would maintain all of its existing programs of goods and services for the population, and strengthen all of the jobs presently given by the Greek government.

After several months of increasing pressure by all the capitalist nations of Europe, plus all of the institutions of the European Union, the new Greek government bowed to the pressure and reiterated the old austerity policy. In return for new monetary bailouts by the European Central Bank, Greece would further restrict governmental goods and services. The new restrictions included large additional reductions in Greek pensions and further reductions in jobs available for teachers. Thus, at one stroke, the new government proposed to reduce education for Greece and to reduce aggregate demand, which would deepen its depression. When this policy was announced in August 2015, the new Greek government of left-socialists split. Those who were actually further to the right endorsed the new austerity program as the only possible program. Those who were further to the left attacked the program, explaining that it would cause deeper depression in Greece. With the help of conservatives, the austerity program passed the Greek parliament.

It is sad that this set of events, where the democratic will is defeated by the bankers and their allies, has repeated itself so often in history.

The mystery of international relations

Some theories of international relationships assume that if there were no barriers between countries, there would be perfect competition in global trade, investment, and finance. Under these conditions of pure and perfect competition, international trade, investment, and finance would all benefit the economic development of all countries. If there is no evidence for this benevolent result, there is plenty of evidence that the effects of global relations are harmful for many countries.

Conclusions

The reality of international relations is that different countries are at different levels of development, so their strengths in international transactions is different. Furthermore, a relatively small number of giant corporations, acting in the best interest of their millionaire and billionaire stockholders, control most of global trade, investment, and finance.

Therefore, it should not be strange that a small country such as Greece has had its economy worsened each time an international group supposedly helped it by bailing it out so it can pay off its previous debts. Even a powerful country such as America has run an international deficit for decades. The trade deficit has grown larger in the last half of each economic expansion in America. The trade deficit has been due in part to the enormous military spending of America in foreign countries. For more information on the topics covered in this chapter, see Joseph Stiglitz's *Globalization and Its Discontents* (Stiglitz, 2002).

12

STORY OF THE INEQUALITY CYCLE

This chapter narrates the most important points about inequality and financial crises. The detailed data are omitted because they were covered in Chapters 5 to 11. The story and the model discussed here deal only with the average economic cycle of boom and bust. The next chapter discusses the different economic behavior in the Great Recession. Chapter 14 examines the financial crisis of 2008.

The story will be clearest if the cycle is divided into the usual four phases: Recovery, Prosperity, Crisis, and Recession. The four phases were defined in Chapter 6 as follows. Recovery is the first half of an expansion, usually Stages 1 to 3. Prosperity is the last half of an expansion, usually Stages 4 and 5. Crisis is the first half of the economic contraction, usually Stages 5 to 7. Finally, Recession is the second half of the contraction, Stages 7 to 9.

Prosperity: why does it end?

The four phases continually repeat themselves, so it is arbitrary where to begin. It is easiest to begin at the midpoint of the expansion, where all the main indicators, including GDP and profits, are moving upward at their fastest pace. What happens in the Prosperity phase of an expansion in the average business cycle in the Age of Globalization? Why does an economy advancing with apparently endless potential slow down and then slide into recession?

First, the inequality of income and wealth increases and reaches a peak at the profit peak of the expansion. At the profit peak at Stage 4, profits have risen enormously, while wages and salaries have moved up only a little.

Second, the stagnation of wages and salaries means stagnation in a large sector of the aggregate economy. What consumers have to spend has risen far less than the production of consumer goods and services. This lack of demand in the consumer goods and services sector is one reason why profits falter while production is still rising.

Third, the existence of rising economic inequality also produces rising political inequality, with the growth of influence by the wealthiest 1 percent. Their influence is used to reduce government spending on the goods and services that might otherwise go to the middle-income groups and the poor. The conservative media are happy that government spending has been held in check, so there is less drain on the pocketbooks of the wealthiest taxpayers.

Total government spending always tends to rise fairly slowly in each expansion. It actually rises only about as much as is absolutely necessary for the government to meet rising needs of a greater population for such items as schools and roads or bridges. Since government spending is rising fairly slowly, it has always been the case since the Second World War that taxes and other government revenue rise faster than government spending. Therefore, government spending as a percentage of GDP has fallen in every peacetime expansion. Since taxes are rising faster than government spending, the annual deficit tends to decline.

This reduction in the growth of government spending, however, means that there is less aggregate demand. It is thus another source of how the growth of aggregate demand is reduced, which then reduces the growth of profits.

Fourth, the inequality between nations ensures that the poorer nations do not have enough money to keep their purchase of American exports growing at the same rate that imports by Americans grow. The result is a rising American trade deficit. This is another effect of inequality that lowers aggregate demand for American goods and services. It is thus another downward pressure on American profits after those profits have reached their peak just before the end of the expansion.

Fifth, rising inequality plus stagnant wages and salaries cause people to use more and more credit. Debt from borrowing becomes a greater burden. The credit allows temporary increase in demand, but once the recession begins, the existence of a large consumer credit means that most people cannot pay their current bills. When consumers cannot pay their bills, corporations may suffer losses. This makes the recession deeper.

Crisis

In a crisis, the economic world of capitalism turns upside down. Aggregate production, aggregate consumption, and aggregate investment all decrease. Real wages and salaries are reduced, so the burden of the crisis falls on the employee class. If the average wage declines 10 percent, then many people can no longer buy their usual food, they cannot make payments on their house, and they may lose their car. Some employees will become part of the unemployed and fall into poverty.

Yet aggregate profits fall far faster than wages and salaries. As businesses cannot sell their goods and services, some profits swiftly become losses. Some businesses go bankrupt. The average income of the wealthiest 1 percent, who receive most of their income as profits on capital, may find that their whole income goes down by 20 percent and that their wealth goes down by 30 percent. Yet this still leaves the average member of the wealthiest 1 percent with enormous wealth. Therefore, they may cry over their lost income and wealth, but the food, clothing, shelter, and recreation of the wealthiest 1 percent remains about as they were. If they already own five mansions, they may decide to be careful and not buy a sixth mansion. They will then have to "suffer" through the recession living in only five mansions.

During the crisis, government taxes automatically decline as income declines. On the other hand, government spending automatically rises to cover some of the costs of the recession, such as increasing unemployment compensation or increasing farm subsidies that go mostly to wealthy farmers. Thus, the government deficit increases. An increase in the government deficit means that the gap between government revenue (mostly taxes) and government spending has widened. For this reason, the net flow of government money above taxes to the economy increases.

American exports decline because in a worldwide recession, the imports of other countries immediately decline. During the crisis, there is a reverberation effect so that all countries reduce their trade, which further reduces the trade of all other countries.

Since production, consumption, investment, exports, wages, and salaries all decline, each sector reduces aggregate demand. Therefore, each causes the demand of the other sectors to also decline further. The most dramatic sequence is that falling production reduces employment, but less employment means less income, less income causes less spending, so production falls further. The result is a vicious circle moving the economy downward.

Recession

During each recession, wages and salaries fall. They do not fall, however, as fast as production of goods and services falls.

In many mild recessions, real wages fall very little or not at all. In a mild recession, since wages and salaries are falling less than production, eventually production will increase to meet the demand by consumers. This provides one of the conditions for a possible recovery.

The fact that government tax revenues are falling, while government spending is rising to meet the payments necessary in a recession, results in a stronger flow of money from the government into the economy.

In a recession, the poorer countries have much weaker monetary reserves than the richer countries. Moreover, to the extent that they rely on selling raw materials, the demand for their goods drops rapidly when the production of the richer countries declines. As a result, the exports of the poor countries decline rapidly, but the whole world is forced to buy some of the necessities sold by the richer countries. Therefore, during a recession, American exports usually fall less than American imports. Thus, the flow of money out of America falls less than the flow of money into America. This also helps provide a floor for American aggregate demand.

Recovery

At the beginning of the recovery, wages and salaries remain low because there is still considerable unemployment, even among professionals. Since labor costs still remain low while there is an increase in aggregate demand, the amount of profits starts rising.

In fact, in an average business cycle, profits increase rapidly in a recovery. At the beginning of a recovery, interest rates are still low and there is a lot of idle money willing to make loans as soon as the economy begins to rise. This helps investment to increase rapidly in the usual recovery.

Production rises rapidly and inequality of income increases rapidly. It is only in a depression, as we shall see in the next two chapters, that aggregate demand does not rise sufficiently in the recovery. The recovery from a depression may remain relatively weak in terms of production and employment growth.

Conclusions

This brief story of the inequality of income and wealth against the background of the business cycle of boom and bust has a few important conclusions.

The inequality of income and wealth grows during the average cyclical expansion. The growing inequality, based on the basic institutions of capitalism, is a major cause of the crisis that follows the Prosperity phase of each expansion.

The crisis is in large part based on a lack of aggregate demand caused by the stagnation of wages and salaries during the expansion. Since tax revenue increases in an expansion while government spending increases more slowly, this also reduces aggregate demand.

The slower growth of aggregate demand is also based on the usual increase in the trade deficit at the end of the prosperity phase of the cycle. Because all of these sectors, plus investment itself, exert a downward pressure on aggregate demand at the end of the prosperity phase, they create a vicious circle downward. It is that vicious circle downward that is felt during the whole crisis and on into the recession. It is made far worse by the fact that the credit boom of the expansion always turns into a credit bust in the contraction, though that may be a relatively small factor compared with the credit crisis in a depression.

In the recession, the conditions for a new recovery begin to emerge. Those conditions include the slowing pace of the decline in wages and salaries, the decline in the trade deficit, and the sharp rise of net government spending above taxes.

This concludes the basic explanation of inequality and cyclical unemployment during the average business cycle. Exceptions to this story are discussed in Appendix 12.1.

Appendix 12.1

The cycle rule and the exceptions to it

The basic rule in capitalist economies has been that growth occurs only through cycles of boom and bust. This basic rule is strengthened by the fact shown in the technical appendix at the end of the book. In that appendix, it will be found that there is a large amount of statistical data and testing indicating that some basic movements are similar in every cycle for almost all variables. In the cycles of a given variable, such as consumption, the sequence of movements and the direction in each phase remain the same; only the amplitude and the duration change.

The technical appendix also shows that a coherent mathematical model of the cycle discussed above can be written in a number of equations and can be solved. The solution shows that the model can be cyclical, rather than moving in a straight line, with a given set of constants.

Nevertheless, there are very important exceptions to the rule that all capitalist economies are subject to these same cycles at all times. The first exception is that economic performance during a war is entirely different from the peacetime cycle. The reason is that governments have a practically unlimited demand for war production during major wars. For example, there are no cycles in major American wars, such as the Civil War, First World War, or Second World War.

A second exception is that major wars change greatly what happens after the war. For example, after the Second World War, the so-called Golden Age from 1949 to 1970 had relatively mild cycles. The reason is that the economy of the United States was not harmed during the war, so it had most of the production and most of the world's trade and production for many years after the war. This situation of plentiful demand in the American economy was the reason for the mild cycles. It also caused a reduction in inequality, as spelled out in Chapter 7.

The third exception is that long-run economic trends may produce a cycle that is three or four times more severe when measured in terms of amplitude and duration. One of these long-run trends is the behavior of economic inequality. The Inequality Ratio rose from 1980 to 2007. As a result, the economy was weakened in such a way that it produced the Great Recession of 2007 to 2009. The details of the performance of the American economy in the Great Recession are discussed in Chapter 13.

The same exception explains the far more violent behavior of the Great Depression in 1929 to 1938. The Inequality Ratio rose to its highest point in the twentieth century in 1929. The worst depression of the twentieth century began in that same year.

Long-run changes in American institutions also helped to explain the fourth exception. In the average cycle, there is usually just a small financial crisis in the recession. The long-run trends in American economic institutions, however, produced major financial crises in the midst of the Great Depression and the Great Recession. Chapter 14 will describe the long-run trends, the financial crisis of 2008 and 2009, and its relationship to the Great Recession.

13

THE GREAT RECESSION AND INEQUALITY

The Great Recession, 2007 to 2009, was the greatest economic catastrophe in America since the Great Depression of 1929 to 1938. The Great Recession should have been called a medium depression, but it was labeled the Great Recession and the name stuck. Whatever it is called, during it, over 11 percent of the labor force was fully unemployed. Millions more had only a part-time job. Millions of other workers gave up completely on finding a job. It meant over 10 million homes were foreclosed. It meant millions of small businesses in bankruptcy. It meant millions of more people in poverty.

More precisely, the so-called Great Recession is a completely misleading term that was coined by a conservative economist. It sounds like merely a larger recession, but actually was a horse of a different color. In terms of its percentage decline of GDP over the whole contraction, it was about halfway between an average recession and the Great Depression. Yet some aspects were even more spectacular. For example, an average of 750,000 people were fired each month between November 2008 and April 2009.

The pace of the contraction was so swift, it is clear that without government action there would have been a major depression equaling or larger than the Great Depression. The unprecedented size of President Obama's two packages of stimulus plus the enormous bailout of the banks was enough to end the free fall into a depression. For that achievement, the Obama Administration should be congratulated. Preventing another Great Depression was not a minor achievement. Yet it will be shown in the next chapter that the rate of decline of GDP was so great that even this large amount of spending was insufficient to get the economy back to a normal, healthy expansion.

Moreover, the expansion under President Obama has mostly consisted of 2 or 3 percent growth in part of the year followed by a growth rate of 1 percent or less for the rest year. It will be some years before there is a complete enough statistical picture to explain this odd oscillation and the harm it is doing to the American economy. It was, however, clear enough by 2016 to say that the wage and salary stagnation, as well as the general uncertainty, has led to unprecedented anger in the majority of the American population.

How does a depression, such as the Great Depression or the Great Recession, differ from the average recession of the Age of Globalization? The basic relationship between different economic variables, such as wages and consumption, remained approximately the same in the average expansion of the Age of Globalization and the expansion leading up to the Great Recession.

The first thing that was different was the far more violent upward and downward movements by most variables. For example, it will be shown below that the Inequality Ratio rose several times as fast in the expansion leading up to the Great Recession as it did in the average expansion of the Age of Globalization. Another difference is that each of these major trends was not only stronger in the Great Recession, but generally lasted longer than in other recessions.

In addition, there were also relatively large and rapid changes in the long-run trends, reflecting major changes in the structure of capitalism.

One such change was the increase in inequality since 1980. There was also a long-run increase in the burden of debt from loans throughout the Age of Globalization. This was caused by a large increase in debt in each expansion, especially in the Bush expansion leading up to the Great Recession. Finally, the gutting of regulations on the financial sector by all the Administrations from Reagan through Bush was an important cause of the catastrophic financial crises during the Great Recession.

Long-run trends leading to depression

Four long-run trends operated for a considerable time before the Great Depression and the Great Recession in order to create the conditions for a depression. The four trends were: rising inequality, a crisis in housing, a fragile financial system, and similar problems in the rest of the global economy.

During the twentieth century, the Inequality Ratio reached its highest point in 1928, just before the Great Depression began in 1929. The highest point reached since the Great Depression was in 2007, the same year the Great Recession began. The fact that the Inequality Ratio was at historic highs and reached its peak just before the Great Depression and the Great Recession cannot just be a coincidence. Rather, it will be shown below that the growth of inequality leads to a falling long-run growth rate of GDP, and is also a major cause of recessions and depressions. This rising trend of inequality was reflected in a falling trend in the employee share of national income.

In the years before the Great Depression of 1929, as in the years before the Great Recession of 2007, housing had a long-run rapid expansion or boom. The massive decline in housing prices and construction that followed was a major cause of both the Great Depression and the Great Recession. The details of the housing crises and of its relationship to inequality will be discussed in Chapter 14, including its effect on the financial crisis of 2008.

In addition to rising inequality during the housing crises, the third trend before the Great Depression and before the Great Recession was toward a more fragile financial system. There were few financial regulations in the years before the Great Depression. One result was that the largest banks took extreme risks to make more profit. Not only did they lend out all of their capital, but they also borrowed more money in order to make even more loans. This process is known as becoming highly leveraged.

As they make more and more loans, those loans also become riskier because of their lending to less and less qualified people. Their capital comes from the money given to them by their depositors. There is always the danger that everyone will want their money back from the bank at the same time. When the banks are this fragile, they often fail, which causes a financial crisis. This process often leads to a worsening of a recession or depression. The problem of financial crises is discussed in detail in the next chapter.

Another long-run trend that causes mild recessions to turn into galloping depressions is when the rest of the world is slipping into similar problems. If America, for example, has a mild recession, then one way to help get out of it is to encourage more exports to other countries, which brings greater demand in America. If all of the countries face a crisis together, then the decline in trade of each of them reverberates around the world to harm the rest. This process of how depressions spread was discussed in Chapter 11.

Investments in the Great Recession

Chapter 6 explained how investment is the most volatile of the major variables, so its behavior has a large effect in postponing or setting off a recession or depression. Investment has a two-sided effect on the economy. On the one hand, new investment means growth in the production of capital goods used to expand an enterprise, such as building and equipment. In addition to expanding possible growth, however, investment is also designed to produce additional profit. If wages and salaries have slow growth, while profits on new investment rises rapidly, then there must be an increase in the inequality of income and wealth.

The Bush expansion took place from the fourth quarter of 2001 until the fourth quarter of 2007. It was followed by a severe contraction from the fourth quarter of 2007 to the second quarter of 2009. The drastic decline in investment led to the drastic decline in production and employment.

The slow rise of investment in the Bush expansion, followed by the rapid contraction of investment in the Great Recession, is shown in Figure 13.1.

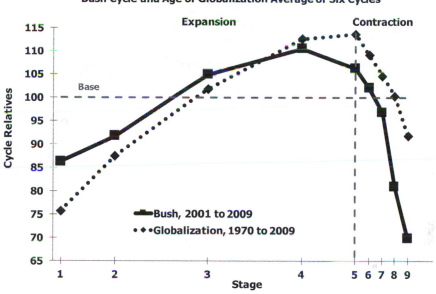

INVESTMENT
Bush Cycle and Age of Globalization Average of Six Cycles

FIGURE 13.1 Investment, Bush cycle, 2001–2009

Investment in the Bush expansion rose 20 percent. Investment in the follow-ing Great Recession fell 37 percent. Thus, the contraction of investment was far greater than in the expansion. This large decline in investment was the direct cause of the decline in all other production in the Great Recession. Of course, the decline in investment was only the final step in a long chain of causation.

Figure 13.1 depicts the increase of investment during the Bush expansion, fol-lowed by the even more rapid decline of investment in the Great Recession. Yet it also reveals that in this one cycle, investment was a leading indicator. Investment reached a peak at the profit peak (Stage 4), and then fell for the rest of the cycle all the way to the bottom during the Great Recession.

In all other cycles on record, investment rose to its peak at the reference cycle peak (Stage 5). The reason investment peaked and declined before the reference cycle peak in the Great Recession is that the economy looked weak even before it actually began to decline.

Investment and profit in the Great Recession

Private investment is driven by the expectation of profit. During the expansion part of the Bush cycle, and in the Great Recession that followed it, profit and invest-ment moved together most of the time. In every other expansion, however, profits peaked before investment peaked. In every other recession, profit reached its trough

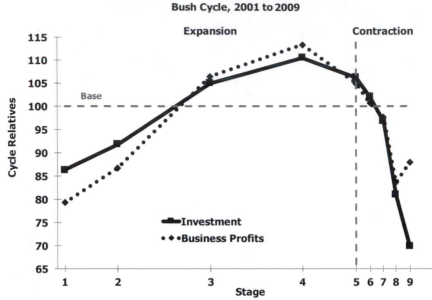

FIGURE 13.2 Investment and profit, Bush cycle, 2001–2009

before investment reached its trough. Profits are usually a leading indicator, but investment is usually a coincident indicator that turns only at the reference cycle peaks and troughs.

The behavior of profit and investment in the Bush expansion and in the Great Recession may be viewed in Figure 13.2.

Aggregate profits fell by 17 percent during the Great Recession. If the Great Recession was fundamentally caused by the extreme decline in profits, one question is why profits fell to that degree. The fall in profits in the Great Recession was much greater than the fall in profits during an average recession.

The relationship between profit and investment in terms of their rise and fall over the Bush cycle is portrayed in Table 13.1.

Table 13.1 shows that both profit and investment rose enormously during the Bush expansion. Profit rose even more than investment, so some of the profit was being used in other ways. It was this rise of profit and investment that fueled the expansion. As shown in Figure 13.2, profit and investment actually rose most rapidly up to mid-expansion, and then rose more slowly to the profit peak in Stage 4.

Both profit and investment began to fall after Stage 4. They continued a rapid fall at about the same percentage down until Stage 8 at the profit trough. It was the rapid fall of profits and investment that was the direct cause of the Great Recession in all sectors. As they fell, unemployment grew rapidly, until about 800,000 people were being fired each month. So profit and investment were the heroes of the Bush expansion, but they were also clearly the villains of the Great Recession.

TABLE 13.1 Profit and investment, specific amplitudes from Stages 1 to 4 and Stages 4 to 8, Bush cycle, 2001–2009

Variable	Expansion amplitude	Contraction amplitude
Profit	34.3	−30.0
Investment	24.4	−29.8

Definition: Business Profit means all corporate profit plus all non-corporate profit, including proprietors' income. Data are quarterly, seasonally adjusted, and adjusted for inflation by the U.S. government.

Source: Department of Commerce, Bureau of Economic Analysis, National Income and Product Account (NIPA), Table 1.12, lines 9 and 13.

Definition: Investment means Gross Private Domestic Investment.

Source: Department of Commerce, Bureau of Economic Analysis, National Income and Product Accounts (NIPA), Table 1.1.6, line 7.

Note: Expansion amplitude is Stage 4 minus Stage 1. Contraction amplitude is Stage 8 minus Stage 4. In stating the amplitudes, if the variable has declined, then a minus sign is used. If the variable has risen, then no sign is used.

Investment usually rises all the way to the cycle peak, so why did it start to decline at Stage 4 in the Bush cycle? It appears that the main reason that it declined at Stage 4 before the cycle peak was the fact that housing construction started to decline considerably before the cycle peak.

Inequality in the Great Recession

At the start of the Bush expansion in 2001, employee income tended to be stuck in the mud, as in all economic expansions under the present economic system. Employees are hesitant to go on strike or take other militant action in expansions if their hours and wages are rising even slightly.

Moreover, both government and public opinion, manipulated by the media, are opposed to employee demands when conditions are getting better in the economy because employees are seen to be still having the same standard of living. The fact that profits are soaring is ignored by the government and the media, so employees appear to be irrational if they are pushing for better wages and conditions.

This explains to some extent the fact that inequality in wages and wealth rapidly expands in the business expansions, but does not grip the public imagination. Figure 13.3 reveals the rapid rise of income inequality in the Age of Globalization and Bush expansion, followed by its decline during the contractions.

The pattern of wages and salaries in the Bush expansion preceding the Great Recession has two aspects to it. During the expansion, wages and salaries rose a small amount. Therefore, conservative economists said that the condition of employees, both manual workers and professionals, did improve slightly in the Bush expansion. Moreover, by the end of the expansion in 2007, it is also true that poverty had declined a little.

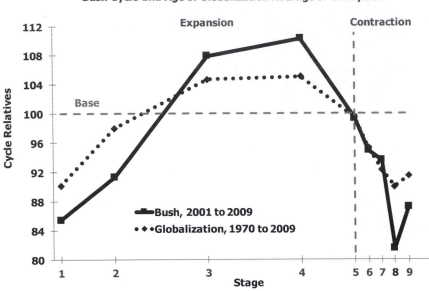

FIGURE 13.3 Inequality Ratio, Bush cycle, 2001–2009

On the other hand, the increase in aggregate wages and salaries was tiny, but the increase in profits was enormous. Therefore, the income ratio of profits to employee income rose by an astonishing 25 percent up to the profit peak in Stage 4. Rising inequality was not only a major factor in causing the Great Recession; it was the largest rise in inequality since the rise on the eve of the Great Depression.

The behavior of employee income in the large contraction, known as the Great Recession, was also two-sided, but the direction was exactly opposite of what took place in the Bush expansion. It is true that both employee income and profits fell in the Great Recession. Thus, employees were much worse off in the recession than they had been in the previous expansion. Millions of employees lost their jobs and were unemployed for an exceptionally long time. The percentage of poverty in the population also rose greatly. The number of people and small businesses going through bankruptcy became larger and larger. Millions of people lost their homes.

Since the rich lost only part of their large income and vast wealth, they were still mostly able to maintain the same standard of living in terms of food, clothing, shelter, and recreation. A few of the wealthiest one percent fell from riches to the middle class. Thus, it is important to say that the brunt of the Great Recession fell on wage and salary employees, not on the wealthy owners of capital who live mainly off profits.

It is also true that inequality always falls in a recession. This was also true in the Great Recession. It just means that while the percentage decline in wages and salaries was significant, the percentage decline in profit income was enormous.

Why do wages and salaries fall less than national income in every recession, including the Great Recession? Employees resist actual cuts in income, and public opinion tends to support them. Thus, in the Great Recession, employee income fell by 5 percent. On the other hand, profit income, including both corporate and individual proprietors' income, fell by 17 percent. For this reason, the inequality index fell during the Great Recession. Remember however, that wages and salaries fell significantly, poverty increased, and that inequality started rapidly rising again toward the end of the recession.

What was the importance to aggregate demand of the extreme increase in inequality during the Bush expansion? The first and most obvious effect was that it limited the growth of consumer demand.

Consumer spending and inequality in the Great Recession

What happened to consumer spending in the Bush cycle? During the Bush expansion, aggregate personal consumption expenditures rose by 15.9 percent. In the following Great Recession, personal consumption expenditures fell by 3.6 percent. By the standards of the preceding nine contractions, the decline in consumer spending in the Great Recession was enormous.

What happened to the consumer share of national income during the Great Recession? What happened to the share of employee income out of national income in the Great Recession? The full behavior of the consumer share and the employee share in the Bush expansion and the Great Recession is shown in Figure 13.4.

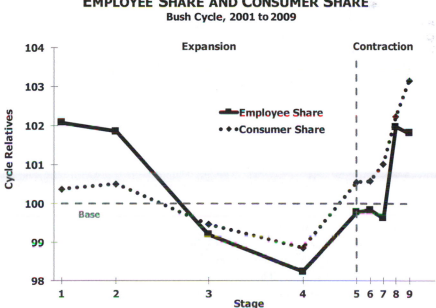

FIGURE 13.4   Employee share and consumer share, Bush cycle, 2001–2009

TABLE 13.2 Consumer share, employee share, and inequality, amplitudes for specific profit peak at Stage 4 and specific profit trough at Stage 8, Bush cycle, 2001–2009, including Great Recession

Economic series	Expansion amplitude	Contraction amplitude
Consumer share	−1.6	3.4
Employee share	−3.9	3.8
Inequality Ratio	24.9	−28.8

Note: Expansion amplitude is Stage 4 minus Stage 1. Contraction amplitude is Stage 8 minus Stage 4. In stating the amplitudes, if the variable has declined, then a minus sign is used. If the variable has risen, then no sign is used.

Source: US Department of Commerce, Bureau of Economic Analysis, NIPA, Table 1.1.6, line 7; NIPA, Table 1.12, lines 9 and 13; and NIPA, Table 1.1.9, line 1.

During the Bush expansion, both the employee share and the consumer share of national income fell from the beginning of the expansion until the profit peak. The falling employee share is another way to measure the rising inequality of income. Concretely, it meant that wages and salaries rose a small amount, although profits soared.

Since the employee share fell, there was a lower percentage of income spent on consumption. The fall in the percentage of income spent on consumption meant that the slow rise of national income contributed little to consumer spending by the time of the profit peak. This behavior was one of the major reasons for the lack of demand that was the main cause of the Great Recession.

The most important numbers on inequality during the Bush expansion and the Great Recession are stated in Table 13.2.

Note again that the Inequality Ratio rose by a large amount in the Bush expansion, and then fell by a large amount in the contraction. The table also shows that the employee share fell in the Bush expansion, reflecting a rise in inequality, then rose in the Great Recession, showing a small fall in inequality. Finally, the consumer share of national income moves similarly to the movements of the employee share of national income. Both fall together in the Bush expansion, but rise together in the Great Recession.

The fact that the inequality measure moved exactly opposite to the consumer share during both the expansion and contraction shows the influence of inequality on consumption.

Consumer credit

In Chapter 9, it was found that both new consumer credit and total outstanding consumer credit rose in the business expansion of the Golden Age and in the Age of Globalization. This increase of credit helped raise consumer spending in the expansion of every cycle. That steady increase in consumer credit was a very important support of all spending on consumer goods and services in the expansion of every cycle. This rise of consumer credit in the business expansion helped to fuel a large rise in aggregate demand.

On the other hand, the great increase in consumer debt led to an increase in pay-ments of interest and principal during the recession. The burden of a small money flow for all of their consumer needs was felt by millions of people. The fact that a higher percentage of their income must be spent on interest payments and debt repayment meant that life was harder for millions of people, and it was far more dif-ficult to get people to increase their spending so as to increase total demand.

The amount of outstanding consumer credit worried people in terms of repay-ment. It also meant that many individuals went bankrupt, while the great majority had less to spend during the recession.

What happened during the Bush cycle and the Great Recession of 2007 to 2009? Wages and salaries rose slowly in the Bush expansion. Therefore, consum-ers felt an urgent need for more cash to meet basic family requirements. If a child needed new shoes, more credit was the only solution.

Outstanding consumer credit rose at a considerable and steady pace both in the average expansion of the Age of Globalization and in the expansion during the Bush Administration. The decline of outstanding consumer credit in the contrac-tion of the Age of Globalization was significant but relatively small. The decline of outstanding consumer credit in the contraction of the Great Recession was considerably larger than in the Age of Globalization.

Figure 13.5 reveals the large rise and fall in the flow of new consumer credit. The picture is far more dramatic than it was for the slow-moving total of the out-standing consumer credit.

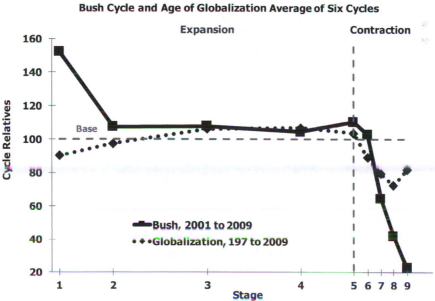

CONSUMER CREDIT
Bush Cycle and Age of Globalization Average of Six Cycles

FIGURE 13.5 Consumer credit flow, Bush cycle, 2001–2009

There was a brief decline of new consumer credit issued each quarter at the beginning of the Bush cycle as the economy continued to be quite weak. New consumer credit was issued in about the same amount from Stage 2 to the cycle peak at Stage 5. After the cycle peak at Stage 5, the amount of new consumer credit issued each quarter falls very rapidly all the way from the cycle peak to the cycle trough at Stage 9. The decline was an enormous 306 percent, or 51 percent per quarter.

This extraordinary decline represented the financial crisis concretely in terms of the disastrous fall of new consumer credit. It tells the story of a huge decline in the spending power of the average American. At the same time that wages and salaries were falling, new consumer credit almost disappeared. This fact not only directly harmed the living standards of millions of Americans; it also harmed the economic system itself, as discussed in the next section.

How were individual Americans affected? It was difficult for workers to make repayments in the Great Recession. Large numbers of people went through bankruptcy. Even those who did not go bankrupt found that repayments of interest and principal forced them to considerably reduce spending on everything else. Thus, consumer debt was one of the reasons for a deep recession.

Banks refused to make more loans to consumers in the recession, which is a common occurrence. This was not, however, another mild reduction of credit. The next chapter will explain how a financial crisis occurred in 2008 and 2009, starting many months after the beginning of the recession in the fourth quarter of 2007.

When the Great Recession lasted for a year and three quarters, it wiped out the incomes and savings of millions of people. With nothing but unemployment compensation, they could not pay back their debts. Whenever someone fell behind, the banks raised the interest rate on that account. Once they fell behind the payment schedule on their debts, people just ended up with greater and greater debts.

Either they continued with heavy interest burdens, or they lost everything in bankruptcy. Inequality was thus greatly increased by both the loss of jobs and the loss of savings.

Corporate credit

Corporations became overly optimistic as profits rose to an amazingly high level in the Bush expansion. It therefore seemed rational to make large new investments using a great deal of credit. Corporate credit therefore fueled the Bush expansion, keeping it going for some years. It also meant a rising ratio of corporate debt to corporate income. The rise and fall of corporate credit in the Bush expansion and the Great Recession, as well as the Age of Globalization, is revealed in Figure 13.6.

Corporate credit had a great rise in the Bush expansion, then, like Humpty Dumpty, it had a great fall. In the Great Recession, the flow of new corporate credit fell by 374 percent, or 62 percent per quarter, from the cycle peak at Stage 5 to the cycle trough at Stage 9. The fall of corporate credit, as part of the financial crisis, played a major role in turning an average recession into the Great Recession.

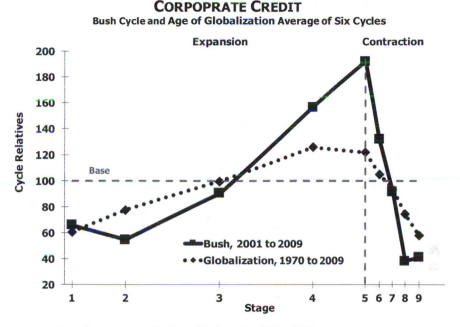

FIGURE 13.6 Corporate credit flow, Bush cycle, 2001–2009

When corporations are unable to get credit, even for a short time, it means that they cannot pay their employees, nor can they pay for supplies. The credit crunch led to a financial crisis, so there was a lot of doom and gloom until the end of the recession.

A great many smaller corporations who could not pay their debts and went bankrupt in the Great Recession. The fact that so many small corporations went bankrupt in the Great Recession, when their best assets were often taken by giant corporations, meant that the inequality among corporations greatly increased. After the Great Recession was over, the giant corporations had become even larger, and a large percentage of small corporations disappeared. The increase of inequality among corporations greatly increased the economic and political power of the giant corporations, benefiting their owners, who are mostly among the wealthiest 1 percent of the income pyramid.

The prime rate of interest

Not only did corporations borrow more and more money as the Bush expansion continued; they also had to pay a higher and higher interest rate for it. The larger corporations mostly paid the "prime lending rate," which is the interest rate paid by the banks' best customers. The rise of the interest rate in the Bush expansion and the fall of the interest rate in the Great Recession are both shown in Figure 13.7.

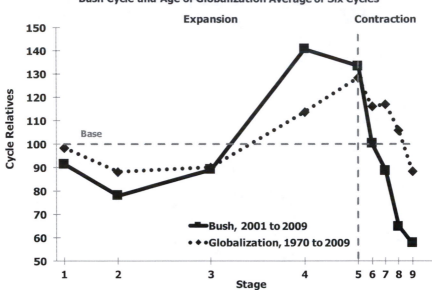

FIGURE 13.7 Prime rate of interest, Bush cycle, 2001–2009

In Figure 13.7, the prime lending rate—sometimes called the prime rate of interest—continues to rise throughout most of the Bush expansion. In the last half of the expansion, the prime lending rate rises rapidly up to the peak of the profit rate in Stage 4. This behavior of the interest rate means that corporations face rising costs in order to borrow money for investment. Therefore, the higher lending rate up to Stage 4 reduces corporate profits. It is thus one of the reasons for the recession that followed the profit peak.

In the contraction, the rapid decline of interest rates created one of the conditions for a possible recovery. Other things prevented that recovery for a year and three quarters. Not only did the economy tend to push the interest rate down; the Federal Reserve also pushed the interest rate down. Because of the financial crisis, treated in the next chapter, neither the falling interest rate nor government policy for further cuts in the interest rate could induce a large amount of new loans.

That chill on new investment for plants and equipment continued through the end of the recession and for many years of the weak recovery that followed. The average employee suffered greatly from lower wages or lower hours, job insecurity, and continued high unemployment. In the recovery, the only thing that recovered rapidly was profits, while wages and salaries fell into a long era of no growth or extremely weak growth.

As inequality once again increased rapidly after the Great Recession, there was feeble market demand for most goods and services. During the recovery, the low demand led to the postponement of most investment for plant and equipment. Corporations instead used their money to buy at least $2 trillion of their own corporate stock. The higher stock value gave executives a large amount of capital gains, with low taxes on them. This corporate policy increased inequality but did not expand the economy.

The high rates of interest at the end of the Bush expansion harmed small business and millions of poor and middle-class people. The increase in the debt burden and the higher interest rate forced consumers to use more of their limited income to pay back their loans. This higher cost of borrowing increased inequality between the average consumer and the financial giants.

Stocks

Since the Second World War, stocks have mostly risen in value. Even in the weak recovery from 2010 to 2015, the rise of the stock market was a major factor once again in increasing inequality. Its actions increased the value of stocks so that the wealth of the wealthiest 1 percent continued to rise. The bottom half of the American population, however, has only 2 percent of the wealth, including a small amount of stocks. This discrepancy increased inequality from 2010 to 2015.

The stock market has generally reflected the rise and fall of profits. The behavior of the stock market in the Bush cycle, as well as the Age of Globalization, will be shown in Figure 13.8.

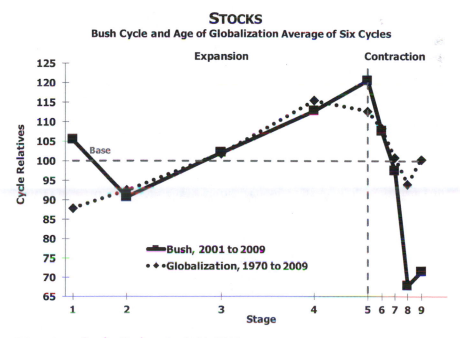

FIGURE 13.8 Stocks, Bush cycle, 2001–2009

In the average expansion of the Age of Globalization, the stock market rose from the beginning trough to the profit peak at Stage 5; then the stock market fell all the way down to Stage 8, the final trough of profit. In the Bush cycle, stocks continued to fall from Stage 1 until Stage 2. Then they rose all the way to Stage 5 at the reference cycle peak. From the peak down to the final profit trough at Stage 8, the stock market fell with much greater violence than in the average recession of the Age of Globalization.

The stock market is usually a leading indicator. In the Bush cycle, however, it did not fall before the business cycle peak. Therefore, there was the strange spectacle of falling profits and investments while the stock market continued to rise. At the end of the Great Recession, the stock market went back to its traditional pattern of being a leading indicator by only falling to Stage 8.

The fact that the stock market does not always follow its usual pattern is one of the many good reasons that most people tend to lose money in the stock market. Only the wealthiest 1 percent, with their crew of experts, tend to make large stock market returns most of the time.

The stock market not only follows the behavior of profits, but tends to exaggerate its movements beyond that pattern. Since a drop in the stock market tends to convince many stockholders that they should spend less money for a while, it tends to reinforce every recession. On the other hand, since the stock market also has exaggerated moves up during expansions, it tends to increase the boom that occurs in most expansions.

During the Great Recession, most owners of a small amount of stock, who had low incomes, were forced to sell their stock at low prices in order to pay for their immediate consumption requirements. The wealthy, on the contrary, simply held the stock and it rose rapidly in the following recovery. Thus, the losses on the stock market were another reason for growing inequality.

Federal spending, taxation, and deficits in the Bush cycle

During the Bush expansion, government spending rose, but tax revenue also rose. During the Great Recession that followed, government spending actually rose while total government taxes and revenue fell. The numbers for the rise and fall of federal spending, revenue, and the deficit are all shown in Table 13.3.

Table 13.3 shows clearly why one should never assume every detail of what happened in past average business cycles will continue to happen in the future. In the average cycle of the Age of Globalization, the amount of government revenue has always risen faster than the amount of government spending. What normally happens is that the revenue from income taxes rises in the expansion at the same rate that national income rises. On the other hand, the rise of government spending has usually been limited to the slowly growing needs of society in a capitalist economy.

In the case of the Bush cycle, revenue from taxes rose at its usual pace. Yet government spending rose even faster. The reason for the more rapid rise of

TABLE 13.3 Federal spending, revenue, and deficit, amplitudes for specific profit peak at Stage 4 and specific profit trough at Stage 8, Bush cycle, 2001–2009, including Great Recession

Economic series	Expansion amplitude	Contraction amplitude
Federal spending	15.3	12.6
Federal revenue	13.6	−9.6
Federal deficit	1.7	22.2

Definition: The Inequality Ratio, or profit/employee ratio, means business profit divided by employee income, in real dollars adjusted for inflation, quarterly data, in annual terms, seasonally adjusted.

Source: US Department of Commerce, Bureau of Economic Analysis, NIPA, Table 1.12 lines 9 and line 1; NIPA, Table 1.1.9, line 1; NIPA, Table 2.1, line 2; and NIPA, Table 1.1.9, line 1.

Note: Expansion amplitude is Stage 4 minus Stage 1. Contraction amplitude is Stage 8 minus Stage 4. In stating the amplitudes, if the variable has declined, then a minus sign is used. If the variable has risen, then no sign is used.

government spending was military spending for new wars during the Bush Administration. The new wars, especially the Iraq War, needed trillions of dollars of additional government spending. Therefore, in the entire time from the initial trough of the Bush cycle to the profit peak, government spending rose slightly faster than government revenue.

This gap meant that the federal deficit did not go down in the usual manner, but actually rose slightly during that time span. The increase in deficit spending by the government slightly helped aggregate demand.

Thus, the increased deficit spending offset a small amount of the decrease in consumer demand caused by the rise in inequality that occurred in the Bush expansion.

On the other hand, in the Great Recession, the pattern of federal government spending and revenue was the same as in the average cycle during the Age of Globalization. The only difference was that the movements were much sharper than usual. The rising government spending under the Obama Administration was larger than usual, because of the stimulus to the economy and the bailout of the banks. As usual, revenue from taxes fell considerably, in fact falling more than during an average recession. The reason for the decline in revenue was that incomes fell considerably, so tax revenue also had to fall considerably.

Federal deficit in historical perspective

The short-run movements of the federal deficit, discussed above, must also be placed in terms of the longer run of the Age of Globalization from 1982 to the present. This historical perspective may be seen in Figure 13.9.

The picture portrayed in Figure 13.9 shows a few major points clearly. First, from 1980 to the mid-1990s, there was a deficit that moved only slightly up and down. The deficit increased on the whole because spending rose faster than revenue. As noted above, this relatively small deficit was one factor keeping the

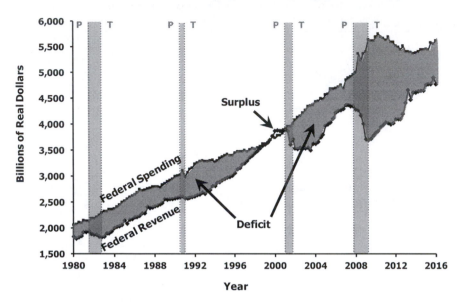

FEDERAL SURPLUS AND DEFICIT

FIGURE 13.9 Federal deficit, time series, 1982–2012

economy in long-run growth because it meant a net outflow of spending from government to the economy. On the other hand, in this era, the continued deficits year after year also meant an increase in government debt. One effect of that increase in government debt was an increase in inequality, since most of the bonds for the government debt are in the hands of the wealthy.

In the late 1990s, under President Clinton, there was a brief period of surplus. The existence of a surplus meant a reduction in aggregate demand, since more money flowed out of the economy and into the government, rather than the other way around. The surplus also meant that it could be used to reduce the debt, in which case there would be less money paid as interest to the wealthy.

Under President Bush, the deficit got much larger. In the early part of the expansion under Bush, the deficit rose mostly because of war expenditure, as well as some extraordinarily large tax cuts, primarily for the rich. As time went on, however, the usual pattern of revenue from taxes rising faster than the growth of government spending meant a declining deficit, as well as a decline in the government support of aggregate demand.

Finally, factors such as the rapid rise of inequality held back demand, while factors such as the rise of interest payments increased costs. This squeeze between limited demand and rising costs reduced profits. The reduced profits, plus the government austerity policy, sent the economy into the Great Recession. Figure 13.9 clearly shows the continued rise of government spending. The spending actually rose faster than in the average recession because the deep contraction of the Great

Recession caused far greater government expense than in the average contraction. At the same time, the picture shows a rapid decrease in revenue from taxes.

Since taxes were decreasing while government spending was rising, there was a large increase in the deficit during the Great Recession and just after it. Eventually, a slowly rising economy during the long slump (a term used by Joseph Stiglitz) did produce enough new tax revenue to start the deficit slowly decreasing. In the long slump that followed the Great Recession, however, the deficit was still historically large, even though it was clearly decreasing under Obama.

Exports, imports, and trade deficit in the Bush cycle

The picture of imports, exports, and trade deficits in the Bush expansion and the Great Recession is given in Table 13.4.

As in most expansions, Table 13.4 discloses that imports rose somewhat faster than exports in the Bush expansion. Since imports mean a flow of money out of America, this was another factor, although a minor one, that led toward lower aggregate demand in America. At the same time that inequality was pushing aggregate demand down, the increasing trade deficit also took more money away from aggregate demand in America. The rise in the trade deficit was a relatively small amount, so it was only a minor villain in the crisis.

In the Great Recession, imports had a considerable fall, reflecting the major decline of aggregate demand in America. Because of the lower prices that resulted from the American recession, there was enough increase in purchasing of American goods and services during the Great Recession to actually increase exports. Of course, the combination of a considerable decline in imports, causing less money to flow out of the country, plus a rise in exports, causing more money to flow into the country, helped create a considerable decline in the deficit. The decline

TABLE 13.4 Imports, exports, and trade deficit, amplitudes for specific profit peak at Stage 4 and specific profit trough at Stage 8, Bush cycle, 2001–2009, including Great Recession

Economic series	Expansion amplitude	Contraction amplitude
Imports	31.7	−10.6
Exports	29.5	4.7
Trade deficit	2.2	−15.3

Definition: Consumer share means the ratio of personal consumption expenditures to national income; employee share means the ratio of employee income to national income. Both variables in real dollars adjusted for inflation, quarterly data, in annual terms, seasonally adjusted.

Source: US Department of Commerce, Bureau of Economic Analysis, NIPA, Table 1.1.6, line 2; NIPA, Table 2.1, line 2; and NIPA, Table 1.1.9, line 1.

Note: Expansion amplitude is Stage 4 minus Stage 1. Contraction amplitude is Stage 8 minus Stage 4. In stating the amplitudes, if the variable has declined, then a minus sign is used. If the variable has risen, then no sign is used.

in the trade deficit during the Great Recession helped raise aggregate demand. This reduction in the trade deficit thereby established the conditions that led to an economic recovery.

The trade deficit in historical perspective

The above section portrays imports, exports, and the trade deficit over the Bush cycle, including the Great Recession. A further understanding, however, is given by examination of the long-run behavior of the American trade deficit.

Remember that the American economy had trade surpluses for most of the 100 years from the 1870s to the 1960s. In the 1970s, American trade shifted from surpluses brought home to the American economy into deficits taken out of the American economy. The picture of the latest era, the Age of Globalization, from 1982 to the present, is depicted in Figure 13.10.

In Figure 13.10, the top line is imports and the bottom line is exports. Imports are larger than exports in this whole time period. The distance between the two lines is the trade deficit.

The long history of trade surpluses helped to finance American investment both at home and abroad. When globalization accelerated, it led to intense competition from Europe, Japan, and China.

The American trade balance changed drastically because of the competition. America soon had a trade deficit that has continued to the present. The long

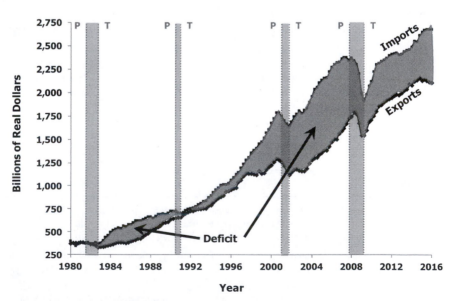

FIGURE 13.10 Trade deficit, time series, 1982–2012

period of trade deficits is shown dramatically in Figure 13.10. This is one source of reduced aggregate demand in America.

Figure 13.10 clearly shows the rise of imports in the late 1990s, when American national income was rising. The rest of the world did not rise as rapidly at that time, so American exports rose slowly. The result was a rapidly rising trade deficit.

In 2001, a recession caused a decline in American national income and imports. The rest of the world suffered a decline, but it was smaller than the American decline in national income. Therefore, for a short time, the deficit was somewhat reduced.

When the American economy took off again from 2001 until 2007, American imports rose because national income increased. The increase in national income for the rest of the world as a whole was far more sluggish, so American exports rose only a small amount. As a result, the American trade deficit increased during this time.

During the Great Recession, American national income fell significantly, so there was a large decrease in American imports. The rest of the world was also affected by the Great Recession, but had a smaller percentage decline. Therefore, the American trade deficit fell during the Great Recession. This was one of the sources that helped set the stage for the economic recovery from the Great Recession.

Impact of the Great Recession on inequality

This chapter has emphasized that a major cause of the Great Recession was the rapid increase of inequality during the Bush Administration. That inequality was in the form of stagnant wages and salaries at the same time as profit rose rapidly along with increased production. This increase in production eventually could not be sold profitably because of the lack of demand due to the lack of a rise in wages and salaries.

During the expansion, the rise in consumer credit eventually caused a shift in income from consumers to banks. This is another way in which inequality increases during expansions. This increase in inequality takes money away from consumers, so it lowers their demand for consumer goods and services.

During the Great Recession, there was an enormous rise in unemployment. There was also a large rise in poverty that resulted from the rise in unemployment. The many workers who gave up and dropped out of the labor force also added to the numbers of people living in poverty. Millions of people lost their homes as well as all of their savings. Thus, this book agrees with Stiglitz (2015a), who emphasizes that the brunt of the Great Recession fell on the middle class and the poor.

During the Great Recession, the Inequality Ratio fell because although wages and salaries fell, profits and stock values fell by an even larger percentage. It was only after the recovery from the Great Recession began that aggregate inequality of income and wealth again increased rapidly.

Since profits are a leading indicator, even before the official end of the Great Recession in June 2009, aggregate profits in the economy had begun to rise again.

The happy faces of the wealthiest 1 percent reflected this new rise in their income. Of course, as noted earlier, only a few of the wealthiest 1 percent actually lost their entire fortune. Most of the wealthy in fact received government charity in various forms, such as the failed bankers who were allowed to keep their bonuses, which allowed them to soon recover most of their fortune.

As soon as the Obama recovery began, while wages and salaries remained stagnant and were given no help by the government, the wealthiest 1 percent found their profits shooting ahead. Some of their profit increase was due to the help received from the Obama Administration, such as all the TARP funds that went to the biggest banks.

During the recovery from 2009 to 2011, 93 percent of the gains in the economy reflected in a higher GDP went to the wealthiest 1 percent. A large part of the gains of the wealthiest 1 percent, about 40 percent of the whole, went to the financial system, especially the largest banks. The economic detail of how the bankers achieved their bailout, and the consequent increase in wealth, is told by Stiglitz (2015a). The political details of the great theft by the bankers from the government are best told by Elizabeth Warren (2014).

The only basic difference between this book and books written by Paul Krugman and Joseph Stiglitz is the difference between the long-run and short-run emphasis.

Krugman and Stiglitz have made a powerful case that over the long run, since 1980, the rise of inequality has led to lower growth. This book has supported their case through picturing the process in precise terms over the business cycle. In that process, it was found that in most cycles in American history, except for war and periods following wars, such as in the Golden Age of 1949 to 1970, a major feature in every expansion was the rise in inequality of income and wealth. That rise in inequality was an important factor in ending the expansion and beginning the economic contraction.

The contractions, such as the Great Recession, were a process in which some of the immediate problems were solved, but always by means that led to an exceptionally rapid rise of inequality in the recovery. This is shown in especially dramatic terms by Stiglitz (2015a, 2015b).

Of course, when the short-run economic movements are added up, they always produce the long-run movement. Vice versa, one can always start with the long-run movements, as Krugman and Stiglitz do, and discuss the short run as fallout from a long-run movement.

The relationship between the short-run business cycle and the long-run trend toward lower growth at the present time is clearly reflected in some studies discussed by Stiglitz (2015a, 2015b). One of these studies, by the International Monetary Fund, finds that both the frequency and the depths of short-run business cycles are clearly correlated with the level of inequality in each era.

14

FINANCIAL CRISIS AND INEQUALITY

What were the main factors causing the financial crisis of 2008 to 2009? The previous chapter has recounted in detail all of the factors that led to the Great Recession. Those same factors set the stage for the financial crisis.

In both the Great Depression and the Great Recession, the real economy turned downwards at least a year before the financial crisis became acute. This point is spelled out in great detail by Stiglitz (2015b). As to the Great Recession, the recession began in the fourth quarter of 2007 (see Table 5.1).

There was a time lag of about a year from the downturn in the real economy until the collapse of credit and the threatened bankruptcy of the largest banks. The financial crisis became acute and was the main point of all economic discussion by the fourth quarter of 2008.

The previous chapter supported the view that the rapid increase of income and wealth inequality during the Bush expansion from 2001 until 2007 was the most important factor causing the Great Recession. Since inequality was a major factor leading to the downturn in the real economy in the fourth quarter of 2007, and that downturn was a major factor leading to the financial crisis, it follows that inequality was one of the major factors leading to the financial crisis of 2008 to 2009. The rise of inequality contributed to the financial crisis both through the reduction of aggregate demand and through the increased political power of the bankers.

There were many factors contributing to the financial crisis. One was the financial deregulation pushed by the bankers. The second was the encouragement of risky home loans by the Bush Administration. The third was the housing crisis. The fourth was the worldwide downturn in trade. All of these causes, plus the single most important factor of increasing inequality, led to the Great Recession.

The housing crisis

The housing crisis began slowly in 2005, but kept rolling along throughout the Great Recession. Why did it happen? The supply of houses continued to rise over many years. Yet the wages and salaries of employees remained constant in real terms ever since 1980. That was the basic conflict that led to the housing crises.

One obvious symptom of the housing crises was that sales continued to be made even though there were not enough qualified buyers. The fact that housing prices rose without sufficient effective demand may be called a bubble. That bubble was encouraged by the government, banks, lending agencies, and even by the wildly optimistic reports of the rating firms.

The housing crisis has been described in many ways and has been included by many writers as the cause that initiated the financial crisis. This section sets the background by exploring the cyclical behavior of housing in the average cycle of the Age of Globalization, as well as in the Bush cycle, including the Great Recession.

What was the behavior of housing prices in the average cycle of the Age of Globalization, 1970 to 2009? The price behavior of housing in the average of those six cycles is portrayed in Figure 14.1.

The average behavior of prices in this era clearly reflects many decades in the long-run rise in prices. The behavior of housing prices in the average recovery is depicted by an almost straight line up during the Recovery phase of the expansion,

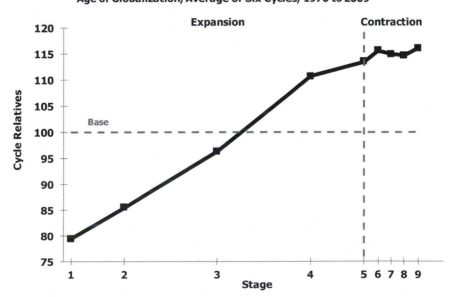

FIGURE 14.1   Housing prices, Age of Globalization, 1970–2009

from Stage 1 to Stage 3. That is similar to the behavior of most cyclical variables in the economy as a whole.

In the last half of the expansion, the so-called Prosperity phase, housing prices rise a little slower from Stage 3 to Stage 4. In the last interval of the expansion, from Stage 4 to Stage 5, the growth rate of housing prices declined, though they did continue to rise slowly until the reference cycle peak.

The interesting point about this graph is that in the average cycle of the Age of Globalization, housing prices did not fall in the recession. Although they bounced up and down a little, housing prices nevertheless ended up slightly higher at the end of the average recession. Since the average housing prices shown here includes the Great Recession, this slightly upward behavior is remarkable. It shows that there was a continuing boom and bubble in housing prices during the average recession of the Age of Globalization. This bubble in the average housing price did not start to crash until just before the Great Recession.

Turning from boom to bust, the picture of housing prices in the Bush cycle and in the Great Recession is quite different. Figure 14.2 depicts the behavior of housing prices during the Bush cycle from 2001 to 2009.

In this graph, housing prices look like the average leading indicator during their rise in the expansion and decline during the contraction. Housing prices rose to the profit peak in Stage 4, and then declined down to the profit trough in Stage 8. Since there was no decline in the previous five cycles, this decline in housing

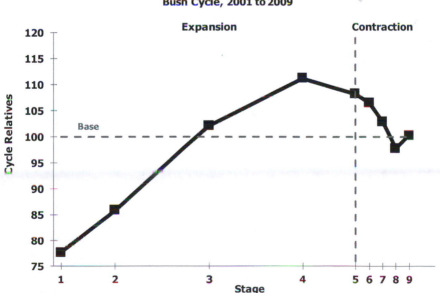

FIGURE 14.2   Housing prices, Bush cycle, 2001–2009

prices during the Great Recession is quite severe. The end of the housing price bubble resulted in a crash. In many areas of America, housing prices dropped by 50 percent.

When the behavior of the banks is discussed below, it should be emphasized that none of the banks and not many stock market speculators ever thought that there could be any fall in housing prices. The long boom in housing prices taught the apparent lesson that housing prices always go up and never go down. That is why almost all the bank officials, as well as the big private speculators, ended up in the intensive care room of the Federal Reserve. The details of the relationship between the housing crisis and the financial crisis are best stated in Pollin (2008).

Housing construction

To this point, only the price behavior of the housing market has been considered. Although this price behavior had an important effect on the financial sector, it was the real behavior of the enormous construction industry that affected the entire economy, even before the turning point in housing prices.

Figure 14.3 sets the background by looking at the average number of housing construction starts during the six cycles of the Age of Globalization.

This graph reveals that housing construction starts typically rose in the recovery rapidly to mid-expansion in the Age of Globalization. After the midpoint of the expansion, housing starts continued to rise more slowly during the rest of the

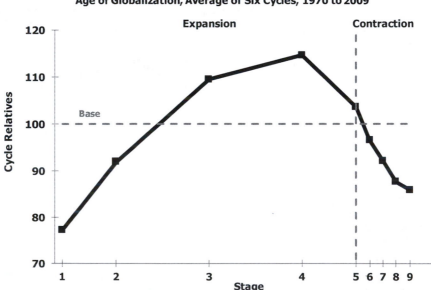

FIGURE 14.3 Housing starts, Age of Globalization, 1970–2009

prosperity phase of the expansion. They reached a peak at the profit peak in Stage 4, and then began to fall. Housing construction declined all the way from Stage 4 to Stage 8, the profit trough, and then remained flat until the end of the recession.

It is clear from this picture that housing construction played a major part in each business expansion, and then contributed considerably to the business contraction. The increase in housing construction during the expansion reflected an increase in the average wage and salary income. The rise in housing purchases was due partly to a reduction in unemployment, but also reflected the ease of obtaining credit.

Rising inequality meant that employee income stagnated during the expansion. The stagnation of income for the bottom 99 percent of income receivers eventually slowed down and then reduced house purchases, even with the use of more credit. Of course, once the recession began, people started to lose their houses to foreclosure, reflecting the rise of unemployment and lack of aggregate demand. Loss of jobs and loss of housing was a bitter pill for millions of people in the average recession.

Now we come to the Bush expansion and the Great Recession that arose from the trends in the Bush expansion. Figure 14.4 reveals the important role of the volatility of housing construction in causing the Great Recession and in making it worse.

Figure 14.4 provides the most dramatic picture of the role of the housing industry in the Great Recession and the financial crisis. Housing starts rose steadily in the first half of the Bush expansion, contributing to more income for additional construction workers due to rising consumer demand.

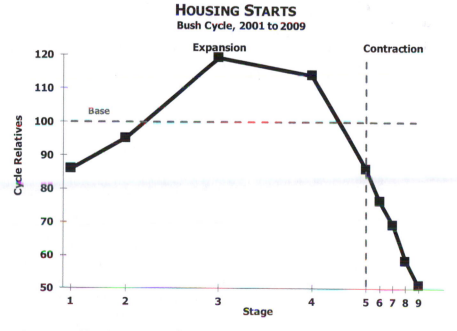

FIGURE 14.4   Housing starts, Bush cycle, 2001–2009

The course of housing construction, however, in the last half of the Bush expansion is all downward. The decline of housing construction in the Great Recession, as seen in Figure 14.4, was far more drastic than the average for all the cycles in the Age of Globalization, as seen in Figure 14.3. Thus, the decline in the housing construction industry was one cause of the Great Recession. Its decline is also the spark that set off the conflagration of the financial crisis.

The decline in the housing industry meant a change from the expectation of continually rising housing prices and construction to the reality of a large decline in that sector of the economy. Since the banks took extremely large risks based on the expectation of rising housing construction and sales, the actual decline led to a catastrophe.

The picture in Figure 14.4 is extremely dramatic in its portrayal of the construction industry going down and down. This meant that the decline of housing construction and prices not only helped to start the recession and financial crisis, but also continued to make the recession much worse and to make the financial crisis become almost the worst in history.

The bankers

There is plenty of proof, in investigative reporting, court documents, and court decisions, that officials at some of the largest banks used every way they could, by both legal and illegal means, to squeeze profit from their customers and everyone else who dealt with them. Their practices included inflicting higher and higher penalties on anyone who paid back loans even one day late, thus managing to keep millions of people in worse and worse debt. They also criminally deceived investors by selling them bundles of mortgages as fast as they could, after they themselves had decided that the mortgages were worthless. They also used every means possible to evade regulations, including the excessive use of leverage to take risks beyond what was rational. A number of banks managed to lend up to 33 times their capital.

All of these harmful machinations and crimes are thoroughly recorded in clear, excellent, prose in several books. Elizabeth Warren (2014) explains how the banks got the bankruptcy laws changed to make it far more difficult for customers to get rid of their debts, got the federal government to give the largest banks hundreds of billions of dollars in bailouts for no good reason, and opposed any protections for the banks' customers. Her book *A Fighting Chance* is a personal and moving story of how she fought these three battles while changing her role from housewife with two children to Senator of the United States.

A more advanced but clearly written book by Joseph Stiglitz (2015b), *Rewriting the Rules of America*, emphasizes the important economic fact that the bailout, called TARP, gave hundreds of billions of dollars to the biggest banks for no good reason, while giving no help to householders who could not pay their mortgages or to workers who were being fired. Most of it is powerful in economics, while written in popular speech.

The Democratic view

Why did the financial crisis of 2008 to 2009 occur, and why did it occur at that time? Most of the Democrats in Congress have argued that the financial crisis happened because some bankers were both greedy and irrational in their expectations of the returns from financial speculations. Such speculations included their purchases of large bundles of mortgages that had extremely weak probability of repayment.

The Democrats followed up their view of the cause of the crisis by passing the Dodd–Frank Act. This act attempted to reimpose strong regulations on the banks, so as to prevent them from taking risks that would result in another major financial crisis.

It is certainly true, as shown in the previous section, that the bankers acted in exploitative, illegal, and irrational ways. On the other hand, bankers have been acting in these harmful ways ever since the ancient Greek and Roman Empires. Why did this financial crisis happen at this time?

It is the nature of their job that bankers are always grasping for profits. Their job puts their interests squarely against those of the bottom 99 percent of the population by income and wealth. Since the bankers act this way all of the time, there is no explanation from this viewpoint of why the financial crisis occurred at this time.

The Dodd–Frank Act, passed by Democrats, had good intentions, but is completely insufficient to prevent future financial crises. This is because, in part, it was watered down at each stage in its progress. The Republicans weakened it before it was passed. The Republicans have further weakened the bill in later years with certain new bills.

Furthermore, an army of lobbyists for the banks have done everything possible to weaken the laws and to weaken the detailed regulations when they are written by the enforcing agencies. Finally, as in past American financial history, it is likely that the regulators will apply the regulations in a way that is most favorable to the big banks. The regulators almost always expect to get good jobs on Wall Street when they retire from the government.

It should be added that some famous economists, such as Joseph Stiglitz, have argued persuasively that monetary policy alone can do very little to prevent the business cycle of boom and bust. To get out of a recession, fiscal policy, including government spending and revenue, is necessary.

The Republican view

Conservative economists have argued that large banks behave in a rational manner on the basis of rational assumptions about the future behavior of the economy. The bankers behave rationally in the sense that they are simply trying to maximize their profits in ways that Adam Smith might have thought would produce optimal growth for the economy. They argue that economic and financial crises will not produce any lack of aggregate demand.

Conservative politicians believe the problem that caused the financial crisis was not the capitalist economy or the behavior of the bankers. Rather, it was financial regulations and the incorrect policy decisions of the Federal Reserve System that held back banks. In order to cure the problems that caused the Great Recession and the financial crisis, conservative politicians and economists have two major policy proposals.

Their first proposal is to get rid of all governmental financial regulations. They claim that if the regulations were abolished, most of the financial system would proceed at maximum growth without any recessions or financial crises.

In reality, many financial regulations were abolished under a series of presidents. This allowed the banks to amass enormous amounts of profit from various types of risky speculation and by gouging money out of their customers.

Thus, deregulation greatly increased inequality of income and wealth in America. The previous chapter showed how this rapid increase of inequality in income and wealth, both in the long run since 1980 and in the short run during every economic expansion, was a major cause of every average recession and the Great Recession.

The fact that wages and salaries stagnated was not part of the banks' future expectations. They assumed wages and salaries would continue to increase and thus support a continuing rise in housing prices. When this did not happen, profits from the housing bubble turned into losses when the bubble burst. Thus, the rise of inequality coming from deregulation was one reason for the financial crisis at that time.

The second policy proposal by conservative politicians and economists to fix the financial crisis as well as the Great Recession has been a policy of austerity. Austerity here means that government spending must be drastically cut. The cuts should be made in all programs and social services provided by the government. They would include cuts in health services, education, infrastructure, and support for clean energy. All of these proposals tend to harm the primary beneficiaries: the poor and the middle class. The conservative argument is based partly on the idea that less spending will mean fewer taxes on the wealthy. If taxes on the wealthiest 1 percent are reduced, then they can invest more in profitable enterprises and stimulate economic growth.

Wherever these policies have been used, whether in America, England, or Greece, they have caused greater unemployment, less aggregate demand, and lower economic growth or recession. This was spelled out to some extent in Chapters 10 and 11. It has been fully explained in powerful prose by Krugman (2012). The process by which austerity causes lower economic growth and more intense financial crises is also spelled out in Stiglitz (2015a, 2015b).

The progressive view of the financial crisis of 2008 to 2009

There are some controversies concerning the causes of the financial crisis of 2008 to 2009 among progressive economists, and the following is an attempt to emphasize the points of agreement.

The story of the financial crisis begins with the rising inequality of income and wealth over the long run from 1980 to the Great Recession of 2007 to 2009. There was an especially rapid rise of inequality from 2001 to 2007 in the Bush expansion. This rise of inequality caused a lack of aggregate demand, especially a lack of consumer demand.

Other factors causing the Great Recession are stated at the beginning of Chapter 12. These included a decline in government deficit spending, higher interest rates, and higher trade deficits.

These causes, beginning with inequality, started a mild recession that began in the last quarter of 2007. That recession, however, also further reduced housing prices. The fall of the value of houses made the housing crisis worse. Houseowners then became unable to refinance their house in order to keep paying the mortgage, or sell their house for enough money to pay back the mortgage. Eventually, the banks foreclosed on the houses. This left the banks with a large number of houses they could not sell for a profit.

A brief summary might say: the financial crisis was brought about by the usual factors causing recessions, including inequality; it also included the austerity policies put in place by the conservative politicians, plus the usual irrational risk-taking by the bankers, compounded by the end of financial regulations.

Global financial crisis of 2008 to 2009

The Great Recession and the financial crisis began first in America before spreading to other countries. For a time, some of the political leaders of Europe laughed behind the scenes at the American financial crisis and commented loudly about their own continuing good economic performance.

Three types of economic processes—trade, investment, and finance—spread the recession and financial crisis throughout the global economy.

The first channel for spreading the crisis was global investment. When there is recession in one country, especially a country as wealthy and powerful as America, investors tend to reduce their investment in all the countries of the world. This is based on the quite rational notion that the recession and crisis may spread from the initial victim to all of the countries in the world.

The second channel for spreading the crisis was global finance. Finance is no longer simply a national industry. Rather, the financial industry dominates every country, with the same giant firms lending in almost every country. In some ways, the top 100 corporations constitute the underlying government of the global economy, while the financial giants control who gets credit.

When a financial instrument such as a package of mortgages turns out to make enormous profits for those who use it, the financial corporations begin to use it throughout the world. For example, American banks made enormous profits from the sale of large bundles of weak and risky mortgages. Some of these bundles of toxic mortgages were sold to greedy banks in many countries. Thus, when the financial crisis began, some apparently strong German banks held bundles of American mortgages. For a while, they made good profits from them. Then, when the financial crisis exploded, the bundles of weak toxic mortgages were no longer worth anything. They were thus one factor sending some of these foreign banks into bankruptcy.

The third factor spreading the crisis was global trade. The American recession reduced aggregate American demand, which included the reduction of demand for imports into America. This reduction of demand by American corporations and individuals reduced the exports of many countries to America. This reduction in trade reverberated around the world. Finally, the reduction in trade by many other countries decreased their aggregate demand for goods and services. They were forced to reduce their imports from American and other countries. Each round of reductions in trade made the next round of reductions in trade still worse in almost every country in the world.

As a result of its spread through the global highways of trade, investment, and finance, the plague of recession and depression hit almost every country and became a truly global recession and global financial crisis. Therefore, any set of proposals to end financial crises, as well as proposals to end recessions and depressions, must be global in nature.

It has been stressed by many economists, including Stiglitz (2015a, 2015b) and Ben Bernanke in his last speech to Congress as Chair of the Federal Reserve (Bernanke, 2014), that recessions, depressions, and financial crises can never be ended by monetary policy alone. Monetary policies and regulations are helpful in preventing the very worst financial crises in the capitalist economy. What is necessary, however, for sustained growth is fiscal policy and major changes in the economic institutions. Fiscal policies and institutional changes are discussed in the next chapter.

Bush, Obama, and the great theft

Toward the end of the Bush Administration in 2008 and the beginning of the Obama Administration in 2009, Congress passed a law to allow the Federal Reserve to give $750 billion to the banks. This had two forms. One of the forms was a loan, while the other was the purchase of common stock.

The loan to each bank was at an extremely low interest rate. There were no conditions on the loan; therefore, it could be used to pay high bonuses to the bank executives. It could also be used to pay dividends to the stockholders. It could also be used for all kinds of financial speculation.

The purpose had been to get the banks to lend money to small and middle-sized business. Yet there were few loans to business at any level, so this type of monetary policy was not much help to the economy. The program was, however, very useful if the purpose was to put money in the hands of the wealthiest 1 percent. On a positive side, the bank bailout did help prevent a major depression.

A second way money was transferred from the government to the banks was the purchase of common stock by the Federal Reserve. This money that went to the banks was never used for productive investment. The government bought the stock of the banking corporations and then sold it when the crisis was over.

This meant that the banks had free use of the money for a considerable length of time. The $750 billion also could not be used by the government for services aimed at helping the middle class and the poor.

The program to give emergency money to the banks, plus the Obama Administration stimulus program, did not provide enough stimulus to the basic economy to get a healthy recovery going. The expansion that followed has had the lowest growth rate of any expansion since the Second World War. Instead of using massive stimulus money through fiscal programs to get the economy moving, the only large-scale program by the government since the bailout program (TARP) has been the "Quantitative Easing" (QE) program of the Federal Reserve.

That program has given money directly to the banks, again without any restrictions on how they can use it. QE meant the Federal Reserve created money by buying securities (such as government bonds) from banks, with electronic cash instead of paper money. The new money increased bank reserves by the amount of assets purchased, which gave the program the name "Quantitative Easing." The total amount spent on the program was at least $2 trillion over several years.

Quantitative Easing sounds like an innocuous monetary program designed to stimulate the economy by encouraging banks to make more loans. This was supposed to help businesses make more investments, which would encourage economic growth. In reality, however, the $2 trillion given to the banks has mostly not been used for traditional investment projects by business to expand the economy.

Instead, its largest use has been in financial speculation that has greatly increased the profits of the banks. Financial speculation does not lead to a healthy economy. Only productive investments in the expansion of equipment and buildings can create economic growth.

When one adds up the total amount of money given to banks by the initial Bush–Obama program, plus other minor gifts to the banks, plus the money given through Quantitative Easing, the total is almost $3 trillion.

This has meant enormous banks profits, including massive profits to the wealthiest 1 percent, who own most of the bank stocks. Yet that money was stolen from the taxpayers, although the process of stealing was covered with legalisms. Taken all together, this is surely the largest theft in American history.

The shift of $3 trillion from the general populace to the financial sector must have had a powerful effect on the inequality of income and wealth. Indeed, it has meant that most of the economic growth in the Obama era has gone as income only to the wealthiest 1 percent, especially to those in the financial sector. It follows that this shift of wealth has greatly increased the degree of inequality of income and wealth in America since the Great Recession.

Was a bailout necessary?

It was absolutely necessary. More precisely, some kind of large, drastic action was required to prevent another Great Depression. One can argue about the kind of measure necessary. But it is clear that some such measure was needed.

Some conservative economists argued at the time that no government support for the economy and no government bailout to the banks were necessary. They saw the Great Recession and the financial crisis as simply the results of forces outside of the American economy. This book has shown that they were wrong. Chapter 13 showed that the Great Recession resulted from internal forces in the American economy. This chapter has shown that the financial crisis was also mainly the result of forces within the American economy.

Before the Great Depression, the primary cause of financial crises was fearful depositors hurrying to get their money out of their bank. Since the Federal Deposit Insurance Corporation (FDIC) was put into effect, the main problem is no longer individual bank deposits.

The main problem is that the current American economy is totally based on credit, not paper or metallic money. In early 2009, when the financial crisis was at its worst, allowing all of the major banks to go bankrupt would have meant an end to credit for most business. If a business had no credit, then it could not pay its suppliers or its workers for more than a week or two.

If they could not pay suppliers or workers, then a large number of businesses would have gone bankrupt within a month. This would have unemployed additional tens of millions of employees. It would have meant the collapse of demand coming from wages or salaries, and the pileup of huge amounts of unsold goods. Therefore, some large, drastic measure was necessary to save the financial system and economic system.

The previous section explained why the bank bailout, adopted by the Obama Administration, produced an enormous increase in inequality of income and wealth, while harming the long-run prospects for a healthy economy. It was harmful in the long run because banks knew that they could take big risks and still be bailed out even if those risky investments turned into massive losses.

So what reasonable solutions were available to solve the problem of corporations and banks "too big to fail"?

More financial regulations

There is a long American tradition of reformers regulating different industries for various reasons, such as safety in the meatpacking industry. The Federal Reserve has many regulations applying to banks.

During the Great Depression, many regulations were passed to help stop the banks from taking too many risky actions that could turn into future financial crises. From the 1970s to the Great Recession, conservative economists, conservative legislators, and conservative Presidents did their best to get rid of all regulations on the banks. They argued that the private enterprise system can solve all economic problems in the long run, so regulations are not necessary. They also argued that all government regulations make banks less efficient, so they are harmful to economic progress.

The conservative push to end all bank regulations was quite successful. Getting rid of the regulations allowed the banks to take tremendous risks in order to make tremendous profits. Thus, deregulation was one cause of the financial crisis of 2008 to 2009.

To remedy the situation, Senator Chris Dodd and Representative Barney Frank created the Dodd–Frank bill to regulate banks so as to make the financial system safe against future financial crises. This bill offered relatively small regulatory improvements. It was then greatly weakened in Congress by conservatives. It was further weakened when the agency wrote its detailed provisions. The regulators are sympathetic to the banks and expect good positions with those banks when they retire from government. Therefore, in practice, the Dodd-Frank Act will not prevent future economic financial crises.

There is a long history in America of breaking up large corporations when they are found to have a monopoly control over a sector of the economy. The solution has been tried a number of times, including the breaking up of the largest corporation in the world in the early 1960s, AT&T. As part of a deal with the Justice Department, AT&T was allowed to keep 30 percent of its business, but agreed to create seven new smaller corporations, known as the "Baby Bells."

From 1996 to 2006, one of the Baby Bells bought three of the other Baby Bells and AT&T, taking on that name. All of the other original Baby Bells were also bought by larger corporations, so that of the original eight companies, there are now only three large telecommunication companies. Breaking up corporations therefore does not seem to be the best way to achieve more equality in the long run.

Democratization: a progressive solution

When conservatives see what they view as too large a government, they argue for privatization. Privatization means that the property of the government, belonging to all the country, is given away to private individuals and private corporations.

On the contrary, many progressives urge democratization when the problem is viewed as corporations that are too large to fail, because their failure would pull down a large part of the economy.

Democratization means that some private property, a large part of which has been exploited from the public, should be taken from private hands and be put under democratic control. The largest banks control so much wealth that their failure may lead to a depression or large recession. In order to prevent those devastating economic events from ever happening again, the largest banks need to be put under the control of democratically elected governments.

This would not be something brand new in America. When the state of North Dakota was under the control of a populist government, it set up the Bank of North Dakota. This bank has over a long time successfully given loans to individuals and small enterprises when they were most needed during recessions.

If a giant bank were democratically run by the American people, then all the executives would be appointed by the American government. The bank executives would no longer receive hundreds of millions of dollars in salary and bonuses. Instead, they would receive a large enough salary so that numerous highly qualified people would compete for these positions.

These banks would be instructed to help expand the economy by loans to individuals and businesses when they were most needed in recessions and depressions. They would also be instructed to be careful to not take too much risk. The net effect of the change from private banks with tens of billions of dollars in profit each year to stable, publicly run banks would reduce the probability of recessions and depressions.

This process of democratization would shift a large amount of money from the bonuses of the corporate executives to the general public. Therefore, it would substantially increase the equality in the economy.

How many banks need to be taken under democratically controlled management? If even only the two largest banks were transferred from private to public ownership, this might be sufficient to control and prevent financial crises. How would that be possible?

In the 2008 to 2009 financial crisis, all of the top banks were close to bankruptcy. If the largest two had been taken over and stabilized, then the rest might have been allowed to go through the usual bankruptcy. What would've happened? Suppose we call this largest public bank the Public Bank of America (PBA).

The PBA would have convenient branches everywhere in the country where they were needed. The Federal Deposit Insurance Corporation (FDIC) could immediately have given the PBA all of the private accounts from banks that failed. People would have then known that their accounts were safe. That would be the first step toward public confidence in the banking system.

Next, the FDIC and courts would give the PBA responsibility for all of the loans that had been made by the banks that failed. The PBA could then, instead of forcing people and businesses into bankruptcy, restructure the loans so individuals and businesses would be able to eventually pay off all of their debt. This would be another step toward public confidence in the banking system.

One of the two largest banks that were now democratically controlled could also be assigned the task of giving new loans and credit where they were needed and could eventually be repaid. Thus, one of the two new public banks of America would deal with depositors. The other would deal with loans.

The new investment bank, by making loans and credit available in the growing areas of the economy, would have the task of promoting investment policy in America. By having such a bank under public control, it could help the economy to stay out of recessions as well as financial crises. The combination of the two banks under public control would also greatly diminish inequality in America. Thus, this solution is a necessary component of any serious policy directed toward a large reduction in inequality and to end most or all economic instability. The next two chapters will explore the other main policies required for these goals.

Conclusions

The two major reasons for the financial crisis of 2008 to 2009 were the rapid increase of inequality combined with the rapid decrease of financial regulations.

A critical point was reached when all of the top banks would have gone bankrupt without immediate financial help. Something major had to be done because otherwise a much larger financial crisis would have led to a Great Depression similar to that of the 1930s.

Some conservative economists wanted to leave the solution to the market. Most economists, however, agreed with economists in the administration that the only possible answer was an immense bailout for all of the largest banks.

To prevent a financial crisis in the future, most conservative economists argue that the capitalist system can prevent it or automatically recover if there are hardly any regulations and almost no government interference of any kind. The economists in the Obama Administration relied on a set of weak bank regulations that both continued the unabated power and wealth of Wall Street, and could not prevent future crises. Some progressive economists would rely on breaking up the largest banks and corporations, but this has had little success when it was tried in the past. Many progressive economists would support a public bank for depositors and small loans, along with a public bank for investments.

For further reading, the best book on the operation and history of all financial crises before the 1990s is *Financial Crisis* by Martin Wolfson (1994).

Appendix 14.1

Financial markets, instability, and crises

These three processes are closely intertwined, so let us look systematically at each of the threads connecting them. Although some of the following points have been touched on in earlier discussions, the intensive and systematic discussion of these issues in recent literature has helped to reduce this material into a clear synthesis, putting all the points in their proper places.

First, rising inequality was a major part of the process leading to the deep financial crisis of 2008 and 2009. For example, although profits soared in 2001 to 2007, wages and salaries stagnated, which greatly reduced the spending power of the middle class. Banks and other financial corporations assumed that continued increases in wages would be sufficient to keep paying the extremely high mortgages owed by people, even when those people had very little savings. Therefore, the banks continued a very easy lending policy that allowed everyone, even people with substandard or insufficient resources, to buy a home with an enormous mortgage.

This model of financing new homes worked well so long as the economy was rising at a rate high enough to allow payment of wage increases. After about 2005, however, the growth of the economy began to slow and became slower each year. The slower economic growth meant that employers refused to pay more than a pittance in increased wages. This declining growth of middle-class income slowed the rise of housing and began to witness less payment of mortgages. This weakened the ability of financial markets to make profits, but the banks continued to assume that growth and wages would still be sufficient to pay mortgages. By the end of 2007, however, the economy came to a halt. When the economy stopped rising, real wages began to decline. The decline was far more than the financial models had allowed to happen. The falling wages turned the few refusals to pay mortgages into a flood of unpayable mortgages and people selling or just giving up their homes. This turned the vast market in buying and selling packages of mortgages from an amazingly profitable level to a rapid decline in the profits from housing and a rapidly increasing number of almost worthless packages of mortgages. This was a major factor in producing the financial crisis of 2008 and 2009.

Another link in the process began to harm the financial octopus as well as its victims through a train of events beginning with rising long-run inequality. The rising inequality gave a higher and higher percentage of all the wealth to the small group of rich people at the top of the wealth pyramid. The wealthy were able to use their additional assets to increase their political power. With vast sums of money, pressure could be exerted on federal, state, and local legislators and government executives.

The increased political power of Wall Street is shown by the fact that the Trump Administration has five billionaires in its cabinet, and the cabinet includes a total of six representatives of Goldman Sachs. President Trump and the Republicans in Congress are using their political power to pass every measure that would give income to the wealthy, while reducing the income of the middle class. To the extent they are successful, this will mean a great increase in inequality in America.

The increased power of the wealthy bankers has already been used to eliminate most regulations on the financial sector. The banks had a stream of victories that slowly tore apart the existing financial regulations, many of which had existed since the Great Depression. For example, the Glass-Steagall Act had reduced financial risk by dividing the banks into ordinary deposit and lending institutions as well as investment banks. When that Act was ended by the political power of the banks, a spree of highly speculative and risky new financial instruments went into action. The new kinds of speculations helped the banks to make immense profits. At the same time, these speculations put the banks into far more risk. The most spectacular aspect of the risky financial maneuvers was the extensive use of borrowing by the banks from other sources so as to make loans and investments many times their initial capital invested in the bank. For example, a bank might have an initial capital of $1 billion, but borrow another $1 billion, then invest the whole $2 billion in high-paying but risky endeavors. Although it sounds impossible, some banks actually borrowed and invested over 30 times their initial capital.

Instead of keeping some money in reserve out of their original capital investment in the bank, bankers borrow far beyond the original bank assets. The process of borrowing and spending beyond their original assets is called "leveraging." The bank uses their original investment only as a lever to borrow many times more money and then make further risky investments.

From the 1970s to the present, Wall Street has used all of its great economic and political power to get rid of financial regulations so that it can make immense amounts of speculative financial investments. These investments do not expand the productive base of America, but they do provide new ways of gambling with other people's money in complex ways that provide the bankers with billions of additional dollars.

Wall Street no longer waits passively for millions of small depositors to increase its base for investment. Rather, by leveraging their own capital with widespread borrowing from other sources, they are able to make hundreds of billions of dollars of additional profit through their control of the shape and volume of investment. Their reach extends around the world. In this manner, Wall Street controls much of the mining and manufacturing investment of most countries. Instead of a primarily manufacturing economy, they have shifted focus to a mainly financial economy. This process of extending financial control to most of the economy may be called "financialization."

How exactly does this new process of speculative investment and financialization affect economic inequality and instability? When the bankers make hundreds of billions of dollars of profit from financial speculation, this profit must come eventually from the output of all employees so as to leave that output in the hands of the billionaires. As the assets of the billionaires grow while the wages of the employee class remain stagnant, it is obvious that economic inequality must grow. This has happened from 1980 to the present. Since the growth of economic inequality leads to further growth of political inequality, which in turn increases economic inequality still further, it is clear that the whole process is a vicious circle of rising political and economic inequality.

How has the rising economic and political inequality affected the movements of the whole economy? In long-run terms, it has led to an increasing gap between the two Americas of the wealthy versus the poor and the middle class. In short-run terms, each economic expansion has increased the inequality. That increase in economic inequality has led to a less stable economy because each business expansion raises the Inequality Ratio, which then leads to an often-violent recession or depression. In fact, the increasing instability is one important cause of the tendency for such minor recessions to turn into roaring depressions.

15

DEMOCRATIC REVOLUTION

A progressive road to economic equality and full employment

Creating economic equality and full employment

A "democratic revolution" is a massive shift of power from the political and economic elite to the great majority of the people through legal and peaceful means. In America, this means a shift of power and resources from conservative billionaire capitalists to a large majority of the population.

Conservative governments have three primary principles: transfer as much political power as possible to the wealthy elite, who are about 1 percent of the population; transfer as much economic power as possible to the same wealthy elite; and do not interfere in the economy, except to cut taxes for the wealthy or cut goods and services for the rest of the people. For example, in June 2017, the U.S. Senate considered a bill to cut $800 billion from medical care for the poor and the middle class, while the bill also cut $600 billion in taxes for the wealthy.

A progressive American government would reduce the political power of the corporations and billionaires, while increasing the political power of the other 99 percent of the people. Factual investigations in the rest of this book show that political inequality results from economic inequality. It is also necessary, therefore, to reduce economic inequality as much as possible. At the present time, income inequality, wealth inequality, and inequality of opportunity are all extremely high and have been increasing since about 1980, so there is a lot of work to do to create a reasonably equal distribution of income.

Finally, the factual investigations in the rest of this book have shown that rising inequality in business expansions is the most important reason for recessions and unemployment. Therefore, economic inequality must be greatly reduced in order to end the cycle of boom and bust.

These principles underlie the specific, progressive policies outlined below.

1. Free healthcare

Free healthcare for every American would enable the average citizen to get and keep a better job. This would lead to a stronger economy and more revenue for the government.

Basic healthcare should also include dental expenses, eye care, and mental healthcare. Unfortunately, Americans presently have a healthcare system based on profiteering by the insurance companies, who then provide mediocre and expensive service.

The reduction in the profits of the health insurance industry, plus a reduction in expenses for patients, will reduce inequality. This reduction of economic inequality would reduce the political power of the wealthy, thus strengthening the democratic process. It would also provide a large economic area in which the government could stimulate the economy when needed.

Conservative critics argue that free healthcare is impossible because it is too expensive. In fact, most other industrialized countries, such as Canada and Great Britain, have free healthcare. Since America is richer than these other countries, it can also afford free healthcare.

Furthermore, public healthcare will be far cheaper per patient than the present private insurance system. The American system is currently at least twice as expensive per person compared to any other developed country (Stiglitz, 2015b). The present system is so expensive mostly because the private health insurance companies use 35 percent of all income for overhead and profit. Government Medicare, on the other hand, has no profit and its overhead costs are less than 4 percent of all its expenses.

How can America afford to pay for free healthcare? First, if the nation is at full employment with no idle resources, then free healthcare could be paid by additional taxes on the wealthy. The wealthiest 1 percent in America own 42 percent of all the wealth, so they can afford to pay more taxes in order to have free healthcare for all Americans. The tax on the wealthiest 1 percent would shift resources from them to the rest of the population. That would also accomplish the goal of reducing inequality in America.

If, however, America is in recession with large-scale unemployment, then those workers could find useful employment in productive projects such as healthcare. The money could also be raised by selling interest-paying bonds to the wealthy. Since the wealthy spend a very small proportion of their money on consumer goods and services, the government would be borrowing and spending money that would otherwise be idle during a recession.

Furthermore, if America is in recession or depression, there would also be another way to pay for healthcare. Just as the Federal Reserve creates money to give to banks, the government could also create money to pay for some of the free healthcare. Creating money causes inflation only when the economy is at full employment, so it cannot cause inflation when there is heavy unemployment. The additional money would only stimulate the economy.

2. Free higher education

A system of free higher education will create more scientists, engineers, and other professionals. This will increase the productivity of America, resulting in a stronger economic growth rate. A higher education level for all Americans will enable the average person to get a better job with better pay. Increased education will lead to more knowledgeable voters. Free higher education will also relieve the heavy burden of debt that millions of students currently have when they graduate.

Conservative critics claim that free higher education is impossible because it costs too much. In fact, conservatives argued in the last quarter of the nineteenth century that the creation of free primary education would bankrupt the government. Later, they also argued that free secondary education would bankrupt the government. Although no such bankruptcy occurred, they now present the same incorrect argument with respect to higher education.

Actually, it was shown above that free higher education increases economic growth, which will provide more than enough new revenue to pay the additional educational costs. If there are not enough funds to pay for the increased educational expenses in the short run, then the funds could be obtained by higher taxes on the wealthy or by borrowing from the wealthy, or through the creation of new money, as discussed above.

3. Infrastructure

Infrastructure includes roads, bridges, airports, and seaports. If the American government pays workers to build a road in a national park, then the workers receive wages. The wages are part of our national income. The wages are re-spent for other goods and services, which puts money in the hands of other people. The process of income expansion continues until the last dollar of the government money is re-spent. This book has shown concretely how government spending can lead directly to productive growth, greater equality, and more jobs.

Maintaining an excellent infrastructure of roads, bridges, airports, and seaports, as well as buses, city subways, and rapid trains, clearly helps raise the national product by improving the transportation of employees, goods, and services. If the workers on these projects were unemployed, this spending will clearly increase equality in America because their pay will be greater than the unemployment compensation that they previously received. These infrastructure jobs will also increase total American employment.

Infrastructure spending must also include projects for clean energy to help fight climate instability caused by global warming. Other projects would include reducing or eliminating air pollution by use of cleaner fuel and more efficient modes of transportation. There would be many other projects to improve the environment in which the American economy operates. One of the many projects would be expansion and conservation of local, state, and national parks.

Under the present system, the government spends enormous amounts of money on infrastructure through private enterprises and subcontractors that receive a great deal of profit from these public projects. Some progressive economists recommend saving money for the taxpayer by having the construction of infrastructure handled by an entirely public department. This would save even more money if positions such as accountant, architect, and engineer were included as necessary parts of the public process of building infrastructure.

The larger and better infrastructure, such as an improved transportation system, would lead to stronger economic growth and more revenue for the government. In the short run, the initial funds for infrastructure could be obtained through higher taxes on the wealthy or borrowing from them, or through the creation of new money, as discussed earlier.

4. A living wage and trade unions

The federal minimum wage was instituted during the Great Depression at a very low level of wages and salaries. Since the Second World War, the real value of the minimum wage has often dropped because wages rise slower than price inflation. What is needed is an increase each year so as to provide a decent living wage for every full-time employee.

If minimum wages were raised high enough to become a living wage, then fewer workers would find it necessary or desirable to change jobs. When the rate of job transfer declines, this helps the overall productivity of an economy because there is less necessity for recruiting or training new workers. For a more thorough discussion of the living wage, see Pollin and Luce (1998).

Conservative economists claim that higher minimum wages harm the economy because the higher wage expense forces employers to fire many workers. Conservative economists conveniently forget that every dollar paid to a low-income worker will be spent on buying goods and services. Moreover, those who receive the money that is spent on those goods and services will themselves spend a large part of it. Since the enlarged revenue from higher demand is greater than the increased wages, the effect is to actually increase the net income of the corporations.

Conservative economists often argue that if a trade union is successful in raising wages, this will cause employers to fire workers in order to stay competitive. Conservatives contend that if they have to pay higher wages, then they would also have to charge higher prices or reduce their output.

Progressive economists, on the other hand, point out that the higher wages to employees are immediately spent to buy more goods and services. Therefore, business as a whole has more money in revenue, so they can easily afford the higher wages.

5. Progressive taxation

So long as there is a capitalist economic system with extreme profits, stagnant wages and salaries, and rising inequality, there must be progressive income taxes, estate taxes, and property taxes, without tax loopholes for the wealthy or large corporations. Progressive taxation means that people with much higher income pay a much higher proportion of their income.

This type of taxation will help reduce the extreme inequality of income, wealth, and opportunity. More tax revenue will also provide funds for many of the progressive programs discussed in this chapter. The increase or decrease of all taxes at the appropriate time can also help stabilize the economy.

Conservative economists claim that the capitalist market provides each individual with an income that reflects the additional product they add to the output of the enterprise. Therefore, a just tax system should require equal tax rates on every individual. They also believe special tax deductions for the wealthy and corporations are necessary in order for them to have more money to invest in the economy.

Progressive economists, on the contrary, point out that wealthy investors, such as the billionaire President Donald Trump, have received income equal to thousands of times their input to the product. Therefore, progressive taxation is needed to remove the extreme inequality that has resulted from this current economic system.

Taxation policies are also needed for the control of cyclical booms and busts. When the economy is reaching the end of a boom, lower taxes for the middle class and the poor would help people to continue spending money on consumer goods. When the economy goes into recession, people still need money in their pockets. Further reduction of middle-class taxes is yet another way to provide more money for consumption.

In addition to the state and federal income tax system, several other taxes are large enough to affect equality and economic performance. The Social Security tax falls on everyone as an equal percentage of their income, but only up to a certain level of income, after which the individual pays nothing.

Because the tax is capped at a certain level, individuals with a very high income pay only a tiny percentage of their income on that tax. Thus, the Social Security tax is regressive because low-income individuals pay a much higher percentage of their income than do high-income individuals. Progressives point out that the Social Security tax could be made a lot less regressive if the present cap was removed.

Another regressive tax is the sales tax. Poor people must pay a significant part of their income for the sales tax whenever they buy any goods or services. A wealthy person, on the other hand, spends such a low percentage of their income on the sales tax that it has no affect on their amount of spending. It would greatly increase income equality if the sales tax was repealed and replaced by a more progressive income tax in each state. Oregon is one state that has abolished the sales tax.

The inheritance tax falls mainly on the wealthy, so it reduces inequality in America. The easiest way to considerably reduce inequality would be to significantly increase the inheritance tax on the wealthiest 1 percent. A strong inheritance tax would be a major tool for progressives in fighting for a democratic revolution to increase the equality of wealth. On the other hand, conservatives wish to abolish the inheritance tax, which would greatly increase inequality in America.

6. End discrimination

The large-scale and institutionalized discrimination against women and minorities must be abolished so that the economic system evaluates people only by merit, and not by other criteria. If women and minorities all received wages equal to their merit, then inequality would be greatly reduced. Once again, the reduction of inequality would strengthen the democratic process.

Some types of political discrimination are mainly used against the poor and racial minorities. A high percentage of people in prison are members of racial or ethnic minorities because of discrimination in the justice system.

There is further discrimination when anyone with a prison record is prohibited from voting. A prison record should not be a barrier to voting. There should also be an equal number of voting places in white, African-American, and Latina areas of towns. All voting discrimination must cease.

Progressive economists maintain that capitalism has continued the racism and sexism of earlier societies. Conservative economists, however, claim that capitalism inevitably ends economic racism and sexism because competition causes entrepreneurs to pay equal wages to all groups. In the nineteenth century, racist attitudes against Native Americans were exploited by the railroad corporations to help convince the government to give them large tracts of land along the railroad lines. In the twentieth century, the American South had far less trade unions than any other part of the country because it had far more racial prejudice than any other part of the country.

In the twenty-first century, racism and sexism were used by one political candidate, Donald Trump, to convince white American workers into voting for him for President of the United States. The fact that he was a billionaire who followed his own economic interests, however, meant that his economic interests and beliefs led him to policies exactly opposite to the needs of all workers: male or female; white, black, or brown.

7. Democratization of corporations "too big to fail"

The American economy has millions of small businesses; however, it is dominated by 100 or 200 giant corporations and a few enormous banks and other financial institutions. In the Great Recession, the worst blows to the economy came from the failure of some of the largest corporations and the biggest banks. At the end of the Great Recession, the government bailed out the auto industry and saved many of the largest financial institutions from bankruptcy through various types of bail-outs. If these corporations had been allowed to fail, then the whole economy and everyone in it would have faced great economic suffering.

The solution is not for the government to give hundreds of billions of dollars to failing corporations, who then give a large part of that money as bonuses to the executives who helped create the problem. The solution is not to rely primarily on a set of regulations that are full of holes or weakly enforced. Nor is the solution to break these extremely large corporations and banks into a few large pieces. Each new piece would continue to have enormous power and soon grow just as large as before they were split up.

If the largest corporations are allowed to fail, it would be a disastrous blow to the economy. A progressive solution would be democratic control of these super-large corporations. Democratization would mean that the federal government, elected by the people, would appoint someone to run each of the firms on behalf of all Americans. Any profit would go to the treasury and be used to reduce taxes and pay for other projects to help create full employment.

The only viable way to end the inequality caused by the largest corporations and the cyclical devastation sometimes caused by them is to create new institutions, which would make them subject to democratic control. Democratizing the largest financial corporations and other corporations "too big to fail" would provide a much higher level of economic equality and a much more stable economy.

The democratic ownership could be exercised through local, state, or federal government agencies. These new institutions would tend to create full employment, income and wealth equality, and a stronger democratic process.

Democratic control of some of the largest corporations would have several other beneficial effects beyond establishment of full employment. First, instead of large corporations using their power to reduce wages and salaries in order to increase profits, publicly owned organizations could help create equality by paying higher wages and salaries. If there is a recession, instead of going bankrupt, public firms could expand employment. Finally, instead of sending numerous lobbyists to influence Congress in favor of inequality, these new public institutions could simply follow the public interest by maintaining greater equality of income, wealth, and opportunity.

Conservative economists mostly argue that no corporation is too big, because their size merely reflects their worth in the marketplace. Progressive economists, on the contrary, maintain that much of the profits of these giant corporations come from their ability to pay low wages and salaries, and to influence the government to give them projects in which it is easy to make unjustified profits.

In addition to democratic control through local, state, or federal government agencies, democratic control by employee cooperatives can also help reduce inequality within middle-level corporations. In this case, the democratic control is not exerted by the whole country or a state or locality. It is exerted instead by all the employees of an enterprise. Employee cooperatives are enterprises in which the employees elect all of the board of directors. This elected board determines the level and type of production, the price structure, and the wages and salaries in the firm. All of the revenue in the firm goes to the workers in the firm, to year-end bonuses for each worker, or to reinvestment to expand the firm. There are no private profits. One example of a worker cooperative is the association of all the taxi drivers of one city into one company.

Consumer cooperatives are for the benefit of the consumers who start them. They are nonprofit and have an elected board of directors. The board sets output, wages, and prices. Any profit beyond the amount spent for wages and supplies is put back into the firm to lower prices or to expand its output. Another type of consumer cooperative is the association of farmers and other rural people to obtain electric power for their district, when the power companies refuse to supply power to more distant districts.

Thus, the employee cooperatives and consumer cooperatives have approximately the same nonprofit structure. The only difference between these two types of cooperatives is that one is directed by the representatives of its employees and the other is directed by the representatives of its consumers. In both cases, they increase the degree of equality by eliminating the payments of profits to private capitalists. This greater degree of economic equality helps produce more political equality as well as creating more demand for products.

8. Democratization of the military-industrial complex

Among the largest corporations, those that sell weapons and services to the military, in return for an extraordinarily high rate of profit, are among the worst offenders among those causing inequality. Their massive profits contribute greatly to the economic inequality between corporations and the average employee.

They use their political power, with an army of lobbyists, to increase government spending for military purposes. In addition, they pressure Congress to vote for war or warlike adventures whenever possible. Instead of leaving them to make their enormous private profits, they should be under democratic control of the public.

9. A strong and democratic global organization

In the Age of Globalization, no country is an economic island. America cannot achieve a high level of economic equality and full employment unless there is a global organization with the authority to deal with global economic issues. For a further discussion of all of the global economic issues, see Sherman et al. (2008, especially the five chapters in Part 4) and Stiglitz (2015a, 2015b).

A large part of the global economy today is owned by a few gigantic multinational corporations and the super-rich billionaires. To end this situation will require enough countries willing to cooperate and build a far stronger United Nations (UN).

What should the UN look like in the future in order to govern the global economy, which is now run by major corporations? In the future, the UN General Assembly will be elected democratically around the world according to the population of each country. The UN, and only the UN, will have an army with major weapons. The UN will have the right to regulate and/or take ownership of any large enterprise that controls major economic activity in many countries. The UN will have the power to tax any nation for any necessary amount. The UN will have a program to help equalize incomes in different countries and bring income levels closer together around the world. The UN will encourage cooperation based only on productivity and merit rather than by race, gender, time in prison, belief, or any other identifier. Finally, the UN will allow free migration or movement of people around the world.

Can equality and full employment be permanent?

The conservative argument is that there are no good or useful government projects. This was answered by the nine productive proposals discussed above.

Another question raised is whether temporary full employment may be made into a permanent feature of capitalism. Conservatives claim that there must always be some unemployment or else wages will continue to rise until there are no profits.

On the contrary, Keynesian liberals such as Paul Krugman (2012) claim that permanent full employment is possible if the government carefully controls its spending so that neither too much nor too little money is spent. The government would reduce its spending if there was too much demand and inflation. In the Keynesian liberal view, the government would increase its spending if there was a lack of demand causing unemployment, but it would decrease its spending if there was too much demand causing inflation.

The possibility of such fine balancing in government spending has been questioned from both right and left. Conservatives claim that any attempt to keep an exact level of full employment would be defeated by the fact that Congress and the President require a long process to reach any conclusion.

Progressives question whether there can be a capitalist system with permanent full employment. The problem is that the wealthy obstruct many government projects for full employment. For example, they are opposed to spending for useful purposes such as education that will benefit the middle class and the poor. Such useful spending will be fought by the wealthy because they will have to pay some of the taxes for these projects. Instead, they strongly support only spending for warfare or police. Thus, the interests of some groups get in the way of action for full employment.

For these reasons, it may be impossible to achieve permanent full employment under our present economic institutions of capitalism. The nine proposals, however, would change institutions in order to enhance democracy in America. Some of the institutional changes would also reduce economic instability. As a result of these institutional changes, it would then be possible to have permanent equality and full employment.

For example, free healthcare changes the healthcare institutions so that Americans have a new relationship to healthcare. A living wage places the needs of people above profit. More schools may be built during difficult economic times. Changing the tax system would institutionalize high taxes on the wealthy, low taxes on the middle class, and no taxes on the poor. Democratic ownership and control of the giant corporations will force them to spend on higher wages and salaries at the right times to help the economy have more jobs. Thus, these changes in economic institutions would create new demand for goods and services to end the business cycle, guarantee full employment, and increase equality in America.

In summary, the proposals given above may contain enough changes in the present economic institutions to encourage permanent full employment as well as a high degree of economic equality. The result of the new laws would be an increase in the public sector, with just enough economic power to control the macroeconomic process and prevent recessions and depressions.

What is a democratic revolution?

As was shown in the previous sections, these proposals would lead to a high level of economic equality. They would provide enough aggregate demand to lead toward permanent full employment. They would greatly reduce the degree of economic inequality. They would greatly strengthen the democratic process. Each proposal has been shown to be practical, yet not extreme or utopian. Their combined effect, however, would certainly amount to a revolution in the economic and political processes of our society.

The result would be an economy with no cycle of boom and bust, with no extreme inequality, and with no strong intervention in the democratic process by the large corporations and the wealthy. On the contrary, the economy would be at full employment, with a high level of economic equality and a strong democratic process. That is a good definition of a democratic revolution.

The process of democratization

In order to achieve these goals, how much change in economic institutions is required at a minimum? Conservatives, such as President Trump, wish to change the economy by pushing history in a backward direction to an earlier era of more elite control. They want to privatize almost all of the government functions, except the military and the police. For example, they want to eliminate most of the social services for the middle class and the poor while greatly reducing the taxes on the wealthy.

On the contrary, progressives wish to change institutions in a forward direction toward an era of more democratic control. For example, all healthcare and higher education would be free. In order to stabilize the whole economy, the public sector would also need to own and control a large number of giant corporations.

Aside from the very largest corporations, however, control need not be governmental. The goal of reducing inequality and helping to stabilize the whole economy could be done mostly by democratization in the hands of the employees of each firm. That democratization would take the form of cooperatives using democratic procedures.

What would be the most practical way to achieve a cooperative process in most of the economy? In 2016, the British Labour Party proposed a gradual means of transferring corporations from private hands to cooperatives (discussed in Wolff, 2016). The employees of a corporation would have the right of first purchase or rejection of the corporation under certain circumstances.

There would be at least three such circumstances. The owners might wish to close the corporation. Second, the owners might wish to sell the corporation. Third, the owners might wish to change from a privately held corporation to a public sale of shares in the corporation by private investors.

In these three circumstances, the employees as a whole would be able to buy the corporation if they wish to do so. In each case, the government would offer a sufficient loan—at little or no interest—to cover the price of the corporation.

Hope

In the election of 2016, Senator Bernie Sanders ran on a strong progressive program. He went from 3 percent in the polls to 45 percent of all the votes cast in the Democratic primaries. This strength of a relatively unknown progressive candidate is one of the many signs that a progressive movement could achieve election success and passage of many of the proposals suggested in this chapter.

President Trump supports policies based on racism, sexism, authoritarianism, and a giant tax cut for the rich. The resistance to the Trump Administration has been increasingly active and unprecedented so early in an administration. In the state and local elections of November 2017, liberal and progressive candidates did extremely well by unseating many long-term conservative incumbents. This presents concrete hope for a strong progressive movement for years to come.

TECHNICAL APPENDIX

Model of the inequality cycle

This appendix was written for economists, their students, and other highly motivated readers with the proper mathematical skills. This appendix contains different parts relating to an inequality theory of the business cycle. First, it examines whether the cycles discussed are within a reasonably narrow range so that comparison makes good sense. Second, it presents a simple model reflecting the data in the book. Third, it presents flow diagrams to illustrate the model. Fourth, it asks whether the model is good not only for a cycle with the average recession, but also a cycle in which there is a depression. Finally, it asks whether one could base a model on exclusively global data.

This model is influenced by a long history of progressive models. The first pioneering example of a cycle model with inequality as an important variable was done by Michael Kalecki in the 1930s (see a more complete version in Kalecki, 1968).

Part 1. Investment cycle and standard deviations

Chapters 5 to 11 spelled out in statistics the basic model used in this book. One question that arises is the degree to which the summary of the factual story told in Chapter 12 applies to all cycles. It reflects the average cycle. How far do individual cycles vary from the average? One way of measuring the degree to which individual cycles vary from the average is to examine the standard deviation at each of the nine stages of the cycle.

The standard deviation is used here because all economists know the standard deviation. Its formula may be found in any text on basic statistics. There are many other measurements that could be taken, but each has its own strengths and weaknesses, so we will merely discuss the standard deviation here.

TABLE TA.1 Investment, cycle relatives, and standard deviations, 1949–2009

This table depicts investment at each of the nine stages of the cycle for the average of the
10 cycles from 1949 to 2009. It also depicts the standard deviation for each stage.

The average deviation for each stage is the average of the absolute values of differences
between the cycle relatives of each cycle and the average cycle relatives of all
10 cycles. The average deviation is what Mitchell (1951) uses in his measurements of
the business cycle.

The quartile range is the net of the 75th and 25th percentiles. It tells how widely spread
the middle half of the data points are.

Stage	Cycle relatives	Standard deviations	Average deviations	Quartile ranges
1	75.8	9.62	8.13	14.69
2	90.5	10.00	7.53	12.53
3	103.8	4.19	2.99	3.26
4	110.7	8.36	5.89	7.71
5	111.8	8.64	6.34	9.07
6	107.4	9.62	6.13	6.67
7	102.8	11.56	8.10	7.75
8	99.2	13.58	9.78	9.46
9	93.6	14.06	9.74	9.32

Source: U.S. Department of Commerce, Bureau of Economic Analysis, NIPA, Table 1.16, line 7, at
www.bea.gov.

Note: Investment is Real Gross Private Domestic Investment, in billions of chained 2005 dollars, 1949.4
to 2009.2. Quarterly data, seasonally adjusted at annual rates.

The pattern for the behavior of the cycle relatives of investment is the usual
rise from Stage 1 to Stage 5 plus the usual decline from Stage 5 to Stage 9. The
standard deviation of investment reveals that, even at its highest in Stage 1, it
is fairly small. The lowest point of the standard deviation for investment is in
Stage 3.

In other words, investment moves in almost the same pattern during every cycle.
In the first half of the expansion, from Stages 1 to 3, the growth rate of investment in every cycle keeps rising. In the last half of the expansion, from Stage 3
to 5, the growth rate of investment declines. The fact that the standard deviation
is at its lowest point at Stage 3 means that the behavior of investment is approximately the same in every cycle at Stage 3.

At the beginning trough of the cycle and the final trough, however, there is
more volatility in the behavior of investment than in the rest of the cycle. This
is one of the reasons that it is hard to predict short-run behavior of investment
around the peak and the trough.

It was shown above that the low point of volatility is reached halfway up the
expansion in Stage 3, where the standard deviation is lowest. The main reason is
that the cyclical expansion is proceeding strongly and the economy is healthy, so
the rate of expansion of investment is fairly stable at that point. This interesting
behavior is found in almost every main variable of the cycle. Since all the major
variables behave similarly, the example of investment will suffice here.

Part 2. Basic model of inequality and unemployment

The model adds no new data, but is based on the empirical analysis of Chapters 5 to 11. The model is not designed for prediction. It is designed only to show that a logical and consistent model can explain the relationship of inequality and cyclical unemployment. The model does not use econometric tests, but merely states the picture consistent with the facts found in this book.

It begins with the statement that national income (Y) is equal to consumer spending (C) plus investment spending (I). Therefore:

(1) $Y_t = C_t + I_t$

Note that t means a unit of time, such as a quarter of the year. Again, this is only for the private domestic economy, so it leaves out government activity and trade at this point in the argument.

The second statement is that national income is equal, on the income or cost side, to profits and wages. "Profit" (P) is defined to include rent, interest, and all other kinds of profit, including corporate and non-corporate, financial and non-financial. "Wages" (W) are defined to include all kinds of wages, salaries, and benefits. The total of all property income, called "Profits" here, plus the total of all labor income, called "Wages" here, is equal to all of national income. Therefore:

(2) $Y_t = W_t + P_t$

Notice that the equation may be turned around so that it says profit is equal to national income minus wages. In this simple model, it is assumed that all other costs, including interest costs, taxes, and imports, are zero. These other costs will be added into the model in Part 3.

The heart of this book is the behavior of inequality during a cycle of boom and bust. The next equation presents this in a simple form. The definition of the inequality ratio is aggregate profit divided by aggregate wages. If the total national income is known and aggregate wages are also known, then the ratio of profit to wages is easy to calculate. Remember, aggregate wages plus aggregate profit equals national income. Therefore, inequality can be expressed in the equation below:

(3) $W_t = g + hY_t$

where g and h are constants. In this equation, h is between 1 and 0.

It follows that wages rise when national income rises, but wages rise more slowly than national income. Therefore, profits rise faster than wages. Since profit is rising faster than wages, the Inequality Ratio is rising. A rising Inequality Ratio in the expansion is consistent with the data presented in Chapter 7 describing expansions during the Age of Globalization.

On the contrary, wages will be a rising percentage of national income in the contraction, so the Inequality Ratio must fall in the contraction. The falling Inequality Ratio in the contraction is also consistent with the data found in Chapter 7.

Equation 3 described the behavior of the Inequality Ratio in the cycle of boom and bust. What are the effects of a rising Inequality Ratio in the expansions? The effect of the rising Inequality Ratio is to reduce the growth of wages and salaries relative to national income.

How does the rising Inequality Ratio affect consumer demand? That depends on the different behavior of wage income and profit income. In this simple model, profit and wages are the sole sources of consumer spending and demand. It was shown in Chapter 8 that a high percentage of wages, often 100 percent, are spent to purchase necessary consumer goods and services.

It was also shown in Chapter 8 that the wealthy spend a much lower percentage of their income on consumption than middle- and lower-income employees. Middle- and lower-income employees must use all of their wages and salaries to buy the necessary consumer goods. The wealthy only need to use a small percentage of their profit income to buy as much consumer goods as they desire. This is revealed in a simple way in Equation 4:

$$(4)\ C_t = a + bP_t + W_t$$

In Equation 4, a is a constant reflecting some minimum level of consumption in the aggregate. The letter b is a constant reflecting the percentage of profit income that is spent for consumption. It is assumed to be between 0 and 1. On the other hand, all of wages are assumed to be spent on consumption; a little of wage income is saved by some people, but many other people go into debt, so they spend more than 100 percent of their income. The result is that the ratio of middle-class consumption to middle-class income is approximately 1.

This is an important point, so some detail may be useful. How much of wages are spent on consumption? It is assumed that all wages are spent on consumer goods and services. This is shown by the fact that the constant indicating the percentage of spending of wages is always 1 in this model. In reality, there are times when more than 100 percent of aggregate wages are spent on consumer goods and services, with credit meeting the difference. There are also times, however, when less than 100 percent is spent on consumption. The average spending on consumption of goods and services from wage income is therefore generally around 100 percent in the average business cycle.

The wealthiest 1 percent, on the other hand, have a far larger income than the average employee. They do not usually find it necessary to spend all of their income on consumer goods and services. They spend some of their income on consumption; they also spend a considerable amount on investment and production; but they also spend some of it on purely speculative, including financial, investment. Note that this so-called speculative investment does not add to spending for expansion and does not add to aggregate demand.

As productivity rises, wages rise much less than profits, as shown in Chapter 7. Therefore, profits are able to rise more rapidly. Since the wealthiest 1 percent, who receive most of the capitalist profit, do not spend all of their income on consumption, it follows that their percentage of spending for consumption is lower than that of employees.

Equation 3 above shows a rising Inequality Ratio during the expansion. Therefore, income is shifting from employees to capital owners. Since the capital owners, who receive the profit, do not spend all of their income on consumption, it follows that the percentage of aggregate income being spent on consumer goods and services must be falling during the expansion. This fact was shown empirically in Chapter 8.

Having explained consumption, the model then explains investment in Equation 5:

(5) $I_t = v\,(P_{t-1} - P_{t-2})$

In Equation 5, the constant v is a coefficient showing the influence of a change in previous profits on present investment. The previous change in profits is calculated by the difference in its value from $t-2$ to $t-1$. Of course, a more realistic equation would show investment as a function of all previous profits from $t-n$ to $t-1$.

Equation 5 says that investment is a function of profit. What does that have to do with inequality? Rising inequality leads to smaller demand by consumers whose income is wages and salaries. When wages and salaries stagnate, then aggregate demand for the entire consumer sector also tends to stagnate.

Therefore, the rising inequality causes slower demand growth (while costs are still rising). For this reason, profits must fall because they are crushed in the jaws of the nutcracker, that is, between slower growth of demand and rising costs. Profits are crushed because rising inequality reduces demand. Inequality is thus the main cause that initiates a recession in this model.

Solving the model

These are five equations for the five variables. By substituting for each variable, it is possible to reduce the five equations to one equation in one variable.

That equation is shown here as Equation AA:

(AA) $0 = a - bg + g + (b - bh + h - 1)Y_t + (v - vh)Y_{t-1} - (v - vj)Y_{t-2}$

Equation AA is a second order difference equation. Such equations can be solved by converting them to a quadratic equation.

The general form of the homogeneous quadratic equation is:

$0 = AY_t + BY_{t-1} + QY_{t-2}$

When Equation AA is put into this form, it is found that:

$A = b - bh + h - 1$

$B = v - vh$

$Q = v - vh$

The solution will be cyclical, represented by a sine curve if:

$$B^2 < 4AQ$$

The values of A, B, and Q are given above in terms of the constants used in this model. Therefore, by substitution, the answer is that there will be a cyclical time path if:

$$(v - vh)^2 < 4(b - hb + h - 1)(v - vh)$$

The only important point the reader needs to remember from this equation is that only three constants are involved. Those three constants are v, b, and h: b is the consumer share, which is the ratio of consumption to national income; h is the employee share, which is the ratio of employee income to national income; and v is the ratio of investment to the previous change in profit.

It is not a coincidence that all three of these constants are ratios. In understanding the business cycle, one sees immediately that almost all variables rise together and almost all variables fall together. What is interesting is not the rise or fall of the variable, but the rise or fall of the ratio of one variable to another. For example, the Inequality Ratio is the ratio of profit to wages. Profit and wages both rise during the expansion, but wages rise only at the pace of a turtle, while profits soar like an eagle. That discrepancy is the main cause of recessions and depressions.

The ratio of wages to national income is the simplest possible reflection of the Inequality Ratio. Since wages do not rise as fast as national income, this means that if consumer goods and services continue to rise at their fastest pace after the midpoints of the expansion, there would be huge amounts of consumer goods and services that are not sold. As it is, some are unsold, but many are not produced at all.

The fall of the consumer share in the expansion is caused by the fall in the employee share of national income. This fall in aggregate demand results in a lower growth rate of profits. Because investment is caused by a growth of profits, the lower growth of profits leads to the recession. This is a verbal explanation of the mathematical functions seen in the model.

By stressing these three ratios within the story of inequality in the cycle of boom and bust, the basic model is a useful analytical tool. Obviously, it leaves out some important information. Most importantly, it leaves out the use of credit and financial income, the role of government in causing or curing the cycle of boom and bust, and the role of foreign trade, foreign investment, and foreign finance.

Part 3. Flow of model

Some readers may find the model clearer when it is illustrated in a flow diagram. Figure TA.1 reveals the flow between the variables in the model.

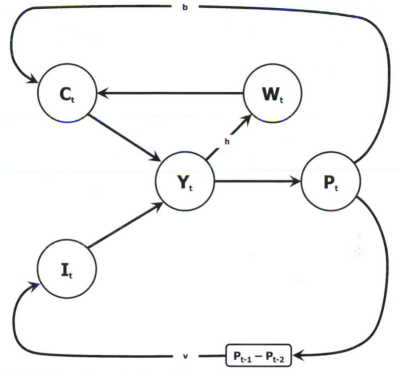

FIGURE TA.1   Flow diagram, basic model

The diagram begins with output (Y) in the center. The flow from output is divided into wage and salary income (W) and profit income (P). The flow from wage and salary income all goes, on average, into consumption (C). Consumption provides 70 percent of the aggregate demand in America, while most consumer spending comes from wages and salaries.

Profit income (P) splits into two flows. One flow sends a small part of profit income into consumption. A significant part of profit income goes into investment. In reality, some of that investment does not go into growth of productive facilities, but into speculative investment (although that distinction is not shown in the flow diagram).

The flow diagram thus explains the amount of consumption and investment. Consumption demand and investment demand together constitute the aggregate demand. The aggregate demand determines aggregate output. Lack of aggregate demand can cause a fall in national output.

Part 4. The general model

The general model is defined to mean: the basic model, plus credit, government economic activity, and trade. As a result, a more complete model of the aggregate economy must include not only the private sector of the domestic economy, but also government spending and revenue, and exports and imports. Aggregate demand must include consumption (C), investment (I), government expenditure of all types (G), and exports (X):

(BB) $Y_t = C_t + I_t + G_t + X_t$

Most macroeconomic progressive economist have a strong focus on aggregate demand. When progressive economists such as Keynes (1936) described the aggregate economy, they also included aggregate supply in their map of the economy. Aggregate cost of supply includes wages and salary income (W), interest income (R), government revenue (U), and import spending (M). For simplicity, rental income is ignored here.

The aggregate supply equation is:

(CC) $Y_t = W_t + R_t + U_t + M_t$

Wages and salaries are the largest single business expenditure for most businesses, but they are also the largest single source of consumer demand. Interest income includes all of the interest paid on consumer credit, all of the interest paid on corporate credit, and all of the interest paid on mortgages, as well as interest paid by government.

The number of variables can be reduced if one defines the net trade deficit or surplus as equal to the amount of exports minus imports. The net trade deficit or surplus may be called net exports (NE). Similarly, net government spending may be defined to equal government spending minus government revenue. The net government spending may be called NG. The net amount of aggregate demand may be thought of as consumer demand (C), plus net investment demand (NI), plus net government spending (DG), plus net exports (NE).

(DD) $Y_t = C_t + NI_t + DG_t + NE_t$

In this framework, aggregate consumption will be determined by all wages and salaries, plus that portion of profit spent for consumer goods and services, plus the consumer part of all credit.

Similarly, in this framework, investment is determined by a percentage of the previous profit plus the amount of credit borrowed and spent by business.

Net government spending, or deficit spending (DG), usually follows the same path in every peacetime business cycle. On the one hand, gross government spending rises slowly in the expansion, and then rises faster in the contraction. Gross government revenue, which is mainly taxes, rises as fast as national income in the expansion, but falls in the contraction because it is a function of declining national income. When one puts these two equations together, including the spending and the revenue of the government, the net government spending falls in each expansion because taxes rise faster than spending. Net government spending then rises in economic contractions because taxes are falling rapidly, while government expenditures are rising rapidly to meet the costs of the recession or depression.

Thus, the resulting equation for net government spending may show it as a positive function of national income, rising in expansions and rising even faster in contractions. As a result, net government spending is affected by total government spending and total government revenue. This causes net government spending to fall in the last half of the expansion, but to rise rapidly during a recession.

What happens to the net exports over the business cycle? Imports rise in the expansion at about the same rate as national income, but exports usually rise more slowly because other countries are not necessarily having exactly the same business cycle expansion as America. In the economic contraction, on the contrary, imports fall as national income falls, but American exports will generally fall more slowly because it takes considerable time for the recession or depression to spread to other countries.

Therefore, net exports have some tendency to fall in expansions and rise in contractions. Thus, net exports are a negative function of American national income in most peacetime business cycles. Of course, the equation for wages and salaries remains the same as shown in Part 2.

This model has shown that each of the aggregate variables in the demand and supply equations can be explained. In addition, investment is still explained primarily by previous profits. Profits are explained by the difference between aggregate demand and the cost of aggregate supply for business. Therefore, it is possible to write a complete multi-equation model of the average business cycle with all the main variables included. Its solution may show a cyclical path, depending on the values of the constants.

Part 5. Flow of general model

Some readers may find the general model clearer when it is illustrated in a flow diagram. Figure TA.2 reveals the flow between the variables in the general model.

The diagram begins with output (Y) in the center. However, the flow from output is divided into three pieces—not two—which are wage and salary income (W), profit income (P), and interest income (R). The flow from wage and salary income all goes, on average, into consumption (C). Consumption provides 70 percent of the aggregate demand in America, while most consumer spending comes from wages and salaries.

As shown in the diagram, profit income (P) splits into two flows. One flow sends a small part of profit income into consumption. A large part of profit income goes into investment. In reality, some of that investment does not go into growth of productive facilities, but into speculative investment (although that distinction is not shown in the flow diagram).

Interest income (R) splits into two flows. One flow sends a small part of output into consumption. Another part of interest income goes into investment.

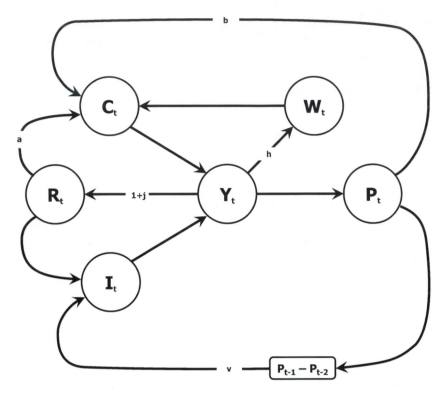

FIGURE TA.2 Flow diagram, general model

Part 6. List of variables

Readers may find it easier to connect the theory to the statistics if they have a complete list of all the variables.

TABLE TA.2 List of variables, sources, and functional relationships

Symbol	Name	Unit	Deflator	Source
I	Gross private domestic investment	Real	–	NIPA, Table 1.1.6, line 7
C	Personal consumption expenditures	Real	–	NIPA, Table 1.1.6, line 2
W	Compensation of employees	Nominal	GDP	NIPA, Table 2.1, line 2 NIPA, Table 1.1.9, line 1
Y	National income	Nominal	GDP	NIPA, Table 1.12, line 1 NIPA, Table 1.1.9, line 1
P	Corporate profits plus proprietors' income	Nominal	GDP	NIPA, Table 1.12, lines 9 and 13 NIPA, Table 1.1.9, line 1

R	Prime rate of interest	Percent	–	FRB H15, RIFSPBLP_NM
M	Imports	Real	–	NIPA, Table 1.1.6, line 18
E	Exports	Real	–	NIPA, Table 1.1.6, line 15
T	Government total receipts	Nominal	GDP	NIPA, Table 3.1, line 30 NIPA, Table 1.1.9, line 1
G	Government total expenditures	Nominal	GDP	NIPA, Table 3.1, line 33 NIPA, Table 1.1.9, line 1
CCR	Total consumer credit owned and securitized	Nominal	GDP	FRB G19, DTCTL.M NIPA, Table 1.1.9, line 1
KCR	Non-farm non-financial corporate business; credit market instruments; liability	Nominal	GDP	FRB Z1, FA104104005 NIPA, Table 1.1.9, line 1
U	Unemployment rate; labor force statistics from the current population survey; 16 years and over	Percent	–	BLS, LNS14000000Q

Abbreviations: NIPA means National Income Product Accounts, from U.S. Department of Commerce. FRB means Federal Reserve Board, from U.S. Federal Reserve. BLS means Bureau of Labor Statistics, from U.S. Department of Labor. CEN means Census, from U.S. Bureau of Census.

#	Equation	Behavior
1	$I_t = f1(Pt \ldots t{-}n)$	Investment is strong function of profit with time lag
2	$P = Y - K$	Profit is revenue minus cost
3	$Y_t = f2(C_t, I_t, G_t, E_t)$	Revenue depends on consumption, investment, government, and exports
4	$K_t = f3(W_t, R_t, T_t, M_t)$	Main costs are wages, interest, taxes, and imports
5	$I_t = f1(P_t \ldots t{-}n)$	Investment is strong function of profit with time lag
6	$P = Y - K$	Profit is revenue minus cost
7	$Y_t = f2(C_t, I_t, G_t, E_t)$	Revenue depends on consumption, investment, government, and exports
8	$C_t = f4(Y_t, (W/Y)_t, CCR_t)$	Consumption rises and falls with national output, wage share of output, and consumer credit
9	$W_t = f5(Y_t)$	Wages rise and fall more slowly than output
10	$CCR_t = f6(Y_t)$	Consumer credit rises and falls
11	$G_t = f7(Y_t \ldots t{-}n) + f8(U_t)$	Government is influenced by output and by unemployment and rises in all phases of the business cycle

(continued)

TABLE TA.2 *(continued)*

#	Equation	Behavior
12	$U_t = -f9(Y_t)$	Unemployment rises when output falls, and falls when output rises
13	$E_t = f10(Y_t)$	Exports rise and fall with output
14	$R_t = f11(Y_t \ldots t-n) + f12(KCR_t)$	Interest rates are a function of output with time lag and with corporate credit
15	$KCR_t = f13(Y_t)$	Corporate credit rises and falls more rapidly of any other variable examined
16	$T_t = f14(Y_t)$	Taxes rise and fall faster than output
17	$M_t = f15(Y_t)$	Imports rise and fall with output

Part 7. The theory of economic depression and economic inequality

Chapters 5 to 11 provided the statistical basis for the story of the average recession and expansion. Chapter 12 told the story in a single, coherent manner. In Chapter 13, the Great Recession was discussed in terms of the factual data on the movements of each variable in that cycle. The cycle of the Great Recession was more like a small depression than a large recession, so some of the movements of variables in that cycle differed considerably from those of the average recession during the Age of Globalization.

There was also, throughout a number of chapters in the book, discussion of the features of the Great Depression. These features had a number of things in common with those of the Great Recession.

By looking in detail at the average recession, the Great Recession, and the Great Depression, it is clear that they are all members of one family. A number of basic traits are found in every cycle for which data exist in sufficient quantity for American history. In addition, however, it is quite clear that each cycle is different. Moreover, the Great Depression and the Great Recession have some points in common in addition to the general features found in all cycles.

What is quite clear in the data is that long-run trends in the institutions of capitalism change the cycle patterns in later stages of capitalism. Both the Great Depression and Great Recession have four long-run trends in common to some degree. The four trends are as follows: first, an extremely high degree of inequality reached just before the Great Depression and the Great Recession each began; second, a housing crisis begins before the crisis phase of the business cycle and continues to get worse within it; third, a financial crisis makes the depression far worse than it otherwise would be; and fourth, the depression, such as the Great Depression and the Great Recession, spreads around the world.

To translate these four features into a mathematical model that included both recessions and depressions would require four long-run equations showing the basic trend of their movement. Then these four long-run equations would have to be linked with all of the short–run equations found in the general model above. If this job can be done, it would require an economist at a genius level of understanding of both the general political economic features of the present economic system, as well as an insightful understanding of mathematical economics.

Part 8. A theory of the inequality cycle in the global economy

It is possible that there now exist enough data among the international agencies to put together a cycle theory, similar to the theories discussed above, which would explain the behavior of the global economy. This would be extremely difficult, however, partly because of the large amount of data that would have to be collected on a global scale. This is partly because the data would have to include historical statistics on inequality at the global level as well as other cyclical variables, and partly because the theory of their interconnections at the global level is not yet written.

REFERENCES

Baran, Paul A. 1957. *The Political Economy of Underdevelopment*. New York: Monthly Review Press.

Bernanke, Ben. 2014. *The Federal Reserve: Looking Back, Looking Forward*. Available at: www.federalreserve.gov/newsevents/speech/bernanke20140103a.htm (accessed November 12, 2017).

Brands, H.W. 2008. *A Traitor to His Class*. New York: Doubleday.

Burns, Arthur F. and Mitchell, Wesley C. 1946. *Measuring Business Cycles*. New York: National Bureau of Economic Research. Available at: http://papers.nber.org/books/burn46-1 (accessed November 24, 2017).

Diamond, Jared. 1997. *Guns, Germs, and Steel*. New York: W.W. Norton.

Economic Cycle Research Institute. 2014. *The Agony and the Ecstasy*, November 7. Available at: www.businesscycle.com/ecri-news-events/news-details/economic-cycle-research-ecri-the-agony-and-the-ecstasy (accessed November 24, 2017).

Friedman, Milton. 1962. *Capitalism and Freedom*. Chicago, IL: University of Chicago Press.

Heilbroner, Robert. 1953. *The Worldly Philosophers*. New York: Simon & Schuster.

Hunt, E.K. 2015. *The History of Economic Thought*. Armonk, NY: M.E. Sharpe, 2nd edition.

Kalecki, Michal. 1968. *Theory of Economic Dynamics: An Essay on Cyclical and Long-Run Changes in Capitalist Economy*. New York: Monthly Review Press.

Keynes, John Maynard. 1936. *The General Theory of Employment, Interest, and Money*. Basingstoke: Palgrave Macmillan.

Krugman, Paul. 2012. *End This Depression Now!* New York: W.W. Norton.

Lewis, Michael. 2013. *The Big Short*. New York: Simon & Schuster.

Lewis, Michael. 2015. *Flash Boys*. New York: Simon & Schuster.

Marx, Karl. 1867. *Capital: A Critique of Political Economy, Volume I*. London: Penguin.

Marx, Karl. 1885. *Capital: A Critique of Political Economy, Volume II*. London: Penguin.

Mitchell, Wesley C. 1951. *What Happens During Business Cycles: A Progress Report*. NBER Studies in Business Cycles, No. 5. New York: National Bureau of Economic Research and Columbia University.

Piketty, Thomas. 2014. *Capital in the 21st Century*. Cambridge, MA: Belknap Press.

Piketty, Thomas. 2015. *The Economics of Inequality*. Cambridge, MA: Belknap Press.

Pollin, Robert (Ed.). 2000. *Capitalism, Socialism, and Radical Political Economy: Essays in Honor of Howard J. Sherman*. Northampton, MA: Edward Elgar.

Pollin, Robert. 2003. *Contours of Descent: U.S. Economic Fractures and the Landscape of Global Austerity*. New York: Verso Books.

Pollin, Robert. 2008. "The housing bubble and financial deregulation: isn't enough enough?" *New Labor Forum*, 17(2), Spring, 118–121.

Pollin, Robert and Luce, Stephanie. 1998. *The Living Wage: Building a Fair Economy*. Abingdon: Routledge.

Sherman, Howard. 1967. *Profits in the United States: Relationship of Monopoly to the Business Cycle*. Ithaca, NY: Cornell University Press.

Sherman, Howard. 1991. *The Business Cycle: Growth and Crisis in Capitalism*. Princeton, NJ: Princeton University Press.

Sherman, Howard. 2001. "The business cycle theory of Wesley Mitchell." *Journal of Economic Issues*, 35(1), March, 85–98.

Sherman, Howard. 2003. "Institutions and the business cycle." *Journal of Economic Issues*, 37(3), September, 621–642.

Sherman, Howard. 2006a. *How Society Makes Itself: The Evolution of Political and Economic Institutions*. Armonk, NY: M.E. Sharpe.

Sherman, Howard. 2006b. "Making of a radical economist." *Review of Radical Political Economics*, 38(4), Fall, 519–538.

Sherman, Howard and Sherman, Paul. 2012. "Recessions and human misery: dating the cycle." *Monthly Review*, 63(10), March, 33–37.

Sherman, Howard and Sherman, Paul. 2015. "Inequality and the business cycle." *Challenge*, 58(1), January–February, 51–63.

Sherman, Howard, Hunt, E.K., Nesiba, Reynold, O'Hara, Phillip, and Wiense-Tuers, Barbara. 2008. *Economics: An Introduction to Traditional and Progressive Views*. Armonk, NY: M.E. Sharpe, 7th edition.

Sherman, Howard, Meeropol, Michael, and Sherman, Paul. 2013. *Principles of Macroeconomics: Activist vs. Austerity Policies*. Armonk, NY: M.E. Sharpe.

Sinclair, Barbara. 1983. *The Women's Movement*. New York: Harper & Row, 3rd edition.

Stiglitz, Joseph. 2002. *Globalization and Its Discontents*. New York: W.W. Norton.

Stiglitz, Joseph. 2012. *The Price of Inequality*. New York: W.W. Norton.

Stiglitz, Joseph. 2015a. *The Great Divide*. New York: W.W. Norton.

Stiglitz, Joseph. 2015b. *Rewriting the Rules of America: An Agenda for Growth and Shared Prosperity*. New York: W.W. Norton.

Veblen, Thorstein. 1899. *The Theory of the Leisure Class*. London: Macmillan & Company.

Warren, Elizabeth. 2014. *A Fighting Chance*. New York: Metropolitan Books.

Wolff, Richard D. 2016. *Capitalism's Crisis Deepens*. Chicago, IL: Haymarket Books.

Wolfson, Martin H. 1994. *Financial Crisis: Understanding the Postwar U.S. Experience*. Armonk, NY: M.E. Sharpe, 2nd edition.

INDEX

Locators in **bold** refer to tables and those in *italics* to figures.

Taylor & Francis eBooks

Helping you to choose the right eBooks for your Library

Add Routledge titles to your library's digital collection today. Taylor and Francis ebooks contains over 50,000 titles in the Humanities, Social Sciences, Behavioural Sciences, Built Environment and Law.

Choose from a range of subject packages or create your own!

Benefits for you

- » Free MARC records
- » COUNTER-compliant usage statistics
- » Flexible purchase and pricing options
- » All titles DRM-free.

REQUEST YOUR **FREE** INSTITUTIONAL TRIAL TODAY

Free Trials Available
We offer free trials to qualifying academic, corporate and government customers.

Benefits for your user

- » Off-site, anytime access via Athens or referring URL
- » Print or copy pages or chapters
- » Full content search
- » Bookmark, highlight and annotate text
- » Access to thousands of pages of quality research at the click of a button.

eCollections – Choose from over 30 subject eCollections, including:

Archaeology	Language Learning
Architecture	Law
Asian Studies	Literature
Business & Management	Media & Communication
Classical Studies	Middle East Studies
Construction	Music
Creative & Media Arts	Philosophy
Criminology & Criminal Justice	Planning
Economics	Politics
Education	Psychology & Mental Health
Energy	Religion
Engineering	Security
English Language & Linguistics	Social Work
Environment & Sustainability	Sociology
Geography	Sport
Health Studies	Theatre & Performance
History	Tourism, Hospitality & Events

For more information, pricing enquiries or to order a free trial, please contact your local sales team:
www.tandfebooks.com/page/sales

 Routledge
Taylor & Francis Group

The home of
Routledge books

www.tandfebooks.com